NEVER EAT YOUR
HEART OUT

The Left Coast of Paradise
(1987)

X
(with Sue Coe)
(1986)

NEVER
EAT
YOUR
HEART
OUT

Judith Moore

NORTH POINT PRESS

FARRAR STRAUS GIROUX

NEW YORK

North Point Press
A division of Farrar, Straus and Giroux
19 Union Square West, New York 10003

Copyright © 1997 by Judith Moore
All rights reserved
Distributed in Canada by Douglas & McIntyre Ltd.
Printed in the United States of America
Designed by Fritz Metsch
First published in 1997 by Farrar, Straus and Giroux
First North Point Press paperback edition, 1998

AUTHOR'S NOTE

In telling my stories, I have wanted to respect discretion as much as truth. I have therefore altered names and identifying details of certain people and places appearing in this book.

I would like to thank the National Endowment for the Arts for the two fellowships that made possible my work on *Never Eat Your Heart Out*.

Opening lines of *A Portrait of the Artist as a Young Man* quoted with permission of the Estate of James Joyce.

The Library of Congress has catalogued the hardcover edition as follows:
Moore, Judith.
    Never eat your heart out / Judith Moore.
      p.   cm.
    ISBN 0-374-22073-5 (alk. paper)
    1. Cookery, American   2. Cooks—United States—Biography.
    3. Moore, Judith. I. Title.
TX715.M82635   1997
641.5'092—dc20
[B]   96–38024

For Jim, who gave me work
For Juris, who gave me hope

CONTENTS

❦

NEVER EAT YOUR
HEART OUT

PIE

*I have simply wanted to show that whenever life
seeks to shelter, protect, cover or hide itself, the imagination sympathizes
with the being that inhabits the protected space.*
RILKE

*As far back in time as we can go, the gastronomic value has always been more
highly prized than the nutritive value.*
BACHELARD

.

ITS FILLING SEQUESTERED BENEATH A CANOPY OF TOP CRUST,
hidden from the eye (if not the nose), a pie (not unlike the body)
offers itself for reverie on the enigma of inside and out.

Even when I was a child, a pre-school toddler, I adored con-
cocting for my dolls mud-crust pies in doll-size pie tins. I filled
them with pansies or nasturtiums or marigolds or yellow china-
berries picked off bushes that grew along the back alley, or with
pea gravel culled from our driveway. With Belinda, my rag doll,
snuggled in the crook of my arm, I would curl up in bed at nap-
time or at night, engrossed—transported, really—in figuring out
what ingredients I could fill pies with next. In my mind I would
roll out mud circles, and more daintily in thought than ever in
fact I would tuck these crusts in pans. In my mind's eye I would
see myself, in passionate imitation of adult pie-makers, layering in
flowers or pebbles, dribbling over them my sandbox sand for
sugar, and adding daubs of wet mud butter. Then, carefully, with
an enormous sigh of satisfaction that comes as one nears a task's
completion, I spread a top crust over my pie's filling, and with the
stubby dimpled fingers I see now in my photographs at that age,

I pinched together, around the pie's entire circumference, the edges of the top and bottom mud crusts. What was in the pie was a secret only I knew.

I so heartily believed in my mud and sand ingredients that falling asleep I smelled my pie baking (it would be a doubled make-believe, because I did not smell mud, I smelled apples, cherries, apricots). While my body gave off that last shudder as tensed muscle let go, I began to arrange in my mind's eye all the dolls on chairs around my playhouse table, even incontinent Betsy-Wetsy, who left wet spots wherever she sat, the cloth rabbit, the woolen Pooh bear come across the ocean from what my father called "war-torn England."

Next to pie, what pleasure cake offers, whether looked at or eaten, seems meager. To wonder about a cake's interior, given a well-made cake's unvarying, uniform web and constant all-chocolate or all-"white" taste (even when lemon or raspberry filling or dark chocolate glistens silkily between its layers) is to have the mind taken nowhere. The simplest breakfast muffin, aclutter with plump raisins and walnuts, seems more a marvel, inciting curiosity in the mind, bonanza for the mouth.

Another person might see this pie-cake distinction in an entirely opposite fashion, and consider cake, leavened as it is by baking powder and by the air-retaining foam of whipped egg whites or whole eggs and baking powder—which means that its volume is significantly increased by internal gas expansion—is far more the miracle. But it seems to me that mere chemistry can explain what makes a cake, while pie demands metaphysics. The opposition between a pie's inside and out, the dialectic, if you will, between crust and filling, can't but set minds wondering. As children and as adults we never lose interest in it. Confronted with turtle or snail shell, high fence, blank wall, lid, door, veil, or wrapping past which the eye cannot go (think of egg rolls, turnovers, pocket bread), the mind proceeds at once to ask, "What's in there?" or, more suspiciously, "What is being hidden?" and, of course, "Why?" If one is in an elegaic mood, this consideration of outside and in may steer one to certain qualities of innerness: tenderness, vulnerability. One may then find oneself filled with emotions similar to the poet Rilke's, in which "the imagination sympathizes with the being that inhabits the protected space."

In my mud-pie days I had a tiny wooden rolling pin equipped with handles lacquered bright red. I had to ask permission, but once having done so, I was allowed to dust the wide lower step of the back stoop with sand from my sandbox and then I'd plop down my mud mix on top of the sand, pat my mud flat, and roll out my crusts on the concrete.

How did I bake my mud pies? Next to my sandbox I built an oven from red bricks left over from some project of my father's. Four bricks made the oven floor, four bricks stood on end made its sides, and for the oven roof I used a piece of corrugated tin. I had more bricks that I stood up against the oven for its door. As my pies (I could fit two in the oven) baked, I would conjure drawings in my mind like the ones in my picture books: pies cooling on wide wooden windowsills, steam rising up out of vents cut in the pies' top crusts and floating in chimney-smoke whorls across blue skies above fairy-tale villages, and I could work myself up into a fret of fear by imagining that the sweet, fruity aroma drifting off my pie had attracted a sharp-toothed wolf. I would remember the nursery rhyme that began:

> *Sing a song of sixpence,*
> *A pocket full of rye;*
> *Four and twenty blackbirds,*
> *Baked in a pie.*

I asked permission to use the back stoop for my mud-pie making from Black Mary, so called to distinguish her from my father's aunt, whom, I guess, we would have called White Mary, had things been equal. Black Mary lived with us, kept our house, washed and ironed our clothes, and cooked our food. She had raised my father and his younger brother from the day they were born, and after their mother died, when my father was six, she became all the mother my father had left. He adored her. Black Mary had what my father called a Queen Mary bosom, by which he meant a breastline carried well forward, like a ship's prow. She was better to me than anybody, better than my maternal grandmother or paternal stepgrandmother, better than my mother, and better even than my father, if only because she, unlike my father and mother, was always home. I loved to bury my nose deep down in the cleft between her breasts, where her smooth skin gave off the fragrance of spices and breakfast bacon and furniture oil and the flowery talcum she dusted her brown skin with, spotting it white. I loved to lay my cheek along the bodice of Mary's print dresses and hear her heart beat. Its thump reverberated through her huge body into my ear, her flesh quivered and hummed, and I would begin to breathe with her. I felt lulled and narcotized, and I wondered if, like Sleeping Beauty or Rip Van Winkle, I might not fall asleep there forever.

I remember a springtime afternoon when a storm came up; bright lightning strokes and a series of thunderclaps—not rolling thunder, but sharp, harsh cracks—woke me from my nap. It was not long after lunch, but outside, the sky looked dark as evening. My mother was at school and my father at work. Mary set me at the kitchen table. Our dog, a black Scottie like President Roosevelt's Fala, lay under the table and whimpered every time another thunderbolt crashed. Mary had her little Bakelite radio turned on to one of her stories about romance, which did not interest me. I touched the dog with my bare toes and he growled.

My father loved Mary's chicken pie, and she was fixing us one for dinner. To make the pie she had to start by stewing what she called an old hen. I remember old hens coming to us (but don't remember from where, or how they got to the kitchen). The hens arrived headless and plucked, with their skinny yellow scaly legs and feet still attached.

That afternoon Mary stood by the stove and held the old hen over a gas flame, singeing off bluish pinfeathers that poked out from the hen's naked body the same way my father's weekend beard poked from his chin. The remains of the hen's broken neck drooped downward, and a long empty sleeve of loose skin hung off it, bobbing. Every time a flame caught at a pinfeather, the burning feather set off a *psst* sound. The feathers burning smelled the same as hair burning.

The storm didn't let up and rain came down so hard onto our roof that I couldn't even hear the voices on Mary's radio anymore. Mary had water boiling by then in her black iron stew pot and had put the hen in the bubbling water and then turned down the flame and covered the pot with a lid. Right away, the glass in the kitchen windows began to steam up, and soon I couldn't see out the window, and then my father called from his office to make sure we were all right in the storm. Mary let me talk to him for a minute. He said if I couldn't see out the kitchen windows I should get in the dining-room window seat and watch the storm from there, and then the line crackled and I could barely hear him and gave the phone back to Mary.

I knelt on the window-seat cushions, which were covered with rough monk's cloth and scratched my bare knees. I pulled back the curtain and looked through the glass Mary kept spotless with ammonia, out into the unnaturally dark side yard. Lightning flared across the sky, leaving behind an eerie radiance. Rain hit the grass and beat yellow blossoms off the forsythia canes and knocked petals off the red Darwin tulips. Low spots in the yard were drowning.

In no time rain turned to hail, and Mary came and stood by

me, hand on my shoulder and dog whimpering right behind her, and Mary said that with so much hail hitting the roof so hard she felt as if we were stuck inside a drum that was being rat-a-tat-tatted with about a hundred drumsticks. She said she hoped the hail didn't ruin our roof or break her windshield, which had happened before, or beat down the lettuce and spinach that had been up just a few weeks out in the garden.

Mary said come along into the kitchen, which by then was hot and smelled of good chicken steam. I helped by shelling peas while Mary chopped onion and carrot and potato to go into the chicken pie. The dog went to sleep, and when I had all the peas shelled and a bowl on the table half full of bright green peas and a pan heaped up with empty pods, I looked up and the storm was over. Sun was shining down in a twinkly brightness onto the yard. I squinted because I had gotten used to the dark. Mary brushed flour off her hands, which had made them all white, and helped me into my shoes and tied them and, telling me not to fall on slick grass or get in puddles, allowed me out the back door to go play.

Right away of course I went out to the sidewalk to see if my friend Janet from across the street was out, but she wasn't. I started looking around to see what had happened in the storm. Hailstones, big as mothballs and as white, littered the lawn, and my father's spinach and lettuce had been beaten down in the rows he'd planted them in, and dirt was on the lettuce leaves. The poplars that stood in a line between our lot and the one next door had their leaves knocked off, and the apple trees along the back fence, too. My foot touched something soft, and I looked down. My foot had touched a dead baby robin.

Maybe wind had blown the bird from its nest; maybe rain had drowned the bird in its nest, or maybe hailstones had killed it. It had no real feathers yet, only fuzzy down, and the down was soaked. Its bluish-pink skin was wrinkled all over its body, and its wings had hardly formed and were more like flippers. Its feet were needle-like and not strong enough to have held it up if it had tried to stand. Its head looked too big for its body and its eyes too big for its head. Its beak was halfway open, as if maybe it had struggled for breath. There was no life left in it.

I wasn't supposed to touch it and I knew I wasn't. It was cold to touch. I felt voracious guilt, the quality of which returns to me even now. I was disobeying Mary and my parents—"Do not touch wild birds; they're dirty, crawling with filthy diseases and nasty lice."

I knew what I should do. I should call for Mary and say, "Come quick, there's a dead baby bird out here." Against my better judgment, against what I knew was right, I felt my will move the other way. I felt myself slide down into the desire to make this dead bird into a pretend-chicken pie. I ran to the door and knocked, and Mary stuck out her head. The smell of chicken pie baking came out. Mary looked up in the sky and wondered out loud if I needed my sweater, and I said no and asked permission to make mud pies and got it, as long as I didn't come in and out and track her clean linoleum. She said soon my father and mother would be home.

So I gathered my pots and pans and used water from a puddle and dug with my old tablespoon in the back flower bed, where my father let me dig, and I got two mud balls, one for the top crust and one for the bottom, just right, not too wet and not too dry, and I put some sand on the stoop and took the red lacquered handles of the rolling pin, one handle in each hand, and rolled and rolled the mud balls out flat, and I fitted the bottom crust into the little pie pan and then looked up at the kitchen window with its blue-checkered curtains and the window in the back door to see if Mary was looking out and she wasn't, and I hurried over

with my pie pan to the fruit trees where the bird was lying with
its beak half open and its feet up in the air and I picked it up and
tucked it on its side in the pie shell and it just fit and then I put
some soft apple-tree leaves over it for vegetables and then I carried the pie pan back to the back stoop and when I looked up
Mary was still not looking out, her big face wasn't smiling in the
window, so I put the pie pan down on the stoop and carefully
picked up the top crust and laid it over the leaves and pinched
the two crusts together all around and carried it to my oven and
put it in and piled up the bricks and sat down on the corner of
my sandbox to wait for it to be done. I never told anyone this
until now.

Of course I knew I couldn't feed the pie to my dolls, because
it didn't seem right, and I wasn't happy, sitting there, with all the
robins by then singing and out in the yard pulling worms from the
wet ground, and I thought that one of them was the one whose
baby was dead and she would fly up to her nest and her nest
would be empty. I undid the door bricks and took the pie out of
the oven and walked to the far corner of the garden and gently
turned the pie over at the back of a flower bed and tipped all of
it onto the ground and covered it up with the dead leaves that my
father stacked there in the fall.

By the time I got my mess cleaned up off the stoop, my mother
and father were home. My father first thing checked his garden
for damage, and Mary let the dog out and he yipped and ran in
circles around my father and got muddy paw prints on his trousers.
My father and mother asked Mary and me if we'd been scared
during the storm, and we said no. For dinner, we had the chicken
pie, served in the high-sided Pyrex pie pan in which Mary had
baked it. I am sure that it tasted as it always did and does now
when I make it: chunks of white breast meat, green peas, squares
of potato, carrot, celery, the rich chicken gravy, which, mixed to-

gether, is like tasting an old-fashioned farm landscape. But I didn't eat much and Mary said maybe I was tired because the storm woke me from my nap.

After that I didn't make mud pies anymore. Not for a long time, or not for what seemed, at that age, like a long time, probably only a week or two. And then I went to nursery school and then my parents broke up, and then we moved and I started grade school. All that was a long time ago. But it stayed with me.

As a child rolling out mud crusts I felt much as I feel now, wearing an apron in my kitchen—that making a pie I'm hand-maiden to a miracle. I will begin, let's say, with pale green and ruby rhubarb stalks, sour red pie cherries, McIntosh apples, butter, sugar, flour, salt, and shortening. I peel the coarse strings off the outer blades of the rhubarb, pit cherries, peel and core apples. I spoon the raw fruit into the bottom pie shell, daub the fruit with chunks of butter, dribble sugar and strew flour, the latter for thickening. I sprinkle all this with no more cinnamon than will lightly freckle the fruit. I fold the second round of pie dough in half and gently lift it onto the heaped high fruit with the fold in the pie's center. One half of the pie's fruit, then, is covered. Last, ever so painstakingly, I unfold the top crust across the pie's other half and crimp the edges of the top and bottom crusts together. With a fork I prick the top crust in several places so that while the pie bakes steam can escape.

A transformation that is almost sorcery begins when the pie is set on a middle rack in the heated oven. While I wash the bowl and knives and dust flour off the pastry board, the baking fruit's aroma begins to perfume the house. Thirty, forty minutes later, I open the oven door a few inches and peer in. The oven's radiating heat rises around the pie in indistinct waves, like the contours of a dream. The heat is insinuating itself into the pie's interior, creating between the sealed crusts its own steamy, primordial climate, a site (to use the French postman-philosopher Gaston Bachelard's translated-into-English words) of "thermal sympathy" and "calorific happiness," in which apple and rhubarb and cherry cell walls break down and sugar crystals alter and butter melts.

Another half hour passes and I lean over, open the oven door. Heat rushes out onto my cheeks. What I take out from the oven (my hands protected by potholders) seems precisely like those childhood pies: born rather than made.

If the weather's right I'll set the pie to cool on the windowsill. I have no trouble, all these years later, imagining that heat floats off the pie's browned crust out the window and sails in stylized whorls out into the courtyard and over the fence into the neighborhood. If I happen to be anxious, I may fear that the pie's aroma may tempt a distant wolf. The wolf will appear decidedly older, leaner, and more vicious than the wolves from my childhood.

As a child with mud and as an adult with crust and apples, in the moment before the first cut is taken into a pie, I often have felt uncomfortable, as if I were about to violate a taboo. Someone has suggested to me that cutting into a pie is not all that different from cutting into a body. So I think it is good to make something of a ceremony of cutting a pie. The table can be laid with a pretty cloth and napkins and the best silver and your favorite plates.

Once the pie is brought to the table, I like to take a moment to admire it. I like to give the pie a chance to wet the mouth with anticipation of its tastes (the mouth's imagination at work). I like to contemplate the lustrous lightly browned crust. I like to think one more time about inside and out. Because the moment the pie is cut, outside will have no more meaning. A new dimension, the dimension of this pie's delectable interiority, opens up.

Gathered around the table, those about to eat will say "Ahhh" and "Mmmmm, doesn't that look delicious." They will lean forward, noses alert. Sometimes you can hear them breathing in.

The first bite rises toward the opening mouth. The sentinel nose having anticipated pie's arrival, a tide of saliva crests in the mouth, pools in the tongue's center, washes over the several thousand taste buds. The teeth bite through flaky, slightly salty crust and then into tart cherries and rhubarb and apple. The fruits' sweet and buttery juices, in a total immersion baptism of the mouth, flood tongue, teeth, cheeks. There is no more outside. Everything is in.

READING TO
CHILDREN

❦

EVENINGS DURING THE LAST SPRINGTIME OF THE LAST GREAT
war, after our happy suppers—gravy, fresh vegetables, plate clatter, talk—my father doffed the jacket of his tailor-made suit and
read the paper while Mary and my mother cleared dishes. My
mother plucked up the white tablecloth by its four corners, carried
it out the back door. The sun by then was down, the grass spinach
green and the shadows purple. She stood on the stoop (where,
when the concrete was wet, my father had scratched a lopsided
heart and then inside the heart *1939: B + C*). She shook the cloth.
Up, down. Flapped it, scattering crumbs. Her teeth gripping one
edge of the cloth, my mother folded the linen into a neat square,
while far down the block, from the army barracks, soldiers counted
cadence. "Sound off, one-two. Sound off, three-four."

"Go to your father," she says. "Go, go, go, go." She shoos me
like her mother shoos chickens.

The living room was long, its oak floorboards smelled of wax.
There was a Steinway parlor grand, a flowered couch, low tables,
Turkey carpets, bookcases stacked with *Fortune*, *Life*, gardening
titles from England, novels, a few of my father's law books.

His chair ruled the room. It was upholstered in nubby rose wool, and next to one of its wide arms stood a table with a Chinese lamp which had been his mother's. He was mad for flowers and, breathing noisily through his mouth, would arrange drooping peonies or lilies of the valley in stoneware jugs.

When I could not get along with my mother, Mary, or my friend Janet, or most often—for I was an only child—when some game of my own abruptly dissipated, when I went numb, null, and lost my way, I would rush in from my room or the yard—where I was trying, that spring, in secret and without success, to salt a robin's tail—and kneel on the figured carpet and lay my head on his chair cushion, my hand in the impress his weight left. No one else sat there, and the cushion smelled, not unpleasantly, of his body. Before I can say "Jack Robinson," I'd tell myself, he will be home.

Every evening, after supper I tiptoed to him. Waited.

The newspaper hid his face. He wriggled his giant shoe, signaling that I might straddle his ankle, grab on to his trouser leg, take a pony ride.

I bounced slowly. I heard my own breathing, heard his tendons whine.

A lazy bounce or two later he spoke—"Giddyap's over!"—and let fall half the newspaper, showing his face: round, lightly freckled, blue-eyed, grinning. He was thirty. His loose red curls had begun to recede.

He puts out his hand. "Dreamgirl." He folds my fingers in his palm. I climb up his blue serge calves onto his knees and fall into his lap. His legs extend miles beneath me.

From *The Poky Little Puppy*'s cover the milk-white mongrel of the title streams light. The puppy's muzzle is blunted, his eyes are brown circles. Above a rusty patch on the puppy's rear flank, his tail loops.

"Take as much time as you need," my father says. "*Never* let yourself be rushed."

At the cover's far corner a green lizard gazes up at the puppy. I don't care about lizards.

"Five little puppies dug a hole under the fence and went for a walk in the wide, wide world." From far above, my father's voice comes down to me, telling how against their mother's orders the five puppies escape their yard and take off. Four of the puppies stick together, but Poky Puppy rushes away "roly-poly, pell-mell, tumble-bumble." His siblings catch up to him, ask, "What in the world are you doing?"—to which he replies, "I smell something. I smell mmmmmm Rice Pudding."

The story goes to its familiar end. My father shuts the book, sighs a big enough sigh that I go up in his lap and then down. His arms around me, my father leans over, momentarily displacing, dizzily tilting me, and slips *The Tale of Peter Rabbit* off the table.

Once upon a time there were four little Rabbits, and their names were—

Flopsy,
Mopsy,
Cotton-tail,
and Peter.

'Now, my dears,' said old Mrs. Rabbit one morning, 'you may go into the fields or down the lane, but don't go into Mr. McGregor's garden: your Father had an accident there; he was put in a pie by Mrs. McGregor.'

Instead of the words he reads I think about Peter's father stripped of his lovely fur, fitted in the pie tin on top of diced carrot, vivid green peas. His skinned body glistens, his blue veins branch out. The pinched and fluted raw pie crust rises up around him like a castle wall. The top crust waits on the floured board and soon that crust will cover him. The oven is heating. I hear it tick—tick—tick. Peter Rabbit's father will cook and his meat will fall off his bones.

"Are you listening?" He reaches round and chucks my chin. My top and bottom teeth hit. I whimper and he pulls me more tightly to him. "Listen," he croons, "listen."

I strain to hear my father's breath, his belly rumble under me.

Flopsy, Mopsy, and Cotton-tail are good. But Peter, who was very naughty, ran as fast as he could run to Mr. McGregor's garden. Peter had to squeeze to get under the gate.

Peter's in the garden. His tummy slumps, sags beneath the hem of his blue jacket. His whiskers droop.

Out from the dining room, my mother walks by in high-heeled shoes, comes to my father's side, reaches down from where she stands in the lamplight (which turns her skin the rich gold of egg yolk), and touches my father's shoulder.

I sink into the shade my father's chin makes, out of her sight. I twist myself tighter, take his heartbeats into my ear, adjust my breathing to his, draw breath when he does, let go when he does.

She is saying something I can't hear. They laugh. The laughter dwindles out into the room. She fools with the flowers, straightens the stems, says, "This bunch is tired-looking"; then leans over, smelling of her face powder, hugs his neck, touches noses with him, Eskimo-style, kisses his forehead, leaves her red lips on the furrows.

The wind works tree branches up and down, scratches branches against our windows. Her high heels click down the hall; she sings, "Have you seen but a bright lily grow, before rude hands have touched it?"

I reach up, grab his nose, then squirm, turn around, get on my knees, put my arms around his neck. I see myself in his eyes, seeing me. I erase my mother's lipstick, rub my cheek against his whiskery cheek, kiss him on his soft mouth. Our kiss tastes of the sheen of dinner still on his lips. I want to climb far back into his mouth where the gold glints, be swallowed in him, drown, be carried forever, swimming next to his beating heart.

He clasps my wrist in his enormous hand, rearranges me— flushed, sweating, even my bare feet are red—in his lap. From the table he slides off and puts up in front of us the largest of the three books. Open, the book spreads from knee to knee across his lap. Along the green endpapers, elephants are tailed up—twenty-seven elephants on each page. We count them.

"In the great forest a little elephant is born. His name is Babar. His mother loves him very much."

The green forest rises toward me, shuts out my mother, the wind, the war, eclipses—finally—Peter Rabbit's father curled atop peas and smothered under pie dough, baking, baking.

"Babar is riding so so happily jiggety-jig on his mother's back when a wicked, *wicked*, oh so *very* wicked hunter, lurking behind bushes, shoots them." Red fire spurts from the hunter's gun. Babar's mother topples. Tears stream from Babar's eyes. My father touches Babar's tears, runs their course with a fingertip.

The story drifts by alive. That Babar escapes the hunter, arrives in the big city, is found by the Old Lady, becomes the story of my life. It is what's happening in our house. When the Old Lady gives Babar her purse and tells him to buy himself clothes, I dress myself in his green suit, derby hat, shoes with spats.

We come too soon to the last pages. My father's curls are damp on his forehead. We are warm from each other. I am limp, am as full of happiness as the glass milk jugs on our porch will be full of milk in the morning.

One arm around my middle, he uses his free hand to push us up, shakily, to his feet, and standing, straightening, he deftly turns me, lifts me up until my head rests on his shoulder.

His penny loafers are far beneath me, and I am nested in his arms many miles above the oak floorboards. I press my forehead into his neck, his breath is humid on my cheek. Bobbing with each of his steps, I am going where he takes me.

I sink into the bed, fall into its deep softness. He wraps me in my blanket. He agrees with me. I do have an elephant trunk. It *must* indeed be unfurled, laid out before me on a pillow we place on my stomach.

That my mother not long after that spring tossed my father out, none of this matters now, or does not matter that much.

Every year on my birthday he would call me from somewhere to say, "Your mother came to me on the steps of the law school to tell me that the doctor said we were going to have a child." He'd add, "Knowing that, I gave my all. I was number-one man in the bar exams." He would recount the circumstances of my birth—how the nuns hovered over my mother while she sweated buckets and how she strained until my head emerged—"You had your lovely curls."

He would say, "You know, kitten, I wept with joy."

For all that, we were not together. But I carried in my ear the memory of his voice reading to me and was comforted.

I read to my own children and did so, for my own pleasure, long after both could read for themselves.

At seventy-five my father still mourned his mother. He dreamed about her often. On his battered IBM Selectric he would type out a letter to me every day. He would write his dreams in his letters. My father has been dead more than a year. Looking at the postmark on an envelope addressed to me in his hand and knowing what time his mailman came, I figure he must have written to me and then, as was his habit, walked, whistling, up the path between apple trees to the mailbox two or three hours before his heart stopped, before he fell over in the cramped office he kept next to the house.

From the emergency room, my father's doctor, a friend with whom he collected fern spores, called me. "He was already down when they found him. He was DOA." He hesitated, and in the ear pressed against my telephone I heard other telephones ring and a distant siren. Then: "He had such an expression of surprise on his face when they brought him in."

Every day, for a week after that, his letters came. I still can't read them.

I carry in my ear his voice reading to me. Verses recited in his supple courtroom basso, stories embellished with his peculiar grace notes told—tell—themselves to me. Seeing a Beatrix Potter drawing places me deep in the burrow of my father's lap, and the evenings when he read to me return. He puts out his hand. "Dreamgirl, Dreamgirl," he says, and folds my fingers in his palm. The Poky Little Puppy, pure white, ravishing, gleams out from the book's cover—a night-light, a lighthouse, guiding my father's voice down to me.

BREAKFAST

❧

I HAVE BEEN THINKING ABOUT BREAKFASTS AND THE NEAR-obsolescence now of extravagant morning meals. Breakfasts were eaten by people on America's farms and in its small towns; they were eaten in the dark in winter and in gray dawn in spring and summer. Fried eggs, yolks straining against tense, transparent membrane; bacon slices cut from sugar-cured rashers, the bacon fat cameo white between dark lean; biscuit that steams: I remember all these. I remember French toast. The egg-and-milk-soaked bread puffs up in the iron skillet. Chilly morning air puffs up, too, swells to an ambrosial ferment the nose can't get enough of: sage-seasoned pork sausage, caramelizing sugars, sliced orange, coffee.

I remember breakfast tables from my earliest childhood; sun-shine spills across a blue-checked tablecloth stiff with starch and fresh air. Cut-glass bowls hold jelly and jam. The Concord grape and strawberry wriggle, seem to live lives of their own, nurtured by slow, hidden heartbeats.

From my seat at the table, my father's law books stacked under me, I saw, out the window, two cardinals flutter in midair. The larger bird was bright red, the smaller dull rust. The larger pecked the smaller. "Stop them," I screamed. Even before a word came from my father's mouth, the birds flew. My father said, Calm down, the birds are making babies. Soon they will lay eggs and their pretty eggs will fill to bursting with baby redbirds. Maybe the birds have built their nest in our poplars or maples or elms. Maybe the mother redbird plucked up your lovely hair yesterday, when we set you on a chair in the yard and trimmed your curls so your neck wouldn't get so hot and sweaty. Maybe she lined her nest with your curls. "Imagine that!" my father said, and smiled.

My mother may have said to my father then, as she often did, "Don't fill her head with ideas. You'll make her wild."

I remember fried green tomatoes and fried apple rings. My father and mother dip a forkful of charred tomato or apple into the lake of marigold yolk. They bite down with huge fierce teeth. Butter gleams on their lips. They spoon yellow cream into coffee; the coffee instantly turns pale, the way people do when they hear bad news. I remember the *glurg-glurg* when they swallow coffee, their enormous heads thrown back, pale white throats exposed. My father leaves a coffee taste on my lips when he kisses me goodbye in the morning. Years later, at the movies on Saturday afternoons, I buy coffee Charms and suck them. Coffee-flavored liquid rises over my bottom teeth, pools on my tongue, floods my mouth with my father's kisses.

These memories seem pleasant enough, even with battling cardinals and the strain between my mother and father. But as I enumerate dishes that weighted the breakfast tables of my childhood, I feel uneasy. One specific morning and a second, also specific, come back.

Sun isn't up, rain hits curtainless windows. The furnace is turned off and the house is cold. I see my mother's heart-shaped face and my grandmother's doughy cheeks. I smell their newly applied makeup and deodorant and Bluegrass cologne. In the dim kitchen their lipstick is greasy red and their rouge unnaturally bright.

My grandmother has spread the morning paper open under my bowl. I dawdle with my oatmeal, pat its stucco surface with the back of my spoon. Oatmeal splats against the paper.

My mother's and grandmother's faces loom, slowly expand, like balloons being blown up. My grandmother says, We don't have all day, we need to get on the road if we're going to get to the farm before bedtime.

I ask, Why can't we take my cat Zoe? My mother says, Zoe stays, period, that's it, no nonsense. The cat will find a good home.

Who will give Zoe the good home? Why can't Zoe go to the farm and chase away mice in my grandmother's barn?

"No more questions," my mother says.

My grandmother grabs the spoon. She'll make me eat. She sticks the spoon heaped with oatmeal in my mouth. I swallow. She sticks in another spoonful. I swallow. Another, another, faster and faster. The bowl is empty. The oatmeal rises up and out my lips and splashes into the bowl, onto the newspaper, the table, down my dress front. My grandmother slaps me.

They drag me into the dark bathroom, pull off my dress, my underwear, scrub, then dress me again, from the skin out, in clean clothes. They tell me if I want to do number one or two, I had better goddamn well do them now, there won't be any stopping every ten miles.

My cheek burns and my teeth ache from the hard slap. I am shaky from vomiting.

My grandmother hustles me out the front door to the driveway. The rising sun breaks through clouds and splashes light across bare treetops and our house's green shingles and bare dirt where my father would have put in his Victory garden had my mother not tossed him out.

The tan Packard sits low on its tires. Earlier that morning, my grandmother and mother had packed the back seat and trunk, heaped the roof with boxes and tied them to the car with clothesline. The boxes are covered with tarp.

Wind blows the last leaves off the poplars and maples and elms. I am knee-deep in wet yellow leaves; leaves stick to my bare legs.

My grandmother pushes me into the Packard's back seat, wedges me between boxes stacked with pots and pans that will rattle all day through the long ride. When my grandmother slams the car door, Zoe tries to jump in. My grandmother's blunt foot thuds against Zoe's ribs.

That was the last meal I ate in that house.

Memories come back to you in your mouth. Decades passed before I ate oatmeal again; to this day, when I become sick to my stomach, I am terrified, fear something more awful than vomiting. As an older child, when, for instance, I ran a 102-degree fever with measles and vomited myself empty into the pan my mother left on my bed, that morning unwound itself. I was back at that table, newspaper opened out under the oatmeal bowl. Always when I was—*am*—sick, my body felt—*feels*—more than ache, sore throat, sick stomach; I feel stuffed with sorrow.

That rainy morning I lost the life I was born to. I never trusted anyone again.

Then there is the second breakfast. After my mother divorced my father, I lived with my grandmother on the ramshackle farm Uncle Carl had bought her before he joined the Navy in the Second World War. Uncle Carl was my mother's brother, my grandmother's only son. He said that if anything happened to him in the war, she would have the farm.

Hands on her wide hips, my grandmother stated, proudly, that on her Arkansas farm she had "more land than the eye could take in." How many acres those were, I don't know.

How a woman, then in her sixties, labored sixteen hours a day as she did, I still do not know. She was rarely in the house, and when she was, she was dusting, scrubbing, disinfecting, swatting flies, washing and starching and ironing and then baking all our bread, pies, cakes, canning and pickling and preserving, and then tatting, embroidering, crocheting.

When I talk about my grandmother and her farm, people sometimes ask me how I remember them so clearly, given that I was three and a half when I went there and almost six when I left. I say I was like someone set down in a Bible story where every event seems about to burst into a moral and every breeze is a wind of prophecy. I point out how alone I was, with no children to play with and my mother and father gone. My only human companions were this old woman and her two hired hands.

Her house sat on a rise that sloped toward the gravel county road. Behind the house, outbuildings leaned in varying stages of repair and disrepair. A wood-framed barn held stalls for the Jerseys and Holsteins that my grandmother and the hands, Bushels and Buckles, milked early morning and late afternoon. A ladder led to the hayloft above the stalls. I never once went there. You could break your neck, be, my grandmother said, "crippled for life."

Between the back porch door and the barn was the well house, where the pump pounded and surged, strong and steady as an athlete's heart. The well water tasted as stone would taste if you chewed it.

A concrete-block milk house stood near the barn. In the milk house my grandmother separated milk and poured the milk and cream into stainless-steel jugs for the dairy truck that, daily, picked up filled jugs and left off empties.

To the right of the barn was the henhouse. Next door to the henhouse stood the brooder house, where baby chicks were let out when they arrived, by mail, in boxes. You could hear the chicks peep in the boxes. And next door to the brooder house, inside a wire fence, was a shack where cockerels were fattened for market or for fried chicken dinners.

One thing you learned on the farm was that chickens would not love you. All they wanted was the corn you scattered. If they thought anything about you, it was that you stole their eggs. I don't think they even thought that much.

Spring and summer, when you stretched out on prickly grass, you knew grass didn't care about you either. Grass had a life all its own, trying to go to seed and make more of itself. The grass didn't flinch when the cows left hoofprints. Nothing cared, not the hens, the cows, the mule, the alfalfa. Everything went about its business growing itself; then my grandmother and Bushels and Buckles came along and turned animal or vegetable into food. This hardened your heart.

Behind the barn Bushels and Buckles lived in a windowless bunkhouse. My grandmother had hired the two old men from the county poorhouse. They spit tobacco on the ground near their boots, chewed cigar stubs and orange rat cheese, the latter kept in the bib pockets of their overalls. In winter they layered on underwear; over their underwear and under their overalls they wore plaid flannel shirts with frayed long-john sleeves sticking out below the shirt cuffs. They tucked their overall legs into unfastened rubber galoshes; the galoshes' metal fasteners clacked with each step they took. You could tell where they'd been by the smell they left behind: sweat, urine, manure, soured milk.

My grandmother traded a hog to a housepainter from town who slapped white paint on the house. In exchange for a half dozen laying hens he also calcimined the chicken house. My grandmother said she put one over on him: those hens' laying days were done. When my grandmother put one over on somebody you should have heard her laugh. She threw back her big head and opened wide her big round mouth and clacked together her false teeth and cackled.

My grandmother tacked up a satin Blue Star pennant in the front window. You got one blue star for each son or daughter serving in the armed forces. If your son or daughter died, you took down your blue star and draped a gold star banner over your window and you wore a gold star lapel pin; the dead fighter's mother was now a Gold Star Mother.

When we drove the pickup to town on Saturdays to sell eggs and buy supplies, my grandmother cruised the residential streets. She said she didn't care how much goddamn gas we wasted, she wanted to count gold stars. She wasn't Catholic, but when she saw a gold star, she took a hand off the steering wheel, crossed herself, and said, "There but for the grace of God go I."

Uncle Carl was forty-one when the Japanese bombed Pearl Harbor. He had never married. Given his age and that he was a teacher of organ in a state college, the Navy made him a chaplain's assistant, as they did many apparently homosexual men. Uncle Carl was homosexual, although he hid his homosexuality. He had his mother's stocky German body, a strong chin, large blue eyes, and a flirtatious manner with both men and women. Single women invited him for dinners and to concerts and parties. He accepted their invitations, and then afterward, talking with homosexual male friends, he made fun of the women, their excessive use of cosmetics and perfume, their coy mannerisms. Sometimes he spoke cruelly, mentioning their unpleasant female odors, terrifying ardor, attempts to kiss him, desperation to catch "anything in pants."

The Navy trained Uncle Carl in Norfolk, Virginia, then shipped him to Okinawa along with an armed forces hymnal and a field organ, a three-foot-high console whose keyboard spanned four octaves. You powered the instrument by pumping its two wide pedals, and the organ gave out a surprisingly robust sound. (I know because during the 1960s Uncle Carl bought at a junk store a field organ precisely like the one he'd played on Okinawa.) Uncle Carl's job was to provide music at church services held behind battle lines. "You had to play loud," he said, "and had to be ready at the drop of a hat to pound out 'Onward, Christian Soldiers.' "

"World War Two," he later would say, "was the best vacation I ever had." Then he'd wink lewdly, add, "All that delicious *fresh* seafood, you know." Years later, someone told me that "seafood" was in-crowd gay slang for sailors.

While Uncle Carl was "fighting in the Pacific," as my mother and grandmother put it, the two women, again to use their language, "worried themselves sick." My mother was at the Eastman School of Music in Rochester, New York, getting her master's degree and taking singing lessons, so I don't know what form her worry took. I do know that my grandmother did much vigorous hand-wringing and twisting of apron corners, that her mood rose and fell with the arrival or non-arrival of Uncle Carl's V-mail.

She kept a world map thumbtacked to her bedroom wall. She'd put her fat finger in the blue Pacific and say, "That's where my boy is, out in all that water." Sometimes she would shake her head, say, "That's a goddamn lot of water."

My grandmother was the oldest of six children. All she ever said about her parents was that her father, A. J. Brooks, beat her and that her mother made her "slave" right alongside her, helping raise the children that came after her. My grandmother never said one kind word about her father or mother, nor did I ever hear her mention her brothers and sisters. Not one word.

Like others raised in her era (she was born in the late 1870s) she did not have a sentimental attitude toward children. Days passed when all she called me was "Youngen."

"Youngen," she'd say, "go get the mail."

To get to the mailbox, you walked down a graveled driveway to the gate and took down the gate rails. Hailstones had battered the mailbox, and cattle rubbing against the pole to which the box was bolted had loosened and tipped it.

If three days passed without a letter, I kept my distance. A disagreeable woman at best, my grandmother turned fierce when she worried. For the slightest slip-up—say, breaking an eggshell when gathering eggs—she'd slap you so hard your ears rang. She was short and fat, and when she had hitting you on her mind she moved fast. So I always hoped that when I stood on tiptoe to open the mailbox, she'd have a letter from Uncle Carl, or at least a letter from my mother, of whom, alas, she was not so fond.

I wanted to love my grandmother. I didn't. When I was older and my grandmother had been dead for years, I said to my mother that I had been miserable with my grandmother. My mother looked up from photographs of my children, costumed for a grade-school play, which she had been studying. She turned her face toward me, the heart-shaped face lined and drawn downward but still beautiful. She scooted to the edge of her chair. She inhaled. I could hear the warm air enter her. A small woman, five feet tall, slender and delicately boned, she was wearing an expensive knit dress, the yarn a clear red. She inhaled and her diaphragm enlarged, as singers' diaphragms will. When I was a child, this slow enlargement frightened me. It was like something an animal does before striking.

She spoke in such moments with the careful enunciation she gave to a Puccini aria or a Schubert *Lied*. She grew cautious with dental consonants, fitted them tidily between the easy, open vowels. She said—sang, really—that I should thank my lucky stars my grandmother took me in. She raised her eyebrows and pursed her lips. "Do you think"—she trilled a thrilling crystalline vibrato—"that your father's new wife would have taken you?"

Evenings after my grandmother and Bushels and Buckles herded cows into their stalls, milked them, strained and separated the milk, filled the cows' boxes with feed and hay, got the chickens gathered in, and hasped the henhouse door against skunks and coons, my grandmother turned on the big cathedral Philco, settled deep into her plush easy chair, turned her hearing aid up high as it would go, and grabbed her mending or fancywork. She'd say, "Shut up. I want to hear what they say."

"They" were Edward R. Murrow, Eric Sevareid, Lowell Thomas, Gabriel Heatter, Richard Hottelet, Walter Winchell. Even young children recognized the voices. We might not know what a world war was, and I didn't, but we knew that the news these sonorous voices carried into our living rooms was about whether Japs or Nazis were going to stick bayonets through you. We listened and watched the grownup faces; their frowns or smiles or tears told you if news was good or bad.

Roosevelt's picture hung on my grandmother's bedroom wall. The hand-tinted photograph had that odd pastel haze you see over pictures of saints. Tucked into a corner was a smaller photo torn from a newspaper: Winston Churchill, flashing the V-for-Victory sign. You read now in history books that Roosevelt was the first President to broadcast regularly over the radio, giving what he called "fireside chats." All over America people sat in their living rooms with their radios tuned and waited for his "Good evening, my friends."

Nights when President Roosevelt gave his chats, my grandmother took down the map and draped it over her knees. "This way," she said, "I can follow along with what President Roosevelt says." She pronounced his name "Ruesevelt." She worshipped him. "Now there's a man," my grandmother said, "who loved his mother." Which was how you knew she was going to tell you the story of Roosevelt's life.

That his father was rich, older than his beautiful mother, that they lived in a mansion high on a hill above the Hudson River in New York in a town called Hyde Park. He was the only child, because little Mother Roosevelt, the doctor said, was too delicate to have more children, she was small in the pelvis. When young Franklin was eight his father had a heart attack and lived for the next ten years as an invalid. Franklin was good as gold, my grandmother said, not wanting to do anything to set off his father's heart or worry his mother. When Father Roosevelt died, Franklin was going to Harvard College, and after the funeral Mother Roosevelt was so lonely she moved to Boston to be near Franklin.

After Franklin graduated, when he was twenty-one, he told his mother he was going to marry his fifth cousin, President Teddy Roosevelt's niece, the homely orphan Eleanor, and it about broke Mother Roosevelt's heart. But he married Eleanor anyway, and that marriage, my grandmother said, was about the biggest mistake in the President's life, except for when he went swimming on a cold day and let himself take a chill that left him open to come down with infantile paralysis.

According to my grandmother, some people claimed that Mother Roosevelt was an "interferer," because she always stayed "right close" to the President, even after he married. "He could have told her to mind her own business," my grandmother said, "if he'd felt like it. But he didn't." My grandmother believed that since Eleanor Roosevelt was such a bad housekeeper and hostess and careless mother, Mother Roosevelt had no choice but to keep close to her son to help raise the six children.

My grandmother didn't have one good word for Eleanor. Mrs. Roosevelt wrote a column—"My Day"—that ran in newspapers across the country. When my grandmother read this column she'd say that "Mrs. My Day" gadded around too much, that she ought to stay home in the White House, look after her children, who got married and divorced faster than you could keep track of. She said the President should make his wife keep her big flapping mouth shut. She thought Mrs. Roosevelt "ugly as sin, what with those big horsy teeth jutting out." She criticized her clothing as "Dutchy-looking," which meant "unstylish" and "country." She laughed at her hats.

But the worst thing about Mrs. Roosevelt, according to my grandmother, was that she encouraged "race-mixing." She brought "colored" into the White House and entertained them "right there in front of God and everybody." She was always trying to get the President to "do for the colored." After the war, my grandmother believed, thanks to Mrs. My Day and her "do-gooder" friends, the "colored" would no longer "know their place." She said that while she knew "good colored people" and "clean colored people," colored did not belong with white.

My grandmother said that the one thing Mother Roosevelt had done that *was* wrong was that after the polio crippled up her son, she had begged him to retire. He refused. He'd already been a big man in government in Washington, D.C., with President Wilson, as Assistant Secretary of the Navy, "and a big man," my grandmother said, "can never go back to being a nobody." He fought the polio and got back some use of his legs, she believed, and became governor of New York. Then when the Depression got bad as it could get and the Bolshies were about to start a revolution, he ran for President against that goddamn cheapskate Hoover.

My grandmother saw FDR as personally responsible for the enactment of Social Security, and when she rummaged through her pocketbook for Tums she sometimes slid her Social Security card from her wallet. "This," she said, "will help keep me from the poor farm in my old age." She'd talk about how although FDR was "rich in his own right," he cared about the little man, the "forgotten man," workers and farmers. She'd say that when he became President hardly a house out in the country had electricity, and now almost every farmer had electric lights. "Me?" she'd say, "I'd follow F.D.R. through fire in my bare feet."

My grandmother liked to tell about when Mother Roosevelt died, a few months before the Japanese attacked Pearl Harbor. Even though the President's mother was almost eighty-seven, she was pretty as a picture. "She blued her hair," my grandmother said, patting her own white hair, which she rinsed with laundry bluing, "the same as I do mine. That way it doesn't turn all yellow." The President knew his mother was sinking and got on the train to Hyde Park and was holding her hand when she passed away. After she died, my grandmother said, he didn't come back to the White House for a long time. He just shut himself up there in Hyde Park. He got out the box Mother Roosevelt had kept with his baby shoes all bronzed up and his toys and some of his hair from the first time the barber cut it, and he held on to that box and cried his heart out.

When I was older and had young children of my own and wanted to understand my family, I read everything I could find in the library about Roosevelt. He seemed as much a part of the people I came from as my grandmother or Uncle Carl or Mother or Father.

When Roosevelt became President he couldn't walk. Heavy braces held his useless legs stiff. But he made it appear as if he could walk. If you look, now, at photographs of Roosevelt, you can see the tricks he used. He always had someone holding on to either side of him, and he'd grip their arms and they'd propel him forward. No one talked much about Roosevelt being crippled, but they must have known.

My grandmother, like most Americans during the Second World War, hated the Japanese. (So you won't think she was unusual in this, here's something Ernie Pyle wrote that appeared in papers all across America. ("In Europe we felt that our enemies were still people. But out here in Japan I soon gathered that Japanese were looked upon as something subhuman and repulsive. I watched Japanese POWs laughing and talking just like normal human beings. They gave me the creeps, and I wanted to take a mental bath after looking at them.") When American pilots dropped ton after ton of incendiary bombs on Tokyo and Osaka, my grandmother beat on her knees with her fists and cheered. "They're setting those Japs on fire," she said. She beat her knees so hard that her fancywork fell to the carpet. But when news from the Pacific theater indicated that Japanese torpedoes had blown up a U.S. ship or that kamikazes had dive-bombed a U.S. patrol boat, my grandmother went to bed weeping. Wearing the nightgown she'd sewn from pink outing flannel, she sat at the edge of her bed, took out her teeth, and dropped them into the glass of water on her bedside table, pulled out her hearing-aid amplifier from the yellowed nook between her breasts and the hearing-aid button from her ear and tucked the contraption under her pillow. She sloughed off her slippers. Those nights her sobs rose and fell, throbbing through our bedrooms' thin walls. She moaned the long, low moans that cows, enduring a difficult birth, moaned. I felt helpless to comfort her and I was.

By 1944, F.D.R. had been President for eleven years. My grandmother studied his photograph in newspapers, in *Life* magazine and *The Saturday Evening Post*. She shook her head, said, "Look at those bags under the poor man's eyes. We've done worn him out." Running for reelection to his fourth term Roosevelt dumped his old Vice President, Henry Wallace, and ran with a senator from Missouri, Harry Truman. His Republican opponent was New York governor Thomas E. Dewey, "a horse's ass," my grandmother seethed, "with a silly mustache." No way would Dewey win, she told Bushels and Buckles. He didn't.

My grandmother hated Harry Truman and looked down on him as a failed farmer, which he was. My grandmother said we should pray that Roosevelt wouldn't die in office and leave us with Harry. Of course, he did. The day in April when news came of Roosevelt's death, my grandmother took to her bed. She didn't cook dinner, didn't milk the cows, didn't gather eggs. Next morning, when she walked into the kitchen, her eyes were swollen from crying.

Pretty soon, my grandmother cheered up, because the war was winding down. "My boy," she'd say, "will soon be home."

Lord, how she loved the A-bomb. The day that the *Enola Gay* dropped the bomb on Hiroshima, my grandmother cheered. She loved the thought that all those Japs were finally getting theirs, she said. She clacked her big false teeth and cackled. "Old Tojo," she said, "I bet his old yellow feet are feeling the heat."

Harry became her hero. We heard no more talk about Harry's inability to farm. Harry became the man who "saved the lives of our American boys." Bess Truman, once castigated as a "bridge-club priss ass" and "plain as Irish potato," became "the good woman behind a good man."

After V-J Day, Uncle Carl was due to be demobilized. In his letters he wrote that he couldn't say when he'd actually get out. "I'll surprise you," he wrote. By then potatoes had been dug and taken down to the storm cellar in gunnysacks. The tight cabbage heads, outer leaves wrapped tightly around the head, veins sticking out, were also down in the storm cellar, with turnips, purple at the shoulder and ivory below, and beets and carrots. The canning was done. Baby chicks, arrived that spring in boxes, were pullets who filled nest boxes with eggs. When you got up in the morning and looked out the window, you saw frost on roofs and pasture.

About four one morning I woke up. I was sleeping under heaped quilts. A dream woke me, I thought, or my grandmother, who called out in her sleep to people whose names I didn't know. My room was dark. I got out of bed and looked out my window, pulling aside the curtain. The sun hadn't come up. The red-combed roosters weren't yet crowing and scratching the dirt with their yellow feet.

I heard a knock at the front door and, a moment later, more knocks against the dining- and living-room windows. A voice I didn't recognize called, "Mother, Mother." I didn't think to go shake my grandmother awake. I thought only of the voice crying, "Mother, Mother," for it sounded like the voice of someone in trouble.

I ran through the house to the front door. The top half of the door was inset with murky glass. I looked through the glass and saw a man with a white sailor's cap tilted to one side of his head. I stood on my toes and snapped on the porch light. "Open the door," the man said, "it's your Uncle Carl."

He didn't look like the face that came to mind when I thought Uncle Carl. Years later, studying photographs of him taken before he joined the Navy and at photographs taken the afternoon of the day he arrived at the farm, I see that Navy life had thinned him down, left him appearing younger than his forty-five years. In the later pictures he looks boyish, hoydenish, and his blue eyes look larger, more open.

I threw the bolt and opened the door. Surely he hugged me, but I don't remember. I do remember that he had a huge seabag slung over each shoulder and that once inside the door he hoisted the bags off his shoulders onto the floor. The bags were filled with seashells from the Pacific.

I told him Grammy didn't hear him knocking because she took out her hearing aid at night. He whispered, "We want to wake up Mother carefully, so the shock doesn't give her a stroke or a heart attack." Both my mother and Uncle Carl worried that their mother would have a heart attack or stroke, because her blood pressure was high.

I don't remember how we woke her up. I do remember she grabbed Uncle Carl around the waist and held on so tight he screamed, "You're going to cut me in two, Mother." Her head didn't come up much farther than his stomach. She cried until the front of her nightie was spotted with tears.

Uncle Carl wanted breakfast. He said that while he was on ships out in the Pacific and on Okinawa, he went to sleep nights thinking about her breakfasts. "The biscuits, Mother, the fried eggs, the sausage, your strawberry preserves. Oh my God!" He rolled his blue eyes and told us that in the Navy they fed them powdered eggs and powdered milk and bacon from cans.

The enormous kitchen, painted bright yellow, had windows looking out to the west and south. Along the west wall was the deep sink from whose faucets poured the medicinal well water. My grandmother was so short she stood on a box to get to the sink, and she often stood there, her fat hard belly damp from dishwater, and gazed out onto her pasture. A four-burner, two-oven gas range was backed against the north wall. The kitchen table and the four chairs around it took up all the space in a windowed nook that afforded a view into the vegetable garden and, beyond the garden, to the barn and henhouse.

I know that table well, because after my grandmother died my mother had it and the chairs that went with it shipped Railway Express to our house. She stripped off the paint, and evenings, wearing a mask, because sawdust was bad for her voice, she sanded the oak smooth. When a guest praised the table, my mother ran her pretty hand over the surface. Tears rose in her eyes. She said, "It was my mother's table."

I would remember my grandmother's ugly face. On her death-bed she told my mother she had never loved her as much as she did Uncle Carl. My mother walked into the hospital corridor and sobbed. Uncle Carl patted her shoulder, he said, "She's out of her mind, she doesn't know what she's saying." I always thought she knew precisely what she was saying and enjoyed the hurt her words caused.

In a pantry off the kitchen that was almost as big as the kitchen, shelves ranked from floor to ceiling around all four walls. My grandmother stored her canning there, canning equipment, extra pots and pans, a fruit jar filled with pencils, mops and brooms, perhaps as many as fifty one-pound cans of Folger's coffee, sacks of sugar and flour and cornmeal, the Sears, Roebuck and Montgomery Ward catalogues.

Next to the stove—my grandmother called it "the range"—was the refrigerator, which my grandmother referred to as the "icebox." Mornings, she kept her percolator coffeepot on the range. She liked coffee burned black, and years later, when she was dying of stomach cancer, my uncle and mother whispered that the burned coffee hadn't helped her any.

You don't see stove-top percolators much anymore. Straight-sided pots, fitted out with baskets at the top into which coffee grounds are ladled and tubes running from the hole in the middle of the basket to the bottom of the pot. You put the water in the pot, set in the basket with its tube, and put on the lid, which had a hollow glass knob in its center. You put the pot on the stove with the flame on high. Once the water began to boil, the hot water rose up through the tube and then down through the coffee grounds that sat in the basket, thus extracting their essence. When this process began, one said that the coffee had begun "to perk." You could see the water jet up into the glass knob on the lid. At this point, you turned the flame low beneath the pot. As the water recirculated, the water you saw through the glass darkened and the circulation increased in speed. The sound was *chug, chug, chug*.

The morning Uncle Carl came back from the war, my grandmother blew her nose and put on the percolator and stuck a match in the oven and lit it. She tied her apron on over her nightgown. She got out flour, baking powder, salt, and buttermilk. She poured flour, salt, baking powder, without measuring, into the mixing bowl. She scooped out lard from the lard bucket with a table-spoon. She picked up the red-handled pastry mixer, the same one she used to make pie crust, and cut the white lard into the flour, until the mixture turned to pea-size balls. Uncle Carl pulled a chair out from the kitchen table and sat down. My grandmother's broad fat back, apron bow tied and flopping above her monstrous, massive buttocks, faced him. Over and over, she'd stop in the middle of blending the dough, turn, and say, "Oh, son, let me get another look at you." She stood, flour on her hands, and smiled.

I sat on the cold floor at Uncle Carl's feet and stroked his dusty black boots. I wanted him to open his seabags and show the sea-shells. I knew better than to ask.

Sun was coming up. A dirty brindle dog trailing behind them, Bushels and Buckles came up from the bunkhouse into the kitchen as they did every morning. They brought their doggy sour-washcloth urinous odors with them.

She fed Bushels and Buckles every morning, my grandmother did, and that morning, too, they would have wanted coffee, their ham or sausage or bacon, eggs and pancakes and biscuits, gravy if she had some left from dinner the night before, slices of the day before's pie. Normally she sat with them while they ate and sipped at her ever-blackening coffee. They talked about which cows were "fresh," which heifers were ready for breeding, a hog who seemed off his feed, a motor that needed oiling, an off-taste in the mor-ning's milk, that sort of thing. They talked, too, about the war.

But not this morning. "My son's here," she told them. Uncle Carl stood, shook the old men's hands. Surely they congratulated him on his safe return, and he no doubt thanked them for being a help to his mother.

I remember that while the three men talked my grandmother

slapped together sandwiches made from old biscuits and thick
slices of bologna. She told them to take their food and coffee on
out to the barn and get started milking.

She had sharpened her favorite butcher knife so many times
that its blade had narrowed to a thin steel sliver. That morning
I'm sure she used that knife as she cut thick slices of bacon off a
smoked rasher from hogs she'd butchered. The rasher's exterior,
rubbed with salt and sugar and spices and smoked with hickory in
the smokehouse, had taken on the burnish of oiled mahogany furniture. She held up a bacon slice for Uncle Carl to see. She told
him about the hog from whose side the slice had been cut. I don't
remember the hog's name, but unlike most farmers my grandmother named her hogs, and out in the hog pen she addressed
them by name—Ben, Abner, Robert E. Lee, Stimson, Pappy,
Daisy Mae are names I recall. (Years later, when I told my father
some of these names, he said that at least two were names of my
grandmother's boyfriends.) She told Uncle Carl about butchering
day, how she and Bushels and Buckles did all the sticking and
bleeding and sawing apart of the bones themselves, that she
worked right along with them like a man. I remember that she
sidled over to the table and bulged up her bicep and asked him
to feel it. She would have said, as she often did, "Feel that, hard
as a rock, huh? Hard as a goddamn rock."

While she cooked that morning, she cried. "For joy," she said,
"for pure-out joy." She reached out so many times to touch her
son that the shoulders of his navy-blue uniform were dusted with
flour and imprinted with floury handprints.

She set the bacon slices to cooking in the high-sided iron skillet.
She sent me to the pantry for red Winesaps that she cored and
cut in rounds. She arranged the apple rings in a skillet whose
surface burbled with freshly churned butter. She browned the
apples and, using tongs, turned them carefully, then tossed hand-

fuls of brown sugar over them and set a lid atop the skillet, so the sugar would caramelize over the tart Winesap slices. The bacon fried, its fat sizzling. After the bacon had cooked the way Uncle Carl liked it—not quite crisp, with the lean still soft—she broke open brown eggs on the edge of the iron skillet. "Come here, son," she might have said, as she often did, "and look how high these here yolks set up." Then she may well have told him which of her hens were the most prodigious layers and how many eggs they laid in a good month.

The biscuit, by then, would have put out its heated high-summer wheat-field, floury aroma into the kitchen. The bacon's salty haze drifted across the kitchen like weather. And the apple rings' caramel sweetness bore down on us like July sunshine. My grandmother stood next to Uncle Carl. Her blued hair stuck out in oily strands off her big head. She placed her hands on her wide hips and she smiled. She'd forgotten to put in her teeth. Her lips encircled the emptiness. Her pink tongue emerged over glistening gums. Tears streamed down her fat face. She said, "Well, as far as I'm concerned, my war's over. My boy's home." She must have been happy many times after that, but never again would *I* see her as happy as she was that day.

SAUERKRAUT AND A
PIG STICKING

❦

A LITTLE POT OF A WOMAN, NO TALLER THAN FOUR FEET, TEN
inches, and big around at the belly as a bushel basket, my maternal
grandmother hadn't always been such a tub. Carl, her only son,
kept photos of her in a Florsheim shoebox, which in the 1940s
had housed the tan-and-white spectator oxfords he wore "for
good" in summer. These photographs show a petite, sparrowish
creature, pitch-black hair marceled into precise creases, and eyebrows plucked and penciled into a high, half-moon arch. In those
old snapshots, she wore dark dresses held together at the bosom
with a twinkly brooch and, on her tiny feet, size 4 high-heeled
shoes. From the time I remember my grandmother, her face
looked enough like George Washington's that she could have been
his sister, and her features seemed hacked from wood by a sculptor whose specialty was cigar-store Indians. She had become so
round that her tiny feet seemed freakish. They made me think of
how overly small the hooves looked on fattened sheep and hogs,
too small to hold up their waddling bulk.

My father, who knew my grandmother in her late forties, during
the Great Depression, said she hadn't been unattractive back then,

but added that she was every bit as foul-tempered as she was in her sixties and seventies. "Why, when she'd call up Carl and tell him she was coming to town"—my father laughed—"your poor old uncle would be vibrating with terror."

Part of why my Uncle Carl, my mother's brother, was always so worried when his mother visited was that he was gay, although they didn't call it "gay" then. "Invert," "pansy," "sister-boy," "pervert," "auntie," "nellie," "fruit," "queer," and "queen" were some of the words. So when Uncle Carl's mother showed up at Carl's house in Oklahoma from California or Alaska or Wyoming— where, according to my father, she'd been off doing "God knows what with God knows whom, because she was a woman of loose, loose morals"—her presence put a damper on Uncle Carl's social life.

"When your grandmother was on the premises," my father said, his eyes narrowing evilly, "there was no running around that cozy little brown shingle bungalow of his, him wearing white flannel trousers tailored to show off his basket to advantage and calling himself Carlotta and arraying himself on his piano bench, sipping sidecars and tinkling away at Cole Porter tunes for the college boys that he and his friend Dan lured over there." Uncle Carl taught organ and theory and counterpoint at a college in Oklahoma. My father would usually add some variant of this: "And I ought to know, he moved in just down the street from us when I was in junior high. We saw it all. The entire neighborhood had some idea what went on over there. My grandmother warned me to stay away from him and his kind."

My mother's story was different. She said my father always hated her mother and brother, always talked of them with amusement and condescension, which was part of the reason she was happy to divorce him. Carl, she'd say bitterly, was not worried one whit about his mother knowing he was homosexual. "Our mother, unlike your father, was extremely broad-minded, very 'live-and-let-live.' She did know. What your uncle was worried about was that while she was there, he gained weight. Your grandmother was such a good cook and Carl and his friends loved so to eat. She'd get in his kitchen, tie on an apron, and night after night, there'd be hot buttermilk biscuit, fried chicken, okra, succotash, pork shoulder and fried apples and fried yam cakes, chicken-fried steak and cream gravy. There'd be peach cobbler and blackberry pie and fudge cake with inches of your grandmother's delicious frosting between the layers. If it was summer, she'd put up pickles and preserves. She'd make up quarts of the piccalilli Carl likes. And because your uncle loves sauerkraut, like as not she'd put him up a big crock of kraut, which he'd dip out of all winter. He'd cook up a batch of blood sausage and then simmer the sausage in your grandmother's sauerkraut, or he'd just eat it in a bowl, cold. Anyway, by the time Mother packed to go on her way, Carl and everyone he knew would be bursting out of his trousers and ready to go back to their Gayelord Hauser wonder-foods diet—vegetable broth, blackstrap molasses, brewer's yeast, skimmed milk, wheat germ, and yogurt."

Gayelord Hauser, Uncle Carl was wont to tell anyone who would listen, was the wizard whose diet kept Greta Garbo and the Duchess of Windsor so gorgeous. Uncle Carl swore by Hauser's *Diet Digest*, and when he was feeling "fattish," he kept himself for several weeks on the Hauser vegetable broth, the odors of which, stewing in his kitchen, were noxious.

My father laughed when I repeated to him my mother's assessment of her mother's knowledge of and attitude toward Uncle Carl's sexual preference. "She might well have preferred he had boyfriends to a wife," he added. "No wife would have tolerated that old doll around the house. God knows, I didn't. Besides, if your uncle had married, then your grandmother wouldn't have been able to soak him for so much dough." My father's grandfather owned the bank where Uncle Carl kept his money, and my father claimed that over the years he saw the checks my uncle wrote. "He'd pay a month's salary," my father claimed, "to get her out of his house and back on the road."

After my mother divorced my father, she sent me to live with my grandmother on the ramshackle farm Uncle Carl bought her before he joined the Navy. I stayed there two years, until I was ready to start first grade.

With help from her two hired hands, Bushels and Buckles, my grandmother grew a two-acre vegetable garden. Bushels and Buckles cultivated the rocky soil with a mule. The mule reluctantly pulled the rusted plow, whose parts were held together by baling wire. One hired hand steered while the other went along behind, holding the plow. The mule didn't have a name. "Mule," they called him, or "Jackass," and while they kicked and beat him, they yelled some of the first filthy language I ever heard. That mule led an awful life. Scars ran along his ribs where his former and present owners had whipped him. He hated humans. When you started toward him, he lifted his hairy upper lip and hissed and brayed, swished his tail and pawed the dirt.

My grandmother grew on her two acres: Country Gentleman sweet corn, collards, early and late English peas, Kentucky Wonder green pole beans, Fordhook limas, slicing and pickling cucumbers, dill, green puller and red Bermuda and yellow storage onions, green cabbages and purple cabbages whose outer leaves turned blue under morning dew, carrots, purple-shouldered ivory turnips, Mortgage Lifter tomatoes, bell peppers, beets, potatoes, okra, yellow crookneck squash, muskmelon, Charleston Gray watermelon, pumpkin, and Hubbard squash so heavy I couldn't carry even one and whose spiny, prickly green vines wound with a will of their own, as a snake will, in among rows of onions and turnips and beets. The vines were thick as my wrist and the tendrils that clasped tight around onion tops and cornstalks seemed likely any minute to wind their way around me. They would lace me in a tight bodice that squeezed out my breath. I would turn blue as the huge red cabbage heads turned after rain, and my eyes would pop, and I would be too breathless to scream.

Bushels and Buckles and I hauled cucumbers in zinc milking buckets into the kitchen to my grandmother. We carried peppers, onions, and cabbages. We heaped them onto sideboards and into the deep sink. On the stove, its burners' blue flames turned high, vinegar and cloves and mustard and celery seeds seethed in my grandmother's dented canning kettles. Every wind, those mornings, carried the sharp tinge of vinegar with it. My grandmother took her butcher knife, a knife probably larger in memory than in fact, and chopped the hard green tomatoes, green cabbage, bell peppers into smithereens for the piccalilli relish that Uncle Carl liked to eat with meat loaf and chuck roast and Polish sausage. She lobbed the four-pound cabbages up onto her chopping block. She pulled off the outer leaves, each leaf wide as an opened fan. The leaves had been chewed by cabbage moths. This undressing exposed the cabbage's inner leaves, smooth as a man's newly shaved cheek. Grunting with each whack, my little grandmother went after the heads with her butcher knife, attacking as an angry peasant would attack the head of a despotic king.

When she had the cabbage shredded, she tossed it into her stoneware kraut crocks and mixed the raw cabbage with salt. She kept adding cabbage and salt until the crock was full. With each addition, she'd tamp down the cabbage so that it would be packed tightly into the crocks. When she'd chopped up every head and filled every crock, she'd call for one of the hired hands to shift the crocks into the dark pantry next to the kitchen. That done, she shrouded each crock with clean white cheesecloth, and then, on top of the cheesecloth, she set dinner plates. In warm weather, the cabbage would start to "work" in a few days, ambient bacteria producing lactic acid that brought a vile scum to the top. The kitchen and dining room would take on the sour, treacherous odor of fermenting cabbage, treacherous because that odor veers so near the odors that precede death.

Egyptians, my grandmother told me, lived on kraut while they carried the bricks that built the Great Pyramids. Not until I was an adult did I learn that it was the Chinese, while building the Great Wall, who lived on kraut. Whenever I saw photographs of pyramids or camels at the zoo, Elizabeth Taylor as Cleopatra, or Nasser or Anwar Sadat on television declaring war or signing treaties, what came to mind was the briny harsh rotting odor of cabbage fermenting into kraut.

As summer turned to fall, my grandmother kept careful watch over the last of the bell peppers. Nights when temperatures threatened to go down into the low forties and high thirties, Bushels and Buckles would be sent to cover the pepper plants with sheets, and as soon as the sun came up in the morning, they'd uncover the plants. By the time my grandmother's cabbage had turned to kraut, and all through the kitchen the principal odor was that of fermented cabbage, the green and red bell peppers would be big enough to stuff. She would gather together several dozen peppers and cut off their tops, pull out the seeds and the pithy white linings to which the seeds cling. She'd parboil the peppers, put them out on cookie sheets to cool. Once the peppers cooled, she'd stuff each shell with a handful of the cured kraut. She'd have ready the hot, sterilized quart canning jars; on two burners water in the two canning kettles bubbled, and in a third kettle a pickling brine simmered. Into each jar she'd place one red pepper and two green, or two red and one green, pour in a soup ladle of pickling brine, pop a lid on the filled jar, and then screw on the metal ring.

When all that was done and the jars wiped clean, she processed the jars in the canning kettles, seven jars to each kettle.

Anyone looking at the jars of green and red peppers cooling on kitchen counters couldn't but think, How pretty! Cooking turned the red peppers' skins to dark ruby and the green to a severe dark olive. The kraut rose in a mound atop each ruby and green pepper and then dangled down the peppers' ribbed sides in ivory strands. When you jostled one of the jars, the kraut strands drifted in the briny pale ocher suspension like the long hair of underwater swimmers.

My grandmother and Bushels and Buckles waited for what they called a "good hog-sticking day" to butcher the Chester Whites and black-and-white Poland Chinas. Such a day would fall after the first hard frost. You wanted cold weather so that the meat wouldn't spoil; you wanted the flies dead, and a good hard frost killed flies.

The trio, dressed in their oldest clothes, killed and butchered two hogs at a time, probably because that was all they could handle in one day, what with farm chores that couldn't wait—feeding stock and poultry, milking cows, separating milk, raking out the henhouse, gathering eggs.

Bushels and Buckles took a rope and walked down to the muddy pig wallow and noosed one of the two chosen hogs and marched it toward a huge tree between the barn and the house. A rope hung off a branch that grew eight or ten feet off the ground. What kind of tree it was I don't know, but it was a tree tall enough and so generously branched that when in full leaf it cast a wide circumference of shadow beneath it, enough shade to keep grass from growing and to make the bare dirt cool even on hot days.

You couldn't help feeling sorry for the hog, grunting and heaving, as the hired hands, sooty hat brims pulled low over their foreheads so you couldn't see their eyes, prodded and harried it uphill on its short stumpy legs and cloven hooves. Brought to a halt beneath the tree, the hog blinked, batted its long hog eyelashes, and seemed to smile the way hogs do, waiting perhaps to have its ears scratched or to be offered some treat. It might root then with its hoelike snout, snorting up melting hoarfrost.

Bushels or Buckles, I don't remember which, drew his finger across his neck, in imitation of a knife cutting a throat, and made a horrible whickering noise. My grandmother and Bushels and Buckles looked at the smiling hog and laughed, and then my grandmother looked at me and shushed the hands, and said they'd need to get busy.

Bushels and Buckles looped and then tied the rope that swung from the branch around the hog's hind legs and pulled until the three- or four-hundred-pound animal dangled upside down. The limb gave off an awful groan while the men pulled, staggering from the effort. Surprised to find itself upended and no doubt terrified, the hog squeaked and squealed. The high-pitched squeals ascended, between branches, into the blue sky.

Bushels or Buckles thrust a long knife into the hog's throat, cutting, I think now, the jugular vein. The hog gasped. Dark blood poured out, gushed really, onto the dirt and fallen leaves. The muddy trotters twitched for a few seconds, the hog's head drooped and its eyes closed, long lashes fluttering. My grandmother would say, "He gave up the ghost."

Did the mule, hens, roosters, Jerseys and Guernseys, the other Poland Chinas and Chester Whites observe a moment of silence? No. But I remember the scene that way, remember that the normally noisy farm, its animal Muzak always playing, for a moment went silent. I remember every cluck and whinny and moo and oink erased. Not even the dog, shut up in the house while they stuck the hog, barked.

After both hogs were stuck and bled, clots and rivulets of blood soaked my grandmother's and Bushels's and Buckles's clothes. My grandmother's strong arms dripped hog blood from the elbows down onto her hands.

The hogs were cut down and dragged across the ground, their black blood leaving trails on the hard dirt, and put to soak in an old footed bathtub filled with steaming water. Pigs are blanketed with coarse hair, and the hot water helped loosen the skin's hold on the hair. My grandmother used her butcher knife to scrape bristles off the ears and more delicate hairs from lips and snouts. She brought her sharpening stone in her pocket; she honed and rehoned her blade. While my grandmother worked on the head, the hired hands shaved the hog's body until the skin was naked and smooth.

With help from one of the hired hands, my grandmother sawed off each of the four feet. The three of them swore while they worked, and sweated, even in the cold air. With her knife, she sliced away the cartilaginous ears, the lips, and the snout. These she saved for pickling.

What did my grandmother do with the hooves? How did she get the hogs' toenails off? I read now that butchers prise them out with pliers. I don't remember what she did. I do remember that in the kitchen she dropped the hooves, ears, and snouts into pots of boiling water set on the kitchen stove. I remember that while the hooves boiled, they bumped against the kettle.

Late afternoon, hawks—or were they vultures?—wheeled and drifted down to the ground beneath the tree where the last of the summer's flies glutted themselves on hog blood. The birds called to their fellows, their calls in a tenor range and more human than birdlike. They grabbed up bits of the Poland China's black-and-white skin; they flocked around the bathtub, filled then with pink water atop which skin and scum and bristle floated as water lilies float. The birds perched on the tub's edge and dipped down their heads and drank and fed. After the hawks or vultures left, black crows flew in over the downed cornstalks and pecked and cawed. Then they, too, flew away.

Hog-sticking nights, while I got ready for bed, my grandmother and Bushels and Buckles, blood dried on their clothing, worked under the kitchen's dim overhead light. Bugs seethed, circling the bulb. Even with the windows and the back door open, the last flies and moths of the season hitting lazily against the screens, the heat was terrible near the stove. The heat was summer-noon heat. Steam rose from kettles set atop every burner. The heat reddened my grandmother's and the hired hands' faces; sweat streamed from their foreheads, dripped off their chins.

The kitchen resembled a butcher shop where a crazy drunken butcher was in charge. Disassembled hog crowded every surface. Hoofless legs and snoutless, earless heads and slabs of fatback and squares of what would be smoked into bacon were puzzle pieces. I reassembled the hogs in my mind back down through the hours to morning, when they seemed to smile under the tree.

The trio worked quickly, to keep the meat from going bad. They ate hurriedly while they worked, cold biscuit in one hand, and nearby, for the men, a brown bottle of bootleg whiskey they called "medicine," which they sipped from. Bushels, who had a finger missing on one hand, massaged rough salt into hind and front thighs and chops for hams and smoked pork chops. Buckles chewed a dead cigar stub stuck in one corner of his mouth and pressed gobbets of pink flesh through the meat grinder. The meat dropped into bowls and milk buckets; every big bowl my grandmother owned was heaped with ground hog. It was for sausage, a mixture she seasoned with sage and hot red pepper, then rolled into balls and canned.

I don't remember what my dreams were, those nights. I had nightmares back then from which I'd wake, screaming, in the high four-poster bed, from which I always feared I'd fall.

I remember that the next morning when I walked into the

kitchen, they would still be working, their bloody clothes hanging looser and stinking from sweat, Bushels and Buckles still wearing their grubby hats. Because all three would be wearing the clothing they'd started out in the day before, because over twenty-four hours stains had spotted their hands and clothing one atop another like stucco, the world seemed to have stood still while the two hogs turned to meat.

From the door into the kitchen I watched them. They drank coffee and ate with their hands from a plate of cold biscuit and sausage and fried cracklin's. They spoke quietly and coughed dry coughs. They did not look each other steadily in the eye. If Bushels, for instance, happened to catch my grandmother's eye, he looked away quickly, looked down toward his filthy overalls. They moved slowly, as if under a spell. I felt newly afraid of all three of them. They seemed like people from a story who together had done some terrible deed and were waiting, fearful, for a knock at the door. But that probably is not how it was for them. Most likely they were tired; "bone weary," as my grandmother said. They were old, too, the men in their fifties and my grandmother sixty-something and, although she did not know it, only six or seven years away from death.

Glass jars packed with sausage balls and pigs' feet, pigs' ears, snouts, and lips lined the counters. More glass jars stood on newspapers laid out on the linoleum. My grandmother pointed to the plate of cold biscuit stuffed with sausage, told me to get myself dressed and then come back and take myself some food and eat it on the dining-room table. "Spread out a newspaper on that table so you don't get my good cloth greasy," she'd say. So that's what I did.

She'd sleep all that morning and afternoon, my grandmother would, while the jars cooled. I listened to her snores, her long stertorous sighs, and to the pings of the cooling jars. I made myself lunch from the breakfast scraps. What else I did, I don't know. I must have played with my dolls, undressed and redressed them, must have gone outside and walked in between the white Leghorn hens that ran loose between house and barn. I may have tossed pebbles at them to make them fly up and scatter, something I did when I believed no one was watching. I may have played with the farm dog, a brindled male mutt who regularly ran after the Leghorns with his penis hanging out of its sheath. I didn't much like him. He didn't care anything for humans, and if he had a name I can't remember it.

Finally, my grandmother got up and put on a clean housedress and her rubber boots and went out to check her cows. She cooked dinner, a pan of the hogs' ribs she'd baked in the night and sauerkraut scooped out of the crock and boiled potatoes. I remember the kraut's sourness mixed with the earth taste of the potatoes. I remember the ribs' seared fat and the charred rib bone sticking out of either end of stringy meat, and I suspect I refused to eat the ribs.

After dinner, my grandmother liked to stand with her hands on her big hips and admire her finished work. "I take a lot of pains with these," she said about her pickled pigs' feet or her kraut-stuffed peppers. She took my hand in hers and maneuvered me around until we stood in front of the two half-gallon jars in which she'd placed the pigs' snouts, lips, ears, and feet. She'd put one set of lips, one snout, one set of ears, and two feet in each half-gallon. The feet were at the bottom of the jar, then the lips, then the snout, and then, at the top, the ears. Peppercorns and whole barbed cloves and bay leaves and dried red peppers drifted through the pickling liquid. The lips, still smiling, and the snouts, the nostrils, round and open, pressed against the glass. "Now, didn't I make those look lifelike?" she asked, pointing with her blunt finger at the ears, which stood straight up above the snout. She glanced from the jars to me, waiting for compliments.

My mother said that my grandmother "had an artistic eye."

She'd add, "If she'd had advantages, opportunities, she might have been a painter."

Winters, when the fields lay fallow under snow, my grandmother sat after lunch at the kitchen table and painted what she called "scenes from nature" on china dinner plates. She ordered the plates and paint and brushes from a crafts catalogue. She took the "scenes" from magazine illustrations. She painted stiff blue birds with orange breasts, awkward pompous robins with overly plump orange breasts setting on a clutch of aqua eggs. For eyes, she painted black circles filled in with yellow. Her beaks were sharper than real birds' beaks and looked dangerous. The birds, with yellow claws, grasped branches off which a few chrome-green leaves, red berries, and brown pinecones grew. You couldn't eat off these plates, nor would you have wanted to. The plates were, my grandmother said proudly, "for decoration."

After the paint dried on her newest "creation"—she called them that, "my creations"—she stood the plates in the hutch in the dining room. She urged you to praise them. But the birds looked dead. Worse, their curious stiffness made them appear as if they'd never been alive, and their eyes looked mean.

She did better with needlework, perhaps because threads were more manageable for her than paints. She drew designs on fabric, then, with a big-eyed needle and crewel wools, she picked out calm lakes bordered by conical evergreens, backed by distant snow-capped mountains over which an ungainly eagle flew. On another canvas a brown bear emerged from a cave door at the foot of a tweedy gray mountain, upright, white teeth bared and front paws opened outward, showing nasty claws. She framed her larger canvases and hung them around the house. She made the smaller canvases, with blocky mallard ducks or pheasants, into pillows.

While she painted the china or pulled the wool-threaded needle through canvas, her harsh George Washington face softened into a beatific puddle. She took on a faraway look. She kept her mouth slightly open and breathed in rapid little huffs and puffs when she dotted a bird's eye with bright yellow paint or pulled through the last white thread in her mountaintop snow.

Anyway, after we got through moseying around the kitchen, inspecting all the filled jars, and saying "That's a real fine quart of pigs' feet" or "Did you ever see such a nice-looking bunch of sausage balls?" and "Don't you know this will taste good when it's winter" my grandmother got me to help her haul the filled jars to the pantry and down into the fruit cellar.

The fruit cellar was where my grandmother stored pumpkins, Hubbards, potatoes, turnips and onions, apples, pears, crocks of finished kraut and pickle crocks, some of her canning and empty canning jars. I think now that the fruit cellar, originally, may have been a tornado or storm shelter. Bushels and Buckles called it the "fraidy hole" and "hidey-hole," and said it was where you should scuttle to when a tornado started toward you. My grandmother disagreed. She said that if we had a tornado or cyclone she'd never go down into that cellar; she'd stay right there, in her house. "I'd rather be blown away," she said, "than buried alive."

From the back porch, you could see the wooden cellar door. When I was told to go the twenty feet or so to the fruit cellar by myself to take or get something, I'd feel apprehensive. You grabbed a rusted metal hasp and lifted up the heavy door, which rose at a slight angle off concrete walls. You wanted to make sure you had the door entirely folded back, especially on a windy day, when a strong gust could lift the door and slam it closed.

When you walked down the concrete steps the air grew cooler with each downward step. The cellar ceiling must have been under a good two feet of soil. The walls were concrete. Shelves built from rough wood rose from the dirt floor all the way to the concrete ceiling. The smell was of mold, damp soil, fermenting sauerkraut, and the sweet rot odor that ripening pears and apples give off.

I carried one jar at a time, my heart beating fast from fear I'd drop it and the pickled pig parts would spill out all over me. To say nothing of the fact that my grandmother, as she put it, would "whip me until I couldn't see straight." The jars' contents jiggled, the pigs' feet, ears, snout, lips bobbing in their fluids. On a low shelf next to jars of greengage plums and pickled peaches, I carefully set down the jar. I sighed, I guess from relief. I stood then, looked at the jar. The pig seemed to smile at me. Outside, I heard the dog bark and the wind pick up. I looked to make sure that the cellar door was folded all the way back. You could, I knew, be buried alive down here and no one would ever hear you scream.

SUMMER

❦

SUMMERS WHEN I WAS YOUNG, I WOULD SEE WOMEN WHO ARE
my age now on their knees in flower beds. "It's sad," I'm sure I
said to my high-school best friend, Joanna, "to have nothing more
to do with your life than care about flowers."

I have become one of those women who care about flowers. As
much as all those summers ago I admired tanned boys who wore
white socks and khaki Bermudas and who sweated lightly when
they kissed, now I admire my blue lobelia. My blue delphinium I
am afraid I have come to love almost as much as my first great
love that long-ago summer when we were still only holding hands.
I go out every morning as excited to see what's happened to the
delphinium as I was when waiting for that boy—crew-cut and
shy—to drive up in the pea-green Chevy Bel-Air on loan from his
father.

Today I was out on the roof, where my four sunflowers, growing
in a big pot, drank five gallons of water over sixteen hot and windy
hours. Really, the big pot is too small and not a good idea. Even
though, daily, I've boosted their water with liquid fertilizer, which
their roots take up as our veins take in an IV drip, the thick green

stalks have stunted. They're dwarfed, cramped up. I'm sorry I planted them there. Blooms that normally would be dinner-plate size are no bigger than dessert plates. I feel guilty about the sunflowers. I kept them from what they were meant to be.

A friend brought me five pounds of unshelled peanuts for the scrub jays that come to my roof and feed. I scattered a pound of peanuts across the roof and listened happily to the dry shells clatter. I went back to dead-heading faded flowers from the huge pansies called Super Majestic Giants. The pansy blooms, particularly the yellow ones that are blotched black in the middle, are strongly perfumed and give off a complex aroma, like a mix of white wine and talcum powder. The lavender blooms, however, hardly smell at all.

When I turned around I saw a jay perched on the edge of the sunflowers' pot. He eyed me with his jet-bead eyes, above which run narrow white eyebrows. He hopped off the pot into the scattered peanuts. He pecked at one, rolling it away from his beak, pecked at another and another, and then stood still and hammered his three-quarter-inch-long black beak into a shell until a nut rolled out. He took the nut in his beak, then tossed back his head and swallowed. He repeated his pecking among the nuts, then picked one up and flew away, peanut in mouth. I say "he" because scrub jay males bring food to the female before, during, and for a short while after egg-setting season. This jay's mate sits her eggs, my guess is, in one of the nearby evergreens. Her nest, according to what I read, is a cup of grass lined with fine roots and hair, supported by a platform of twigs.

I edged the sunflower pot and two wooden tubs of blue hydrangea with a trailing blue lobelia called Sapphire, whose three-quarter-inch deep-blue blossoms are centered by two tiny white stripes. The dark, almost severe blue flowers have bloomed in such profusion as to cloak the plant's deep-green foliage. Its stems trail

down a foot and a half over the tub's wood slats and make the
plants seem a miraculous blue cloud. The pot that holds the delphinium Belladonna I filled with lobelia called Cambridge Blue,
whose flower is a sky blue even paler than the delphinium. The
latter, this year, has put out three-foot-high stalks covered with
blue florets.

Back all those summers ago, now way more than half the summers I'll be granted, I didn't know any flowers' names except rose
and daisy and Easter lily and the orchid boys gave for corsages. I
spent summer days at Joanna's air-conditioned house, where we
lay buffered against the hot sun in her father's dark bedroom and
watched soap operas and ate sandwiches the maid Annie Mae
made us. Annie Mae sliced meat off a real ham with a white bone
in it. Sitting on Joanna's father's big bed (which in memory may
be bigger and softer than it was), we watched the half-hour *As the
World Turns* on the black-and-white Philco. We slid off the bed
and turned up the volume when Annie Mae turned on the vacuum
cleaner. We turned down the volume when the organ music announced the end of a scene and the beginning of a soap commercial. We became obsessed with the romantic intrigues between
the Hughes and Lowell families on *As the World Turns*. We even
found ourselves occasionally sympathetic (as we weren't to our
own mothers) to young Don and Bob Hughes's worried mother,
Nancy, as she paced her kitchen linoleum in the fictional Oakdale,
Illinois, and offered her visitors coffee from a percolator she kept
on the stove. (This was years before countertop coffeemakers like
Mr. Coffee.) What Mrs. Hughes (Joanna and I called her that,
just as we would have anyone else of her age) was worried about
was that her teenage son Bob was dating an inappropriate girl. A
wild girl. A girl who "permitted liberties."

We were not wild girls. We lay propped up on Joanna's father's
fat pillows and polished our toenails with Revlon's Fire and Ice.

We talked about what we'd wear when we got married. We wanted lace gowns. We wanted four bridesmaids and each other as maid or matron of honor. We wanted June weddings. We wanted a soprano with a warble in her voice to sing "I Love You Truly." We looked at pictures of silver patterns in Joanna's mother's *Ladies' Home Journals*. Joanna wanted Chantilly. I wanted Melrose.

We expected to be virgins on our wedding night. I know that I knew the physiological definition of the word "intact," but do not recall how I learned it. I believed that to become "un-intact" would involve great pain and leave a thin trickle of darkish blood on the honeymoon sheets. I believed that after the vows and that first night I would be as irrevocably changed as bread and wine at the altar were changed to flesh and blood. I would be a new and different person, *named new with my new name*, myself no more. Even though my own parents were long divorced; even though Joanna's mother and father, while they sipped martinis (the titillating scent of the gin's juniper making me sneeze) and ate blanched almonds in their living room, spoke tensely to one another; even though I heard Mr. and Mrs. Hughes argue in their Oakdale kitchen, I believed I would remain unendurably happy. I would belong to my husband in a way I could never belong to myself.

Shyly, Joanna and I talked about how our lives would be in a future we expected was two or three years away. Our shyness grew not from modesty before an intimate subject but from spacious ignorance.

What kind of man did we want our husband to be?

"Cute," Joanna would say.

"Tall," I would add.

"Well, at least six feet tall," Joanna would suggest.

Where would we meet him?

"In college," one of us would say. A campus greensward, mottled by sunlight, stretched out in my mind, and a tall boy dressed in crew-neck sweater, cords, and dirty Spaulding tennis shoes walked toward me, smiling.

Either Joanna or I would then append, "Not in high school!" We would laugh. Maybe Joanna would say, "Be careful, you're laughing so hard you almost knocked over the nail-polish bottle. My dad will kill me if we mess up his bed."

Most boys we knew in high school seemed barbaric. We must have imagined that these husbands who awaited us rose fully grown on ivied-brick campuses. It never occurred to us that these prospective husbands would be boys who had attended other girls' high schools.

And after we met one of these college boys, what would happen?

Love.

Nothing, of course, came out as we planned. Nothing. We made dreadful mistakes there was no escaping. But that is another story.

I watched *As the World Turns* the other day, now shown in bright color for an hour rather than thirty minutes. Oakdale has gone from a small town to a big city, and it boasts a yacht casino, with gambling. After all these years, while Joanna went on with her real life and I with mine, many people we watched during our high-school summers still live their lives in Oakdale. Lisa, one of the wild girls Mrs. Hughes disapproved of, has bleached her hair a post-menopausal pale blond. Her face is lined and gutted. She has had, I read somewhere, thirty-three lovers, five marriages, half a dozen children, and been put away twice in a mental institution. Bob Hughes is a doctor and has aged well. Mrs. Hughes, who has been on the show since it first aired in 1956 (and is older than either Joanna's or my mother), is now truly old, her back bowed and her stomach pooched out.

None of Oakdale's women any longer hover over coffeepots or wear flowered housedresses and wait at home for people to show up and tell their troubles or bring bad news. They have glamorous jobs and babies out of wedlock. They connive at business deals as readily as at affairs of the heart. The organ music has been replaced by computer-driven orchestral sounds, and commercials offer products that cure yeast infections and tell you if you're pregnant.

A shadow falls over summer now that for me never fell before. Even before June was over, even before the blue dropped off the jacaranda trees and my thwarted sunflowers bloomed, I began to dread summer's end. I kneel down in my flowers. I'm like those women I used to feel sorry for. I am those women.

WATERMELON

❦

*Life was to be enjoyed with the same pleasure
and certainty as the evening breeze that always carried the smell
of lilac and magnolia and watermelons in a distant field.*
JAMES LEE BURKE, A Stained White Radiance

MY LIFE WAS A MESS. IF ANYONE ASKED, I SAID, "I'M EIGHTEEN."
The seventeen I'd just turned made me jailbait to men over
twenty-one, and men over twenty-one were the men I liked. I'd
been in college a year. Before I got ready to go back for my
sophomore year, my mother and I stood in the sunny yellow
kitchen of her new house in Oklahoma City and screamed. She
told me, (*a*) I couldn't go back to the school I'd been attending,
and (*b*) I'd better major in something more practical than English
lit; I'd better get myself some shorthand, for instance, or she
wasn't paying my goddamn tuition. I got red in the face and said,
"I won't."

I usually didn't tell her, "I won't." I was too scared of her.

Even now this episode refuses to stay tucked back mutely in
past tense. My feet seep sweat in my Capezio flats. My armpits
prickle. That's how scared I am. This is too much. I want to go
back to the college where I went last year, where I've got friends.
I can't believe she's doing this. I don't want to learn scraggly-
looking shorthand. I want Shakespeare's Festive Comedies, I want
The Modern Novel, I want Byron, Keats, and Shelley.

Mama gets her pretty heart-shaped face right up in my face so close I see specks of her custom-mixed Merle Norman face powder standing on the ends of her face hairs. What *she* sees is the red sweating female version of her ex-husband, because, as she's always telling me, I look just like my goddamn father. She's right. I do.

I stand my ground. Sort of. I whine. I beg. I say again, "Mama, I just won't."

Mama's Eastman School of Music–trained breathing-for-singers revs up. Her diaphragm heaves. She breathes hard, fast, like a movie madwoman. I smell coffee and cream in her open mouth and watch spittle float over the dark fillings that pit her bottom back teeth. Poor little thing, she manages barely five-one in her high heels. She rises up on her toes, so that our eyes meet. She yells at me in pure scratchless lyric soprano, "Then get out and earn your own goddamn living."

If she'd been speaking Italian, you'd have thought, Here's a diva working out kinks in an aria. But she wasn't a diva. My worthless father had come along and convinced her to elope, and next thing you knew, she was fat as a tick with me, and her life, she said, "turned to shit."

Anyway, we stand there nose to nose, we stare meanly into each other's eyes. I think, You hate me, you old bag, and I hate you, too. The kitchen clock ticks. I suck up a deep breath, hiss, "Okay, then, I will. I'll get a job," and know I've just done something to change my life.

"Cut off your own nose"—Mama laughs—"to spite your face." I grab my purse and head out the front door into merciless Southwestern heat. Which is how I would meet Sam, in the bookstore where he had a job and I got one, and how I came to grow my first watermelon.

Mr. X's horrible bookstore took up the middle of a dirty block in a dirty, horrible state capital.

Somebody my mother loved for five years jilted her, is how she and I got to this town. In a heartbroken huff Mama quit her tenured job as a teacher of voice, sold her house, packed up, and moved her Steinway parlor grand and her flowered furniture and her crates of chipped Wedgwood and her cachepots of African violets to this place where she had a not-so-good job in a Methodist college (which was where she'd planned to enroll me). She was forty-two, a high-breasted, perfervid little green-eyed redhead with no bad habits other than violence and running an adult life on the emotions of a lovesick teenage girl. She'd hated me for so long that dislike, disgust, distaste for me came as a reflex built into her nerves. To see me was to want to slap me across the face that she claimed never stopped reminding her of my worthless lazy father, whose physiognomy and sulky, dreamy, impractical ways I'd inherited.

In this new town, where neither she nor I knew anybody, she started running around with two gay men she met through my Uncle Carl, her brother. (Although no one said "gay" then. "Interested," is what my mother said, raising her eyebrows, "*in men.*") The older, an ugly, rodent-toothed, fat and squat Moon Pie–faced toad named Colin, served as husbandly boss to Jimmy, the tall, skinny, younger boy bride. Colin taught piano to rich people's children; Jimmy played the organ and directed the choir at a big Methodist church. Jimmy's face oozed acne pus, and his big Orphan Annie eyes looked out from dandruffy lashes. Nightly, these two characters pulled up to my mother's dining-room table. They gobbled her excellent fried chicken, her cider-sweating pork roasts, her shiny molten gravies, her by-hand-mashed potatoes, her repertoire of pies. The whole five years she'd cooked for the jilter, she'd figured sooner or later he'd marry her. But here she was, dumped for a younger woman who could neither cook nor hit high C and didn't even, according to my mother, wear clean underwear. Plus, her life had come down to teaching Methodist girls to sing the Wesley brothers' anthems and watching vile Colin, who chewed with his mouth open, and pathetic Jimmy chug down pork chops and buttery Parkerhouse rolls and peach pie with lattice crust. All that fall my poor little mama spent perched at the edge of her spindly antique dining-room chair, wiping tears on the corner of her apron.

We'd never gotten on that well, Mama and me, but this year the hostilities intensified. When I told her one Saturday that I had a date and wouldn't be home until midnight, my curfew, she screamed, "You're a cheap tramp. And you're going to wind up pregnant, and when you do, don't come home crying to me. You make your bed, Sister Sue, you lie in it."

True, though, I was no virgin. The very moment after I did it the first time, I thought, Already I've ruined my life. Nice girls in Eisenhower's last term didn't lose maidenheads as carelessly as I lost mine, and for sure they didn't lose them when they were barely out of their white cotton training bras.

Anyway, that Saturday afternoon, standing in that sunny yellow kitchen, Mama had hurled at me green bell peppers she'd already parboiled and stuffed with ground beef, chopped onion, and rice. Cooked rice and onion had gotten between my bare toes, whose nails I'd just polished with Revlon's Cherries in the Snow. Rice stuck to the damp polish. She had kicked at my ankles with her tiny pointed-toe pumps. She had heaved in a big breath and shrieked, "I'm sick of the sight of you." Tears had flown from her eyes. "I wash my hands of you."

This sounds worse than it was. If she'd cooed over me, the way my friends' mothers cooed over them, I'd have sniffed her breath to see if she'd been drinking. She drank infrequently and liquor led her to wild giggling and demonstrations of the Charleston. And if she'd warmed up to me, I'd have had to warm up to her. It was too late for that, between her and me.

I don't remember what I said to get the job. Probably "I read a lot." I do remember I was frightened. I'd never had a job, not even baby-sitting. I didn't like babies. I liked men, books, music, in that order.

I don't know how I got to work. I didn't have a car. My mother's house wasn't within walking distance of the bookstore. I do remember walking down the street toward the bookstore. I remember the din of a downtown starting the day. Behemoth garbage trucks belched black smoke, fat flies buzzed above overflowing garbage cans set out the night before. A one-legged man played the harmonica and begged coins outside a mom-and-pop diner. In front of a cigar store, no matter the hour, a flock of slack-jawed, ducktailed young men slouched against bricks. "Drugstore cowboys," people called them. They whistled. They made lewd suggestions.

Sometimes they called, "Sooey, sooey, pig." I wasn't fat and I wasn't ugly, but I wasn't somebody whose photo got passed around to kindle hard-ons. Fairly flat-chested, short in leg, low in rump, I was mildly freckled, blue-eyed, and, like my father and mother, red-headed.

Mr. X opened at 8 a.m. and closed at 10 p.m. Usually I worked the eight-to-five shift; sometimes I worked the two-to-ten. Pay was one dollar an hour, forty dollars a week. Ten percent off on books. We got two ten-minute coffee breaks and half an hour for lunch. No medical. They didn't have medical then.

Mornings out in front of Mr. X's bookstore, guys paced, waiting for the bookstore to open. They spit gobs of mucus and ground out cigarettes around their feet. Big guys, little guys, old, young, bums, rich guys, many *Guys and Dolls*–type guys rushed in and out all day. Ten at night, when we closed, they were still arriving.

They headed up a flight of stairs where Mr. X had his office. About half the guys, when they came down the stairs, carried white paper sacks with Mr. X printed across them. And about half the guys' faces were lost under wide-brimmed fedoras, because men still wore hats then.

Mr. X couldn't have carried more than 140 pounds on his six-foot-plus frame. Maybe he was fifty years old. His office hung off a second-floor mezzanine. His office windows looked down onto the store, onto its rows and rows of bookshelves. Mr. X smoked cigars, which, back then, right before Batista fell, still came from Havana.

Smoke unfurled from his windows all day. He coughed wrenching coughs we could hear downstairs. The torment in his coughs made me sick to my stomach. Mr. X told us he had a "bad chest" from TB he picked up in the "Jap concentration camp" in the Second World War. He tossed wadded bloody Kleenex balls in the downstairs trash. He barked out orders from his windows. He called me "Girlie."

I wish I remembered the first time I saw Sam. Probably I didn't pay him much attention. I like big men, and Sam hunched himself down even smaller than he was. Hunkered-over shoulders and white-blond hair, long white eyelashes and pale skin gave him a weird wizened albino-dwarf look, a Frog Prince you'd see in a children's picture book, the monstrosity put in the book to teach children that looks aren't everything.

I do remember the first time Sam and I went to the drugstore next door for coffee. This was the third or fourth day I worked for Mr. X. We took a booth. He sat with his back to the door. September sunlight came in behind him and blinded me. I shaded my eyes. He asked if I wanted to change places. I didn't. My feet ached and I felt way too tired to move. Mama's right about my being lazy, is what I thought.

"Mr. X," Sam said, "he's a bookie."

"Bookie?"

"Bookmaker," Sam said.

"Book maker? Him?" Because we joked that Mr. X never read a book in his life, didn't know Hemingway from the Hofbrau on the corner where they made up Mr. X's take-out dinners on scratched Melamine plates. Mr. X sent me to pick them up.

"No, no, no." Sam laughed. He had a crazy, careening laugh. "Not book maker as in 'one who prints, publishes, or binds books.' Bookmaker as in 'one who takes and pays off wagers, bets, as on a horse race or football game or cockfight or prizefight.' He's also a bit of a bootlegger."

The state was dry. Even my mother had a bootlegger. She got his name from Colin.

Compared to what I knew about the world, Sam knew everything. He'd been discharged from the Army six months before we met. Same as Elvis Presley, he'd gone to Germany. But he never saw the Pelvis, as he called him and didn't care about Presley one way or another. Sam said all that in a way that let me know I was younger than he was.

Sam got out of the Army early. He had got drunk, thrown himself out a second-story window, and hurt his back. He had done it on purpose, so they'd let him go with an honorable discharge and access to the GI Bill for college. He wanted to get back home to his wife, Janie, because he was crazy in love with her and believed she was going out on him with her old boyfriend.

Sam and Janie had married before he went overseas. "We hardly knew each other," he said, pushing his blond forelock off his forehead with a trembling hand. Sam had an almost Parkinsonian tremor. When he felt on edge, his hands quivered and his head bobbed arrhythmically. "And she thought she was pregnant. She was just an awful nice girl."

I'd known people near my age who'd died, but I'd never known anyone near my age who'd got married. I tried to imagine Sam and Janie in their apartment, where I went once, with Sam, to pick up his raincoat. Brick-and-board bookshelves lined the tidy living room. Sam's books—Dostoevsky's diaries, Grove Press paperbacks, New Direction editions of Dylan Thomas, City Lights editions of Ginsberg and Corso—were stacked on the boards. The lid stood open on a suitcase record player set atop the coffee table. LPs were stacked everywhere. On the oil-cloth-covered kitchen table, bananas, apples, and pears rose up out of a cobalt-blue pottery bowl. A white Olympia typewriter with a half-finished page in the roller sat at one end of the same table.

After he grabbed his raincoat, Sam opened the refrigerator and pulled out a fried chicken leg and two 3.2 beers. "Janie," he said, offering me cold chicken, "is a terrific cook." At the end of the hallway I could see the high double bed, neatly made up under an ivory chenille bedspread. This all appeared so settled, pacific, lovely, and Janie, when she came to the store to pick up Sam, seemed more cheerful and bubbly than the Janie Sam portrayed as tragically torn between Sam and her old boyfriend. I couldn't imagine the migraines Sam described that kept Janie in a darkened bedroom through weekends, Sam bringing pans for her to vomit into. I couldn't see in my mind's eye—Sam standing next the kitchen table, Janie frying chicken—the violent fights that caused downstairs neighbors to call the police. I didn't know much.

Some mornings Sam came to work with liquor on his breath and his lips blue, as if he lacked oxygen. He often cut himself shaving. Medicinal odors from alcohol and the styptic pencil he rubbed into his cuts wafted off him. Toilet-paper scraps clung to his cheeks and neck, sopping up blood. But he always dressed neatly, in dark creased slacks, white oxford-cloth shirts, and skinny spotless ties.

Four other clerks, men under thirty; an elderly woman with an arm shriveled by polio who kept accounts and ordered books; and a man in his fifties who unpacked books—they all worked at Mr. X's. Only two of us at a time, though, were on the floor, while a third ran the cash register. Sometimes an hour passed and we didn't sell one copy of that year's bestsellers—Taylor Caldwell's *Dear and Glorious Physician*, Allen Drury's *Advise and Consent*, Boris Pasternak's *Dr. Zhivago*, Saul Bellow. We didn't sell a *Better Homes and Gardens* cookbook or a Jerusalem Bible or an Emily Post etiquette, a *TV Guide* or *Racing Form*. Nothing. We let people steal. We didn't care. Once Mr. X saw a shoplifter from his window. He rushed down the stairs, grabbed a broom, and beat the shoplifter around the head with it. He beat him so hard the man fell down in a corner. He covered his face to keep broom straws from blinding him. "Coward!" Mr. X shouted. "Coward!"

On the Road was already famous, and young women, including myself, were dressing all in black. *Howl* was out. So was Samuel Beckett's *Waiting for Godot*. So was a book I saw Sam reading, a Grove Press edition of Amos Tutuola's *The Palm-Wine Drinkard*, which still after all these years I keep meaning to read and don't.

Sam called himself "an ignorant country boy," but he'd read everything, and when one of the rare well-read persons came into the store, asking after an arcane title, Sam could put title together with author. He could quote, and did, swatches of Eliot, Auden, Dylan Thomas, e. e. cummings, William Burroughs, Kerouac, and, giggling as he recited, the melodious first page of Joyce's *Portrait of the Artist as a Young Man*:

> Once upon a time and a very good time it was there was
> a moocow coming down along the road and this moocow that

was coming down along the road met a nicens little boy
named baby tuckoo . . .

His father told him that story: his father looked at him
through a glass: he had a hairy face.

He was baby tuckoo. The moocow came down the road
where Betty Byrne lived: she sold lemon platt.

> *O, the wild rose blossoms*
> *On the little green place.*

He sang that song. That was his song.

Sam, happy, or melancholic in his cups, called himself Baby Tuckoo. It would be, when happy: "Baby Tuckoo scored himself some
good reefer." When sloppy after a day of vodka: "Baby Tuckoo
isn't a lovable fellow, he's not."

The reefer came from a guy named Terry. Sam spoke of Terry,
when he spoke of him at all, as "my connect." I never saw Terry.
The reefer arrived in the big boxes wooden kitchen matches were
sold in. Sam sometimes carried a tight joint tucked in his pack of
Camels. He'd say, "I'm holding," and be careful to stop at red
lights and stop signs. You could go to state prison for one joint.

You could tell when Sam was smoking, because his speech took
a bop, sprung-rhythm, improvisational turn. Only occasionally did
I smoke. Dope scratched up my throat and my mind took turns
that scared me.

I really didn't have any plans, once Mama and I had fought over
college. I'd intended to hide out in college for four years and see
what happened. I thought if I kept walking forward I would bump
into what I was supposed to be—wife? English professor? whore?
actress?

Actress, I thought, because in high school I'd been Emily in
Thornton Wilder's *Our Town* and still sometimes comforted my-

self with Emily's famous speech. "Goodbye, world. Goodbye, Grover's Corners and Mama and Papa. Goodbye to clocks ticking, and Mama's sunflowers, and food and coffee, and new-ironed dresses and hot baths, and sleeping and waking up—oh Earth, you are too wonderful for anybody to realize you. Do any human beings ever realize life while they live it? Every, every minute?"

I thought "whore," because of the maidenhead loss. *Cherry* loss is what we said then: "She lost her cherry." I used to see my cherry hanging up there in the dark of me, a red maraschino with a jaunty stem. I didn't even like sex that much. Almost the first person who tried, I let him. I'd known for a long time that all somebody had to do was ask and I'd give myself away. I was one of those gifts men get, like ugly ties that they don't even take out of the box. They just slide it up on the top shelf of the closet. I knew that about myself.

After Christmas Janie left Sam and filed for an annulment. "She doesn't want any trace of me in her life," Sam said. She went home to her parents. Sam was almost inconsolable, his eyes in the morning pink as a rabbit's from crying. I was surprised. I didn't think anything to do with romance upset men enough to cause tears. But then, I was seventeen, I'd never heard about love from a man's point of view. I'd heard my mother weep over the jilter's betrayal, I'd read *Madame Bovary*, I'd read *Anna Karenina.*

Sam loaded up his Volkswagen Beetle with his record player, cartons of LPs, typewriter, clothes, books, an electric skillet and electric percolator. Two guys from the store and I helped him haul all this up three flights into a room in a downtown hotel. The room had a grimy curtain fluttering at one window and a single bed with a sprung mattress that Sam said was going to kill his back. After we got him moved in, somebody went for 3.2 beer and potato chips. We sat on the crummy rug and drank while Sam swiped off "Nina Simone Live at the Village Gate" and set the needle down on Nina's singing "I Loves You, Porgy." The line he liked best, for reasons I never knew, was "Don't let him handle me with his hot hands."

I'd had a few dates with bookstore customers, bookish young guys, one a rosy-cheeked, bespectacled pianist named Vinson, who after our third date mailed me a sweet love letter. I didn't love him back and felt guilty that I couldn't. Nothing much came of the rest of these dates. I accepted them mostly because I felt so fiendishly lonely, not knowing one soul in town, and so I wouldn't have to spend evenings at home with my mother and Colin and Jimmy. They'd become the Three Musketeers. They called themselves that. From my upstairs bedroom I heard them, Jimmy and Colin spelling each other at the Steinway, my mother singing. After music hour, Mama served hot pie and ice cream. Colin's pop-out stomach was popping out further than ever.

Sam and I sprawled in downtown coffee shops until ten, eleven at night. We told each other our life story. Sam told me his parents had divorced when he was still in diapers. His mother—"a man-hater," he said, "a castrator"—taught school; his father was an architect and engineer, a designer of freeway bridges who lived in San Francisco. Summers, when Sam was a little boy, he stayed in the country with his maternal grandfather. "I loved that old man more than anybody," Sam said. By junior high Sam began cutting school and running away. His mother enrolled him in a second-rate military school, where he stayed until he graduated. Janie was the daughter of one of the school's instructors. After Sam got home from Germany, he and Janie moved to this city so Janie could go to school at the college where my mother was teaching. They didn't know a soul either.

I told him that my mother had thrown my father out when I was three and a half, that I never saw my father, that my mother had gone off to New York to study music. I'd fallen for a boy in my freshman English class, we had an affair, nothing came of it.

I wrote poems that even I knew were no good. I didn't know what I wanted to major in if I ever got back to college. After I left out all the embarrassing, shameful parts, I didn't have much else to tell.

Weekends, we saw black-and-white French and Italian movies—*Hiroshima, Mon Amour, The 400 Blows, La Dolce Vita, Breathless*. We drove out into the country where farmers were plowing and seeding fields and new lambs and calves suckled their mothers. Sam showed me where, as a teenager, he and his buddies had picked marijuana that grew wild, seeded and reseeded year after year since the 1930s, when farmers grew hemp. All the while we drove, Sam talked. How could he get Janie back? Where did he go wrong? What would have happened had her parents not interfered? If her old boyfriend hadn't been sniffing after her all the time Sam had been in Germany? If she hadn't been so afraid of getting pregnant? I tried to give advice. But I didn't know much. I suggested mailing her a copy of *Lady Chatterley's Lover*, the unexpurgated version of which had just been published. I suggested sending her flowers. Somebody sent me daisies once.

One day that spring, after I'd been at the bookstore seven months, I had cramps so bad I asked Sam to drive me home at lunch. I was going to take aspirin and go to bed and plop the peach-colored heating pad on my stomach. Jimmy's black Ford stood in the driveway. I turned the key in the front door, walked in, and there they were, doing it on the Oriental carpet. She's my mother. I can't describe the scene.

She turns her head toward me and yowls, "Get out!" I can't describe how wild her face looks.

I close the door and put my hand up to get Sam to stop. He is just backing down the drive. I run and get into his Volkswagen. Sam asks, "What's wrong?" He says, "The color's gone out of your face."

People didn't talk the way people talk now. For instance, "fuck." I'd never said that word. I say to Sam, "Mama and Jimmy are having an affair." I say, "She's somehow managed to pull Jimmy away from Colin."

I spent the night with Sam in his bed with the sprung mattress. I wore my slip, and he wore green-striped pajamas that were way too big for him. He set an ashtray on his stomach and smoked. I was embarrassed because I was having my period. I was terrified I'd bleed on his sheets. I got up to go to the bathroom and knocked over the fan that sat on the carpet. When I punched on the bathroom light, roaches skittered across the tiles. I was dripping blood on the floor. I'd cut my ankle on the fan.

Up until then, I hadn't cried. Sam, pajamas billowing, rushed in. I had plopped down on the floor. Between sobs I said, "I don't know what's going to become of me." I said, "I don't want to go back there. I can't stay here."

Sam kept patting my head, saying, "Now now, everything's going to be okay." He got me to sit on the toilet seat and he knelt next to me and poured the last drops from a pint of vodka over my cut. He blew my nose for me with toilet paper. He said, "Let's get you back to bed."

Sam tore open a box of Oreos. We lay there in the dark and Sam split Oreos apart. He fed me the side that was slathered with white filling and ate the naked ones himself. "You get the good side," he said, "because you're the guest." He made a pallet on the floor and slept there. When morning came, we got up and took showers and rushed off to Mr. X's bookstore. If anybody saw I was wearing the same skirt and blouse I wore the day before, nobody said so. I don't think anyone paid enough attention to me to notice.

When Mr. X shouted down from his aerie, "Telephone, girlie!" I knew it was my mother. Telephones were black and heavy. You could've knocked somebody out if you'd conked them with the handset. Mama started right off yelling that I'd walked in on them on purpose, that I was spying on her, that I'd damn well better not tattle to my Uncle Carl about what I'd seen. She said I was just like Carl, I didn't want her to have any happiness of her own. The truth, I now realize, was worse than that: I didn't think one way or another about her happiness. She said, "I expect you home tonight." I didn't say yes and I didn't say no. She slammed down the phone at her end and I heard nothing but flat silence up against my ear. I went off and gift-wrapped Robert Service's poems for a woman whose father was in the veterans hospital with a bad leg, which, maybe, the lady said, he'd have to have amputated.

During coffee break Sam said, "Why don't *we* get a place? You and me?"

This never would have occurred to me. I said, "Yes, why not."

After work, we rented a two-bedroom furnished basement apartment ten blocks from the bookstore. Forty bucks a month. We told the landlord we were sister and brother. We each handed him two ten-dollar bills.

Mama sang in Jimmy's choir, and it was choir practice night. Sam and I drove over and gathered my books and clothes. I left her a note saying I would give her a call but not to expect me home for a while. We had everything I owned out in ten minutes and heaped into the Volkswagen's back seat. We moved in my stuff and then went to Sam's hotel and got his.

Sam worried what my mother would do. I had told him the truth about my age, and he was worried, even though we weren't having sex, about my being jailbait. He said he didn't want to find himself locked up for statch rape. I said I figured that as long as Mama was involved with Jimmy she wouldn't do anything. It turned out I was right about that.

A white frame two-story Edward Hopperish house stood above the basement. A retired seaman rented the top floor, the bottom was occupied by a wide-hipped middle-aged secretary to a local judge. When prairie winds blew across this flat city, the house creaked. You entered the basement through a fenced back yard, going down cement steps into what served as the front door. The apartment was basically one big dark living room and two small dark bedrooms and a bathroom where mold grew in the rusted-out shower stall. In the dismal windowless kitchen, an old refrigerator throbbed, and roaches ran from the four-burner gas stove. We had Sam's electric skillet, coffeepot, and some dishes. We had a dinette set, a sofa, an old easy chair, and a coffee table. In the bedrooms were beds, nightstands, chests of drawers, lamps. We had the basement damp that never left and, for a view, the feet of occasional passersby as they walked past our windows.

After I'd been gone two days, my mother called again at the bookstore. I stood there, black phone cord coiling around my index finger, listening to her voice worm its way into my ear. She asked me where I was living. I said, "With Sam and his wife." (She didn't know they'd broken up.) She asked if I intended to stay there. I said I did. She said there'd better be no funny business. She asked for their telephone number. I said they didn't have a phone. I didn't care that I lied. I didn't want to go back. She said, "Well, suit yourself," and then there was a dial tone.

I couldn't cook much. Sam couldn't cook at all. Sam stole a Betty Crocker cookbook from the store, carried it out under his jacket. We read recipes to each other, but it all sounded too difficult. We went to the supermarket and bought a Kool-Aid pitcher and a bag of sugar and every Kool-Aid flavor they had. Lime was my favorite. We bought hamburger meat and dill-pickle slices, and buns. Down in our dark kitchen that evening, I patted the cold meat together to make burgers. The gristly meat with its bit of white fat and red flesh stuck to my palms, and I thought I probably

wasn't ever going to amount to anything, my mother was right. I
didn't know enough, nor did Sam, to warm the buns. While the
meat fried Sam watched and scratched at his head where his hair
was already thinning on top. Mostly, after that, we ate toasted
cheese sandwiches that we made in the electric skillet or fried
bologna or tuna-fish sandwiches (we made ashtrays from the tuna-
fish cans), scrambled eggs and apples and doughnuts and coffee
and Fritos. Weekends, Sam drank vodka and orange juice and ate
doughnuts.

Right from the start, we lived a reasonably orderly life. Five
days a week we went to work. We gave silly nicknames to co-
workers and customers. Like "Nazi Joe," a clerk who carried
around *Mein Kampf*, and "The Four-Flusher," a braggart real-
estate salesman who wrote Mr. X hot checks. We talked about
what went on in the bookstore. We took turns sweeping. Sam
scrubbed the kitchen and bathroom on his hands and knees—
"dirty work," he said, "that women shouldn't do." He said he always did dirty work for his mother. The dishes he washed, I dried.
Fridays, after the lady with the withered arm handed us our pay-
checks, we lugged laundry to the laundromat, we bought groceries. We didn't have a telephone or a television. Most evenings, I
went to my room and read in bed; Sam stretched out on the
couch, sipped vodka or 3.2 beer, played records, read, wrote letters to Janie. He printed her name and address on the envelopes
in thin, tall majuscules. He printed our grocery lists the same way;
they looked like telegrams. Sometimes he typed out poems.
"Pomes," he called them, and recited them to me. They were full
of lost boys and sad girls and unhappy loners who walked suburban
streets and looked into windows where families sat at tables, eating
dinner. He was reading Camus and Beckett; he was never quite
drunk and never quite sober. I didn't know much about liquor. I
thought, He's drowning his sorrows.

I slept in my bedroom, Sam in his. He treated me as I guessed you'd treat a kid sister—ruffled my curls, patted my cheek, complimented an outfit, teased me by saying this man or that couldn't keep his eyes off me. He'd say, "You want me to fix you up with him?" and I'd blush and say I didn't. Sam, who at best ate powdered sugar doughnuts for breakfast, and more often only coffee and Camels, or bootleg vodka and orange juice, regularly said, "Why don't you make yourself a bowl of Cheerios and sit down and eat it this morning?" And then: "Why don't *I* stir you up a bowl of Cheerios?" Drunk or sober, Sam was all "Please" and "Thank you" and "May I?" I was so accustomed to Mama's screaming, tossing stuffed peppers, and calling me "Sister Sue" that Sam's simple good manners and courtesy sometimes left me almost giddy, like someone who travels rapidly from boggy sea level to high altitude.

We acquired lawn chairs from a junk store and set them out in the back yard. Weekends, and days when we didn't go to work until two, we sat outside and read. Sam's pale skin burned and began to tan; the color on his face made him look more Prince, less Frog. Afternoons when we didn't have to go to the bookstore, Sam made beer runs, carting home two six-packs. After a few beers, he dragged his suitcase record player out in the yard, attached to a long umbilical of extension cord, and played records one after another. Mostly what he had was jazz and classical.

One Saturday morning in mid-April, Sam's twenty-third birthday, we decided we'd plant watermelon. Sam's grandfather had grown melons—muskmelons, honeydew, Charleston Gray watermelons. Sam helped him.

Sam's grandfather, year after year, won the county fair watermelon competition with melons that sometimes weighed more than a hundred pounds and measured three feet long and four feet around. He grew big gardens, but he was obsessed with watermelons. He dug holes and filled the holes with rotted cow manure from his dairy herd. After the melons came up, sometimes the night would be cold and he would go out and lay quilts over the plants. They were like his babies, Sam said. After melons set on the plants, he pulled off the runts of the litter and left only the best-looking melons on the vine. The other guys, Sam said, just leeched off water and food from the big guys. Sam's grandfather carried a tape in his overalls to measure melons. When the weather turned hot, melons grew two or three inches a day. He'd lay watermelon vines over the melons, to shade them. He'd set up card tables over the melons he chose as potential blue-ribbon winners, to keep them from getting sunburned. And he paid Sam to pick off bugs. Along in late July, early August, when the melons thunked with that hollow sound that meant they'd ripened, the melons were so heavy it took a wheelbarrow to truck one out to the pickup. "The melons," Sam sighed, "looked like green blimps."

Why, when neither of us fretted over even a Boston fern or a Wandering Jew on our basement windowsills, did watermelon-growing fever strike us? I don't know. Perhaps Sam missed his grandfather. Perhaps it was that on either side of the board fence around our back yard, neighbors put in gardens. Sam rushed next door and knocked on our neighbor's door and borrowed a shovel. He ripped off his shirt and began digging a hole in the middle of the yard. When I asked, "Why there?" Sam said, "Because you want it to get full sunshine is why." Hole dug, we drove to a suburban seed store and bought Charleston Gray watermelon seed and sand and steer manure. Back home, we mixed sand and manure with the red clay soil in our watermelon pit. We built a hill of dirt, sand, and manure. In the top of the hill, Sam scooped out a hollow, a "seedbed," he called it. He was smeared with dirt. Sweat ran down his chest and stood in drops on his forehead. We carried water in the Kool-Aid pitcher from the spigot on the side of the house, pitcher after pitcher. Sam made a circle of seeds in the hollow. He said that after the seeds came up and grew a little, we'd keep the two strongest plants and pull out others. We patted down damp soil over the seeds. Sam covered the seedbed with a white plastic Wonder bread wrapper and set rocks around the wrapper's edge. "So the dirt won't dry out," he said, grinning. That night Sam crawled into bed with me, and for the first time, we made love.

I'd never slept through the night next to any living creature except my gay uncle's cocker spaniel and two tomcats. I curled up next to Sam and listened to his heart bang against his thin chest. I sniffed his skin, taking in the tobacco and deodorant smells. He smelled old. I wasn't in love with Sam. I didn't want to be. We'd made a mistake, I thought, going all the way. While I lay awake and considered what we'd done and worried about who I would be when I grew up and how I would live, because I knew I could not do nothing more than sell *Lolita* and *Dear and Glorious Physician* and *Racing Forms*, Sam kept an arm thrown over me. If I moved even an inch away, he roughly pulled me back to him. I needed saving. Sam couldn't save me. Deep asleep, he muttered, "Janie, Janie," and spittle bubbled in the corners of his mouth.

Next morning, when Sam awakened he grabbed his underwear off my floor and hurried to the kitchen. Faucets whined, water whooshed, the pot clattered. He'd started coffee. I heard the shower. Minutes later, he stood at my door and said, "I'm going for doughnuts and the Sunday paper." I pretended I was sleeping.

The Volkswagen churned. When the engine whine faded, I got up out of the messy sheets and slung on my bathrobe. I shivered. Even on hot afternoons the basement was chilly. I poured coffee.

Sam had tacked the seed packet on the kitchen wall. I pulled out the tack and looked at the picture. The artist had drawn the oblong melon with a slice cut out of it. Whitish stripes ran through the dark green skin, and where the cut had been drawn, the flesh was painted pale red and dotted with black seeds. According to the instructions on the back of the packet, watermelon required 110 to 120 days of hot, sunny weather and plenty of water to reach twenty pounds. The seeds were supposed to take five to ten days to germinate. I wondered if Sam and I could grow something that weighed twenty pounds.

Sam and I kept to ourselves that Sunday. He slouched down on the living-room couch and sipped his vodka and juice and ate doughnuts. He stubbed out one after another Camel, and put the needle again and again on Nina Simone singing "I Loves You, Porgy." I stayed in my room and tried to read.

By late afternoon, I couldn't take it anymore. I walked into the living room and plopped down on the floor. "So," I said, "I read that it takes 110 days at least for a watermelon to grow. Do you think it will take that long?"

Sam coughed, studied me, his brow furrowed. "Well, we've got to pray for hot weather." He coughed again, one of those nervous dry coughs. "Listen," he said, "I didn't hurt you last night, did I?"

"No," I said, fidgeting with my hands, "but I think you think I'm a tramp."

I bawled, and Sam lifted the needle off "I Loves You, Porgy." He sat on the floor and put his arm around me and told me everything would be all right. After a while, when I'd calmed down, Sam got the plastic calendar out of his wallet and he counted, slowly, as you would for a child, how many days until the melons were ready. "That makes it middle August," Sam said, standing up and stretching out his hand. "Come sit on the couch with me." At his direction I lay down and put my head in his lap. He played with my hair, twirling and untwirling a curl on his finger. He spoke in a low murmurous storytelling voice. "We're going to have to guard our melon patch. Coyotes might come from outside town and sneak in and see our melons and bite big holes in them. I remember one time wild hogs got into Grampa's garden and ate up all his melons, the muskmelon, watermelon, everything. Lord, he was POed."

Sam asked me, "Did you ever watch a watermelon grow?"

I had, when I was a little girl on my grandmother's farm. My grandmother thumped them early in the morning, to see if they were ripe. She set them to chill in the milk house, where the milk cooled. When we ate them she told me not to swallow the seeds or a watermelon would grow in my belly and fill me up until I popped.

Sam laughed. "Well, you didn't believe that, did you?"

I did.

My mother called me at the bookstore every few days. I never saw her. We might as well have been living in different countries. I think she telephoned just to make sure I wasn't thinking of coming home. But I don't know that.

The last few letters Sam wrote to Janie all came back to the apartment stamped in red REFUSED. Sam tucked the letters in Volume I of Dostoevsky's *Diary*.

A hot spell, ninety-degree days and sixty-degree nights, settled over the city. The next Sunday morning, when we went out to look at our melon patch, four sets of green leaves had popped out of the ground. The black seed casing was still stuck to one set of leaves. Sam sat on his heels and carefully removed it. "See," he said, handing the casing to me, "that's what we planted." And he giggled wildly and jumped up and down and yelled, "Whoopee!"

The following week, the nights turned cold. Sam grubbed through the laundry basket and took out two of his shirts. I held a flashlight and Sam covered the plants. Next morning, we lifted off the shirts. We did this three or four nights. Then the air warmed again and stayed warm.

Every morning when we headed out to work, every day when we got home, even before we walked down into the basement, we checked the watermelon patch. "Is anything happening?" we'd ask each other, and "Do *you* see any progress?" Sam sat on his heels and yanked out tiny weeds. After a few weeks, the plants put out leaves that resembled an oak tree's. Sam bought Vigoro and mixed Vigoro granules in water in the Kool-Aid pitcher and poured the liquefied Vigoro into holes in the ground that he'd made all around the plant. He did this, he said, to encourage the plants to root deeply and reach for underground water. We loved the word "Vigoro," and said it again and again. "Vigoro, Vigoro." "James Joyce," Sam said, "would have liked the word 'Vigoro.' "

Days passed when the plants hardly seemed to grow at all. "Patient, patient, patient," Sam hummed, stirring Kool-Aid pitchers of water and Vigoro. In late May, the oakish leaves formed clumps. The clumps grew bushy. By mid-June the clumps threw vines. The vines grew out into the lawn, an inch, two inches a day. Curly tendrils grew off the vines, "wanting," Sam said, "something to hold on to." By June tiny buds had formed in the leaf axils, and from those buds yellow flowers bloomed.

Watermelon, Sam said, has male and female flowers. You can tell them apart, because there's a small swelling on the stem just below the female flower. The bees that I was always running from, he told me, would now get busy carrying yellow pollen from the male flower to the female, and when the female was pollinated, then the melon would start growing. Which is precisely what happened.

Temperatures rose past 100. Sam rushed home at lunchtime to water the melons. At night, moonlight angled into our dark basement, glistened on the white refrigerator. Our skin dried from heat. We woke up and drank water. I expected to walk outside in the morning and step onto scorched grass, to look up and see gray ash floating upward. That's how hot it was. Within a week of these days, days in the bookstore when we mopped our sweating faces with Kleenex and Mr. X yelled down from his office window, "Girlie, go next door and buy me iced tea!" and the men who in winter wore felt fedoras wore dapper straw and rumpled seer-sucker suits, our vines grew two feet and our melons swelled to the size of hen's eggs. Sam said, "We have seven healthy babies!"

Sam and I, after supper, stretch out on our stomachs in the grass in the violet evening. We scratch at the chiggers that jump on us and bat at the whining mosquitoes. We watch the water-melons grow. As the sky darkens, our faces take on a milky glow. We listen to the man next door hose down his patio and the sec-retary upstairs run her bathwater. We talk, talk, talk. I stroke a nearby melon. Sam tells me, "Don't touch that baby so much, you'll wear him out," because I can't keep my hands off the hard green skin.

I wonder what color the melon's flesh is under that hard green. Sam says the flesh is still green and the seeds white, and no bigger than a pinhead. He lights two Camels and passes one to me. We are careful not to hug and kiss, because we are supposed to be brother and sister. He tells me each melon is a womb and each seed a baby. I imagine photographs of babies curled up in utero. He tells me watermelon seeds are there so that there will always be watermelons on the earth, that the watermelon wants it that way. He pulls on a blade of grass and tickles my nose with it. He says he believes fruits and vegetables and this grass have deep in them a will to live and to keep making more and more of them-selves. He says maybe we should get married.

We didn't. I didn't want to.

Our watermelon plants produced five melons. The curly green

tendrils yellowed and the shiny green melon skin turned dull. Sam rapped them with his knuckles. "The more hollow it sounds," he said, "the riper it is."

We ate three melons and gave away two, one to our landlord and one to Nazi Joe. That fall, I moved back home with my mother, whose *affaire* with Jimmy had broken up, as had her friendship with Colin. Sam packed up his Beetle and drove to San Francisco. Sam and I still talk sometimes on the telephone, and in those same tall thin majuscules he writes long letters. If I'd said "Yes" when Sam said maybe we should get married, and had I saved the seeds from those Charleston Grays, I might have planted generations of melons by now. Those melons, I told Sam not long ago, by now would have great-great-great-great-grandchildren.

COMPANY DINNER

❧

THE FIRST TIME I INVITED COMPANY TO DINNER I WAS NOT YET twenty, was newly wed and "house proud." I was impatient to set out Reed & Barton's even then old-fashioned, heavy Melrose on my pretty blue-and-white-checked luncheon cloth. I was eager to use my white-with-cobalt-rim, made-in-France stoneware dishes. I imagined the rare roast-beef slices, asparagus tips, and red-jacketed new potatoes I someday would arrange on them. I imagined a Thanksgiving dinner, a Christmas feast, a New Year's Day banquet for twelve. Lord knows, I had enough cookware, china, stoneware, silver, crystal, and linen.

Alas, for all my wedding booty and imagining of grand meals, I couldn't cook much but frozen vegetables, grilled cheese sandwiches, and breakfast. For the latter I could rarely coax a fried egg from the skillet without breaking its yolk, and the morning I'd learn to do this appeared as impossibly distant as a snow-capped Everest. Also, because my mother had kept me out of her kitchen, fearing I'd make "messes," almost every cooking implement I'd received as a shower or wedding gift felt unfamiliar. Even my new measuring spoons—the quartet of quarter-teaspoon, half-teaspoon, teaspoon, and tablespoon jingling on their metal ring—caused my small hands to feel overlarge and inept. And I was terrified the old four-burner gas stove in our apartment would blow up, afraid I'd burn down the kitchen and singe away my hair.

I was lucky, because I could invoke flavors of everything I'd ever eaten and in my imagination smell and taste, say, moist breast meat carved off a roast turkey or a boiled turnip and that turnip's green leaves or the difference between a Bosc and a Bartlett pear (the Bosc tastes more of honey and the Bartlett feels grittier against the teeth and offers a lesser range of flavor "tones"). Some people seem particularly gifted at fact memorization or easy recollection of faces and names that go with them; I was and am, as are many people, gifted at what James Beard called "taste memory." So, while I could not make my way through even simple food preparations, I could lie in my newlyweds' double bed, stroke the knobby chenille bedspread, and let flavors coalesce in my empty mouth.

I like to believe that nowadays, when a young woman utters her "I do," her promises spill out as a consequence of love and respect for a person who to her seems singularly desirable. When I married, not long after John F. and Jacqueline Kennedy moved into the White House, young women readily, even greedily, gave themselves up to matrimony for reasons quite apart from the husband who shakily agreed to love and honor. Perhaps I idealize women now in their twenties, presume that the world treats them better than it treated me. What brought me in a white brocade gown to an altar was not simple love for the person who stood pale-faced there with me: I wanted to be a wife because I couldn't conceive of anyone else to be; I wanted to escape my mother; I wanted a home of my own.

I didn't know much about how to cook, but I knew enough to know I'd better keep it simple. What I fixed the evening I first entertained company was a meal I'd eaten at my friend Joanna's parents' house: beef and kidney-bean chili, cole slaw, and ginger-bread studded with raisins. (If your taste memory seems to you fairly accurate, try these flavors and textures out in your mouth.) I telephoned Joanna's mother for her chili recipe, a simple prep-aration that began with chunks of round steak and onions browned in olive oil, to which one added garlic, chili powder, cumin, canned tomato paste and tomato sauce, red wine, and several cans of kidney beans. She warned me not to scorch it. Coleslaw I made pretty much as my mother did—grated cabbage, carrots, green bell pepper mixed with a dressing concocted from Best Foods mayonnaise, vinegar, sugar to taste, and celery seed. Gingerbread I stirred up from a recipe in my still-unspotted *Joy of Cooking.*

I wish I still had that blue clothbound tenth edition of *Joy,* co-authored by Irma Rombauer and her daughter Marion Rombauer Becker. Mrs. Rombauer and Marion were my companions during my first years in the kitchen; it was to their book that I turned to learn how to fold egg whites into cake batter (carefully), how to peel a tomato (dip it into hot water and then cold water), and the distinction between quick and light breads (quick breads need baking powder or soda to expand dough; light breads need yeast). I'd used the tenth edition *Joy* for some ten years plus when my husband, who'd begun to take an interest in cooking, urged me to throw it away. Why he wanted it tossed was that its pages were so gummed with ingredient splats as to be in certain spots un-readable. Some pages, particularly in the baking and canning sec-tions, stuck irreparably together. We replaced that *Joy* with a newer edition. When I look through this copy and stop at corn relish or butterscotch brownies or Wiener schnitzel, dishes I cooked often, or pie crust, with which I unsuccessfully struggled for years, I miss the innocent, hopeful girl I was then. In fact, I mourn her.

For that first company meal, I could as easily have prepared some dish of my mother's. She was a far better cook than Joanna's mother, who relied almost entirely upon Annie Mae, who let herself in the back door at dawn and did not leave until she had washed, dried, and put away the dinner dishes. My own mother, long divorced and hardworking at the university where she taught singers, by herself conjured up lovely and complex company meals; her preparations faithfully steered taste buds back to the ingredients on which these dishes were built. She set out on the table little pewter pitchers bearing blue hydrangeas or a wide water-filled bowl where lit flat candles floated among lilac sprigs. She piled records on the changer; all through an evening Bach two-part and three-part inventions, Mozart horn concerti, and Puccini arias filtered as naturally as breezes through guests' conversations.

Marrying so young I see now that I was anxious to put behind me all that my mother and her life represented to me. Most of her friends were unmarried or divorced and many were "gay," although that word was not yet in use. People she knew, primarily university professors, lost jobs if their same-sex romances came to public notice. My mother was not gay, and I liked her gay friends; it was not "gayness" I wanted to escape. I wanted to enter into the life that appeared to me in my friends' homes as the "regular life" of husbands, wives, and children.

I had invited a couple several years older than myself who'd been married two years—George and Carolyn. Their two years seemed an immensity of connubial experience. They'd already, some six hundred nights, cuddled to sleep under blankets and sheets beginning to show wear from weekly washing. They gazed at one another with unblinking calm; nothing, I thought, any longer lay secret between them; even their bare feet must know each other's every callus in the dark.

As soon as I tendered the invitation, I was frightened. In all these years, as many meals as I've made for guests, I still get scared. Not ravening, heart-pounding terror, but a mild anxiety takes over that must be akin to the stage fright a seasoned actress feels. Once guests accept my invitation, the prospective event begins to rehearse itself in my mind. I calculate menu combinations. I consider flavors, colors, textures, and what, that season, the market offers. I ask myself, What if John drinks too much and chokes on a tiny bone in the bluefish? and Can Pamela, who's felt iffy, stomach peppers and garlic? and Would they really like the muddy dark taste of black beans or simply vow to eat them because they thought them nutritionally chic? I pull cookbooks from the kitchen bookshelf. I study recipes. A constantly changing flavor river runs through my empty mouth. Then, rather as I guess the muse visits poets, a menu visits me: I know what I'm going to cook, and I know how. I begin, then, to fantasize the table. I try out a grape hyacinth bouquet set in an old sugar bowl bought at a tag sale and beeswax lavender-infused candles someone gave me for Christmas. I place this guest and that next to each other. I speculate on their likely talk. Everything else about which I should be thinking—moving laundry from washer to dryer, bills, letters, overdue library books, work—gets put on idle. I'm obsessed.

We tend to think sexual intercourse, momentarily joining two bodies, is the most physically intimate human act. Preparing meals for another person, in its own way, is more intimate, so much so that I sometimes wonder that we dare eat what strangers feed us. Bare hands rub and finger the cabbage and carrots and raw meat. Sweat on your palms, so slight that not even you feel it, carries your body salts and other castoffs into everything you touch. Skin flakes so small you'd need a microscope to see them drift off your hands and arms and face, down onto the dinner's ingredients. Eight-legged skin mites, for whom your shed skin is a perpetual feast, ride atop these skin flakes, munching and defecating and copulating and giving birth and dying. Breath and entire kingdoms of submicroscopic creatures alive in exhalations scatter and make camp across the ingredients' surfaces. The foods you prepare, together with these outfalls, cross the threshold of a guest's mouth (which in the case of most guests you would never consider kissing, other than lightly, on the lips). All this then enters the digestive tract and begins its passage from esophagus to stomach to duodenum to small intestine to colon. By the time you proudly bear your dessert of poached pears to the table, the lamb chop, the spinach and blood-orange salad, the rye rolls, together with you and the creatures who feed off you, have traveled deep into your guests' bodies and made a new home there.

When I am invited into someone's house, what I immediately want to do is look out windows. My need to pull aside a curtain and peer out onto lawn and trees and parked cars rises from my dis-ease, almost embarrassment, at having entered private space. The odors of homes—foods and bodies and sleep and pets—or the attempts to conceal those odors with pine aerosol, seem almost unbearably personal, as do even the newest unspotted sofas or chairs from which the imprint of a host's buttocks has been smoothed away. I want to hide my eyes. Every object, no matter how impersonal, hints at its owner's life. Tables, bathmat, wallpaper, lamps, leatherette Our Wedding album on a bottom shelf, Japanese screen, armoire, jade plant, unbitten apple alone in the footed glass bowl: all this might as well be a cry overheard from a confessional. Everything we own tells too much about us. I want to stop up my ears.

My first company dinner proved enormously successful. I bloodied my hand on the grater when I shredded cabbage and carrots, but I didn't scorch the chili or burn the gingerbread. I poured the harsh red jug wine that in those years we all drank into my new crystal wineglasses, whose slender stems and ballooning bowls so pleased me I almost wept at the pleasure of them. George and Carolyn praised what I served and seemed genuinely to like it and took more when more was offered. George was a doctoral student in American history; discussion centered on his reading in Charles A. Beard, a historian who had opposed U.S. entry into the Second World War. I said I had thought everyone was for that war, and he turned to me and said, "Oh no," and went on to tell stories of 1940 antiwar demonstrations on the nearby campus. Carolyn, George's wife, typed in the philosophy department office, for money to keep them going. We moved into the living room. I served coffee. For dessert I had only more gingerbread to offer. Carolyn and I talked about laundromats and her gray wool jumper, which she'd sewn for herself, and what it would be like when our husbands graduated and we had babies and money in the bank and cars that started without having to be pushed downhill.

After midnight, my new husband and I, he giddy from drink and I from accomplishment, stood at the door in starlight and thanked our guests for coming. They invited us to dinner at their house, and we set a date.

Looking back, I realize that it was an awkward, funny little meal. Carolyn, whom I grew to love for her kindness, may have wondered at chili, coleslaw, and gingerbread served on a fortune in tableware. For me, my first company dinner was as much a milestone as a wedding ring, new last name, double bed.

RHUBARB

❦

THIS IS A STORY ABOUT RHUBARB, BUT IT TAKES A WHILE TO GET
to the rhubarb part.

The children's father was in his last year of graduate school. We
were dirt poor. Some mornings I was so depressed I could barely
turn on the flame under the coffeepot. No matter how hard I
scrubbed, the stove stayed dirty. The linoleum stayed dirty. Hems
undid themselves on the girls' dresses. They scribbled in their
Little Golden Books. One morning Sarah hit Rebecca in the eye
with a hammer. "I want her to watch me and not Captain Kangaroo" was why she said she did it.

I had married too young. I was still wild. How would I tame
myself? He couldn't. Meals cooked, pots scrubbed, floors swept,
Jack's huge shirts ironed with no creases on the difficult plackets,
vegetable gardens, canning, pickling, preserving, sewing the girls'
dresses, scrub, scrub, scrub: I made myself do it. I made myself
figure how I'd stretch a puny on-sale chicken to three suppers
plus soup from the bones and rags of skin. I wanted to scream. I
wanted to flirt. I wanted to take ballet lessons. I made myself keep
my mouth shut. I scribbled bad poems about an old boyfriend;
the poems ended "If only" and "Where, where are you now?"

Weekdays, my husband came home late in the afternoon. He got the television going and slumped down in his easy chair. The chair's former owner had greased his hair; he'd left a head-size black stain on the upholstery. Jack watched the tail end of *American Bandstand*, then local news, and then Huntley-Brinkley. He did not smile, he did not frown. He only got up to adjust the rabbit ears and vertical hold. He said, "Can't you shut those kids up?" and sighed, "When's dinner?" I'd try to guess why he had ever said, on his knees, the old-fashioned way, "Marry me," why I'd said "Yes." I couldn't. I wasn't even twenty-one; already I was an old woman. I stooped and cowered. Out in my garden, the Country Gentleman corn stunted in July. I believed that when my husband looked at me, he thought, One more mouth to feed.

We had been living in a series of two-bedroom rented houses. All three had been the final homes of elderly widows. Two died in the houses and one fell on the back-porch steps, hit her head on concrete. An ambulance took her to the hospital, where she died without ever coming to. "Just think," her next-door neighbor Mrs. Forrest said, "Netta must have lay there curled up with rain coming down on her for an hour before I looked out my curtain."

The houses we rented stood in neighborhoods established during the 1920s before the Great Depression hit. They'd been built for working-class folks who had jobs in planing mills, for small-business owners and traveling salesmen, for Union Pacific men who got lifetime railroad passes and fat pensions. Women stayed home in these houses. You could feel their traces.

We rented the houses soon after their owners died. The rent was cheap. Nobody papered over the stained wallpaper and rectangles on walls where mirrors and paintings had hung, nobody fixed the warped windowsills or windows sealed shut with paint. I never asked them to; repairs could raise the rent. The widows' children cleaned the houses hastily. When you opened the refrigerator, you smelled soured milk; you touched knobs on kitchen cupboards and a last meal's grease came off on your hand. The widows' children left behind dented kettles, pink scuffs worn down at the heels, a tattered nightgown, dust balls shining with the widows' white hairs. Dark back bedrooms, kitchens, cramped bathrooms with footed tubs ringed with shed skin and soap fats—these had never quite let the widows go. The women seemed still to circle the rooms, as in late fall wasps seethe in circles around lightbulbs.

The shrubs around the houses were forty years old; nobody had pruned them for years. When it rained and the wind blew, and it always rained, because this was the Pacific Northwest, the shrubs' skinny branches scraped our window screens. At the farthest edges of the back yards, decades earlier, men had heeled in asparagus crowns and rhubarb. Blackberries and huckleberries they planted took hold and spread and grabbed on to plum and pear trees and rail fences. So did the arborvitae and the small evergreen salal that in fall put out purple-black berries. "Blackberry," Mrs. Forrest told me, "it's as much weed as fruit."

Pacific Northwest coastal rains don't so much pour as weep. The skies stay gray. The clouds hang low. Had Southern California's intransigent sun lit those three years, I'd not have been happier. Glare off outgoing tide, off parking-lot asphalt, off oncoming traffic would have hurt my eyes. It's never weather's fault, I would have told you, "light causes sadness." I would have told you anything if you'd promised you'd take me away.

Don't get me wrong. This wasn't that hard poverty you knew would never end. This was exile, and temporary. On a calendar the milkman left, I marked off days until graduation.

Where money was concerned, I was spoiled. I got mad when the twenties my father folded into my birthday card went to pay an overdue light bill. I wanted to buy Pete Seeger and Oscar

Brown, Jr., and Odetta LPs. I wanted to buy up whole flocks of chickens and tell Rebecca, "You can eat every drumstick," because that was the piece she liked, none other. I wanted to waste soap flakes and leave on lights in every room and throw away washcloths when the terry thinned in the center.

Each time, after we'd lived in a house for a year or so, the widows' children would sell it. I'd search classifieds, call landlords, and in late afternoon leave the girls with their father, staring at Fabian or Freddy Cannon or the Shirelles in fuzzy black-and-white on *American Bandstand*. I'd go look at houses.

A son or daughter would come to the door. "I grew up here," they always said. I followed behind, through bedrooms, bath, kitchen, front room. The rooms smelled damp. The son or daughter began sentences, "I remember the time, right here in this house . . ." As they talked, they twisted faucets off and on, flushed the toilet, raised and shut windows. They turned and showed me faces broken by smiles and bad teeth and eyes widened behind bifocals. They said their mother had been a saint, that they worshipped the ground their father walked on. They said, "They made a good life here, Mom and Pop." They pointed a finger out the back door and said, "See, there's the plum trees (or the Seckel pear, or the three McIntosh apple) my dad planted when he came back from the war in '45 (or before the Crash, in '29)." I half-listened; I was interested, then, in the future, not the past.

I tried to foresee our lives in these rooms, where paint had blistered and peeled and broken and mildew had turned blue an old pair of shoes at the back of a closet. What it would be like to get up in the morning here and go to bed at night. I thought, Sarah's goldfish will swim in this corner, Rebecca's red rocker can go there. I'll put the couch against that wall. I thought, I'll love him again in this house, he'll love me.

We'd strike a deal. I handed over crumpled bills, usually forty dollars. The most we ever paid was fifty. They never asked me to sign anything.

I could pack us up in a day. We moved on Saturdays, when guys from school had time to help. They made a party of it. Somebody had a joint, and the men hunkered over and passed it. The green odor hung on their jeans and jean jackets all day. They lifted the big couch and grunted while they hauled it onto a pickup bed. Then they took a breather and handed around a quart of Oly. I heard the beer go down their throats. Moving days, with his buddies, my husband was talkative. He seemed young again and muscular. He laughed so hard he choked. "Want to make us some sandwiches?" he called to me from the living room. I spread Miracle Whip and French's yellow mustard across Wonder bread and I slapped on bologna and American cheese. I tore open the potato-chip bag.

From the kitchen where I stood, Rebecca and Sarah tugging my skirt, I looked at Jack. We gave each other little comfort. I was too afraid of getting pregnant again to enjoy lovemaking.

With each move, I made new resolutions: Be more cheerful, get dust from under beds, give Big Dog a weekly flea bath. I liked fresh starts.

We rented this last house from Netta's son. We got settled by mid-January. I had the concrete block–and–board bookshelves restacked, dishes set in shelves, the pink Maytag chugging out its daily loads. I found new walks to take, pushing Sarah and Rebecca in their stroller. I met Mrs. Gib (for Gibson) Forrest, the eighty-four-year-old widow who told me how Netta slipped and fell. Mrs. Forrest was immensely fat and propelled herself forward with help from two thick rubber-footed canes.

Rebecca got sick a lot. I sat up nights and watched her sleep. I'd open the spiral notebook where I scratched "If only" and "Where are you now?" I multiplied 3 × 365 × 52 to figure out how many times during her married life Netta had filled the dish-pan. I closed my eyes and guessed where the bed had been when Netta's Union Pacific husband, shy and rawboned and full of love, scraped the day's beard against her breasts. Netta lived on alone twelve years after he died. She tossed birdseed out the breakfast-nook window. I knew that because, when we moved in, her birds were waiting for us.

The last year my husband was in graduate school, we were down to no money. A friend of Jack's, an older fellow named Orville who was getting his Ph.D. in philosophy, said he got government farm surplus food—"commodities," he called them—for his family.

Orville's wife—I can't remember her name—had put a match to an oven that leaked gas. It blew up on her and set fire to the house. Her beautiful blue eyes stared out from bumpy scar tissue and shiny skin-graft patches. For fingers she had stubs that ended at the knuckles. She wore her wedding ring on her left thumb. I felt sorry for her, not so much because she'd been scarred and chewed aspirin, three at a time, for pain, but because Orville was such a jerk. He was always telling younger guys like my husband how to manage a wife so as not to be pussy-whipped. He criticized my coffee as too weak, said I should take in typing, and, more than once, when drunk on tequila with the worm in it that he bought in Mexico, suggested he could give me a tupping I'd never forget. I thought I knew what tupping meant, but I looked it up anyway.

When you look rhubarb up in the dictionary you find that the word also means "a quarrel, fight, or heated discussion." Lexicog-raphers don't know why the pretty red-stemmed plant ever came to mean quarrel or squabble. Lexicographers do know that back in Shakespeare's day, rhubarb was the word bit players used in scenes when crowd metamorphosed to bloodthirsty mob. Actors muttered, over and over again in the background, "Rhubarb, rhubarb, rhubarb."

I would have thought that if rhubarb had any family, it would have been cousin to celery; rhubarb blades look like celery dyed red. But rhubarb is a member of the buckwheat family (buckwheat itself is best when added, as flour, to pancake batter) and, like buckwheat, is native to northern Asia and China. Waverly Root notes that it was mentioned in the *Pen-king Herbal*, believed to date from 2700 B.C. The *Herbal*'s author described the rhubarb root as a purgative. By the early Christian era rhubarb had reached the Western world. Its Western name, from the Latin *rhabarbarum*, describes the route the plant took on its way to the Romans, for the word roughly translates as "the vegetable of the barbarians, or foreigners, beyond the Rha." The Rha is the Russian river now known as the Volga, along whose banks, by the early Christian era, rhubarb apparently was growing.

Through the Dark Ages, monastery gardeners cultivated rhubarb in their medicinal gardens. The plant's beauty also made it sufficiently attractive as an ornamental that it occasionally was taken indoors and grown in conservatories. Monastery gardeners also used the huge leaves to cover baskets. In the fourteenth century, when bubonic plague began to spread across Europe and Asia, ground rhubarb root increasingly came into demand as medicine.

Until the sixteenth century rhubarb was grown solely as a medicinal and ornamental plant. Food historians suggest that it took so long to enter the culinary domain because Europeans initially tried to eat the leaves, which, loaded with oxalic acid, at the very least will bring on violent stomachaches, at worst can kill. But given the evidence in cookbooks, by the mid-1500s Western

Europeans were eating the rhubarb stalk and making rhubarb wine. The Italians took rhubarb wine–making one step further and made a liqueur called *Rabarbaro*. Even after rhubarb stalks began to be eaten, rhubarb continued to gain popularity as a purgative. Cervantes mentions, in *Don Quixote*, "a little rhubarb [will] purge their excess of bile." Macbeth asks, "What rhubarb, senna, or what purgative drug / Would scour these English hence?" In London, on March 2, 1784, Samuel Johnson, troubled by stomachache, was thanking a friend for his promise of rhubarb. Dickens's 1850 novel *David Copperfield* suggests for illness "a little tincture of carda-moms mixed with rhubarb, and flavored with seven drops of the essence of cloves."

Russia sold rhubarb root to Western Europeans, as did the Chi-nese; rhubarb, together with Chinese porcelain, pepper, silks, and tea, was standard cargo in the China trade. In England alone, by the end of the nineteenth century, more than 50,000 tons of dried rhubarb root were imported annually.

Colonists brought rhubarb roots to America. Thomas Jefferson planted rhubarb in his Monticello garden, but one wonders if he did any more than admire its beauty and resilience, because in his *Garden Book* he describes the leaves as "excellent as spinach," which of course they're not. The 1838 *American Frugal Housewife* lists recipes for rhubarb, also calling it "pie plant" and "Persian apple."

Rhubarb root's use as medicament continued in the new colo-nies. In *Moby Dick* Melville writes that "spermaceti, used as an ointment, was only to be had from the druggists as you nowadays buy an ounce of rhubarb." Mark Twain mentions that because he was the family pet, he was fed cod-liver oil to keep him regular, while the rest of the family had to get along with rhubarb. Not until the early twentieth century, when new chemical laxatives came onto the market, was trade in rhubarb root discontinued.

Lydia Pinkham recommended spearmint leaves steeped in water with sugar, rhubarb, and baking soda for gas and belching.

Rhubarb root's purgative quality carried over in early-American housewives' minds to rhubarb stalks as food. Rhubarb was one of the first perennial plants to produce in springtime, and often the first fresh food brought to table after long cold winters. A bowl of stewed rhubarb or a thimbleful of rhubarb wine therefore was considered to have a general "spring tonic," blood-clearing effect.

As to Orville, I was happy to hear, years later, that once their two boys graduated from college, Orville's wife left him. The way I heard the story, one morning Orville went off to teach, and that afternoon when he came home his wife was gone. Plus, she stripped their bank account, took savings and checking, stocks and bonds. The person who told me the story said that Orville, that very afternoon, had a heart attack. I'm sorry about the heart attack, but I wish I knew where Orville's now ex-wife is so I could congratulate her.

Orville sent his wife over to take me down to the county courthouse to apply for commodities. I can't remember what I had to say or do, I only remember I was so embarrassed I broke out in a sweat on a day that was so cold I was wearing one of my old cashmere sweaters as underwear and that the lady at the desk said sure, we were below the poverty line. Once a month Orville's wife and I picked up cardboard boxes packed with brown sacks filled with cornmeal and flour and bulgur wheat, kidney beans and dried milk, pound blocks of butter and lard and Cheddar cheese, cans of dried eggs and two-pound tin cans of boiled beef in gravy. The cheese was good, the butter a luxury, the beef stringy and greasy. I mixed it with catsup and vinegar to make sloppy joes. The girls liked sloppy joes.

Every house we lived in, I dug a garden. At the first two, the elderly ladies hadn't gardened for years. Netta had, right up to the day she cracked open her head. So I didn't have to dig out patches of turf and stack them to clear ground for a garden plot.

More than ever that last winter and spring, we needed a garden. The commodities held out for the first two weeks of the month, and silver smelt were selling five pounds for a dollar and fat hamburger three pounds for a dollar. If the girls and I got to the store early in the morning, the butcher had bones he'd give me free. Red flesh still clung to the bones, and sawdust from the floor where the butcher had tossed them. I washed off the sawdust and made broth for beef-vegetable soup. After I boiled the bones clean, I hurled them out in the back yard to Big Dog. We had peaches and purple plums and pickled beets I'd put up the year before. But the last two weeks, every month, we ran short on money for milk and fresh vegetables and fruit. Nights, I lay awake figuring how I could mix dried milk into the girl's oatmeal to get more calcium and vitamin D in them, or what I could do to make them eat cabbage.

You must wait until soil dries before you spade a garden plot. If you turn over wet, cold dirt, you end up with hard clumps. I was bad at waiting.

My gardens were pitiful. All my faults were writ into these plots dug out of back lawns. I planted too soon. February, I put in Bermuda onion sets and peas and beets. March, I knelt by furrows edged in with my hoe. I dribbled radish and carrot seeds into chilly soil. If seeds germinated and produced leaves, the plants dwarfed. They needed warmer soil, sunshine, frost-free nights. They needed somebody with better sense to plant them.

Old yards surprise you. Daffodils and purple crocus buried decades earlier pop out of dirty snow. A forsythia bush that looks dead puts out yellow flowers. Daffodils, crocuses, and forsythia do what they are impelled to do. You don't have to do anything right.

Mrs. Forrest liked to lean on her canes at the garden's edge and talk. She showed me where, along the edge of Netta's garden plot, two rhubarb plants for twenty years had been growing up in early spring and in midsummer dying down. She laughed, said, "You can't kill rhubarb." Netta's husband planted the rhubarb, Mrs. Forrest said, adding, "Lord, that man liked his mess of stewed rhubarb," and "That man liked a slice of rhubarb and strawberry pie."

Every day I went out under gray skies to Netta's garden patch and sat on my heels and looked down at the rhubarb. This is my life, I thought, I'm hunkered here in it. I wished I could plant and grow myself into someone exotic and brave.

From the rhubarb plant's fist-size heart, red-veined green leaves unfurled out of membranous sheaths. The sheaths that covered the leaves looked almost like skin covering some internal human organ. I expected to see thumping, hear a heartbeat. The leaves split the membrane, and then, every day, the leaves lengthened. Red veins ran through the leaves and soon turned blood red, then burgundy. By the end of March, when my radish leaves yellowed and the radish root did not swell at all, when not one carrot seed gave out its feathery first leaf, when I had not kept to my resolutions to be more cheerful, to give Big Dog weekly flea baths, the rhubarb leaves had grown bigger than two big hands.

TWO MOUTHS,
ONE SPOON

❦

SARAH WAS BORN WHEN REBECCA WAS FIFTEEN MONTHS OLD.
Rebecca could walk by then, steadily, although the dog we called
Big Dog, a dog-smelling, sinuous, long-bodied half-beagle mutt,
mottled black and tan over his white coat, could knock her down
if he stood near her and wagged his ropy tail. Breakfast and lunch,
I fed Rebecca and Sarah in high chairs in the kitchen. Big Dog
stationed himself between chairs. Any dropped food, Big Dog
grabbed, delicately, between his front teeth. Spilled soup, spilled
milk, he licked up with his black-spotted pink tongue. His tongue
voluptuously scraped against the linoleum tiles, each of which, one
black and then one white and then one black, I knew from scrubbing, on hands and knees.

Rebecca's mouth kept open house. Rebecca, you could spoon
oatmeal into with her baby spoon, down whose silver handle big-
footed ducks ran. Rebecca would give you such a smile while she
smacked her milky gruel. She showed her baby teeth and the hard
nubs of new teeth about to erupt that pushed under the glistening
gums. She ate any vegetable, red beet or green bean, or spinach,
which when cooked turns the green of lawns darkened by summer
twilight. She ate any of Gerber's bottled baby meals. She sucked

sections of tangerine from whose tight skin I'd popped out the seeds. Meticulously, she dipped toast corners into chopped-up three-minute eggs whose yolk shone out from the hollow of her blue bowl. She chewed her yolky toast and grinned. She grew round as red apples and beefy in the legs. Even her strawberry-blond hair grew prodigiously, into an extravagant electrified halo. We called her a Dylan Thomas baby because she had that cherubic Christmas-morning look Thomas had on covers of his books. She had Dylan Thomas's ardent pouting mouth and full cheeks. If between mother and child, food is love, Rebecca and I were joined at the heart.

Rebecca was born at the end of a cold January that got colder through February. In the Pacific Northwest, the icicles grew long on leafless branches. To look out any window those first months was to shiver and be thankful for the heat pipes knocking. From early morning the sky stayed gray and steepened; twilight lasted a few pink minutes. Blizzard wind from the north rattled windowpanes in the second-floor bedroom where Rebecca's bassinet, next to the double bed where she'd been conceived, reigned high on four white legs. She was sunshine sleeping there. The whole gray world clung to her; she made the short winter days shine.

Outside, where I would go to hang diapers, the wind was so cold I couldn't walk ten steps without mittens. Clothespinning Rebecca's diapers on the line, even through mittens touching what touched her, my breasts blossomed milk. Out in that arctic wind, I thought steam should rise from my breasts as if from a comic-book Mother Wonder Woman. Someone had only to say "Rebecca" and milk bloomed. Rebecca put her lips to my bare skin, milk started. The milk was bluish-white, and while she suckled a line of milk foam settled on her lips. My body was all hers, in love with her, more awake to her cries and her mouth than ever with any lover.

Rebecca and I those winter, spring, and summer months lived

animals' lives, lived as I guessed lions lived in lairs, licking skins, or bears in caves, breathing each other's bear breath, growing rugs of fur that warmed each other over winters, growing shaggy, getting muzzles. We owned a fortune in time, uninterrupted hours of each other. A big rocking chair stood in a corner of the bedroom. I rocked while I nursed Rebecca, the only sounds those of the rocker's treads against the bare floor and Rebecca's greedy swallows. I wanted to rock into a new millennium, rock forever. Late mornings, mid-afternoons, we often went to sleep together after she nursed, my blouse still open and her mouth suckling in sleep as puppies do.

While Rebecca slept I cleaned house, did laundry, fixed meals, changed the murky goldfish water for clear, put Big Dog out and brought Big Dog in, read books, read *Family Circle* and *Woman's Day* for household hints and baby hints and menus. I entertained the girl friends who came by. I was the only girl any of us knew who had both baby and husband. My girl friends regarded me as an exotic. They said so, but did not use that word. I had survived the rigors of childbirth we had been taught by horrendous movie scenes to fear. I had stretch scars across my belly and smelled, I'm sure, of milk, and after three months had gotten back my figure.

Evenings, while Rebecca's father leaned over his living-room desk, drinking black coffee and learning science, I shopped for groceries, I went to the library, I looked in windows of stores closed for the night. I studied the mannequins, dressed in those days in Jackie Kennedy pillbox hats, and thought about dresses I would buy when I had money. I always came home sooner than I needed to. I missed Rebecca.

That second time I did not want to be pregnant. We were too poor. I was not yet twenty-one. When our family doctor, the same woman who delivered Rebecca, looked up and told me, my heart sank. I felt lost and alone. I did not know how to tell her father, who had years of school ahead. I did not know how to tell our parents, who would think me careless. It would be my fault, someone so busy with our happiness that I forgot.

September was when I found out. I remember lying alone in the middle of an Indian-summer afternoon in the hot bedroom, from which Rebecca's bassinet had long been moved. I remember wasps seething against the ceiling. I remember I had not yet that day made the messy bed. I cried; then I cried some more.

Evenings, all fall, I was sick to my stomach. Downstairs in the bathroom, while Rebecca sat in her high chair and my husband at the table finished his dinner, or after dinner, when I was in the middle of washing dishes, and Rebecca, who was beginning to crawl, thumped across the kitchen floor, her diapered bottom high in the air, I would go into the downstairs bathroom and be sick. I tried to do it quietly. I sounded to myself like a cat with fur balls stuck in its throat. Afterward, I rinsed out my mouth with Listerine and mopped my face with a cool cloth and leaned against the cool lavatory rim. I saw my face in the mirror, chalk white and eyes gone huge with terror, and thought, I will never forget this.

After the fourth month passed, I opened the lid on the hope chest I'd kept in bedrooms since I was twelve and unfolded the maternity smocks I'd last taken off the year before. They smelled of mothballs and brought back memories still recent enough I knew them day by day. I washed and ironed them. By then we had a clothes dryer my father had bought me for Christmas. I did not have to go outside, where during Rebecca's second winter, rough wind again blew down from the north, rattled windows on which snow settled along the ledges, and hungry birds pecked at the seed that Rebecca and I, she riding my hip, tossed out, birds whose names for years I would not learn. I pointed to the ice formed along the windowpane and said to Rebecca, "Jack Frost has been here." She smiled and put her hand against the cold window. She had passed her first birthday. She could not yet say "Jack Frost." She could say "Mama," "Dada," "dog," "cat," "bottle."

My stomach got larger. I became slower. I limped under the huge ship my belly became. Late afternoons I was tired. Nights I slept so deeply I dreamed I climbed stairs, tumbled down, was dying. Rebecca crawled, then walked. She cut teeth and drooled down her checked gingham dresses and cried unceasingly; I carried her back and forth on my hip across the living room, twenty-five or so pounds of her, while Big Dog followed, wagging his big tail.

I began to dream my new baby. Son or daughter, I did not care. A boy we would name after my father and a girl we would call Sarah because we thought the name was pretty. When I was pregnant, women passed on old wives' tales about how to determine the sex of a baby. If you carried high, you carried a girl. If the baby kicked a lot, it was a boy. Or perhaps it was the other way around. A baby still in the womb seemed to me like presents shining beneath a Christmas tree, gift-wrapped boxes I was not to pick up and shake, whose contents I was forbidden to guess at.

When I was alone I put my hand over my stomach and touched hard knots I guessed were elbow or knee or shoulder. This baby, more active than Rebecca, stirred rapidly, surprising me so that now and then I'd put a palm against a wall to steady myself and flinch from the sudden pain.

By April, afternoons were warm enough that I sat on the porch and knit while Rebecca, who could walk by then, pulled her wooden PlaySkool truck by its dirty rope through thick grass dotted with dandelions I hadn't dug out. Rebecca crawled up wooden steps from the lawn—the risers were too high for her to step up— and stood next to me and put her head on my knee and pointed to my huge stomach and said, "Baby." I put her hand where the new baby kicked. "Baby, baby," she said, and she smiled, showing many teeth.

She will not be smiling soon, I thought, and went through again what little I'd heard about helping the first child adjust to the second. I was an only child. I tried and could not imagine what Rebecca would feel when the new baby arrived. I asked friends who were from big families. "Oh, I hated him" or "Oh, I loved her" was all they said. I didn't believe it would be that simple.

That last month, I withdrew. My attention focused on Rebecca, for whom I no longer had any lap, who had to sit on my knee, and on the mysterious baby whose arms, legs, knees fattened under my heart. I read to Rebecca from one after another of her tattered Little Golden Books. I prepared tiny sandwiches—slices of bread cut in quarters—for her and her growing doll and bear families. Evenings before she went to bed, I got down on my knees by the bathtub and rubbed shampoo in her turbulent curls and scrubbed up bubbles. Her yellow rubber ducks bobbed atop her bathwater. She splashed and laughed. I soaped her husky arms and legs, big ribs, tight stomach. Water pooled in her stomach's deep nook where we'd been attached. I admired her the way people who have stood in line all day outside the Louvre, when they finally get inside, admire the *Mona Lisa*.

My private joy clashed with the realities of no money, a big ancient house that increasingly I had trouble keeping clean, a refrigerator that needed defrosting, a husband getting ready for final exams, disapproving parents. I kept being happy anyway. When I pushed Rebecca in her stroller along the bumpy neighborhood sidewalks and graveled alleys on our daily walks, walking, as I was, slower all the time, my stomach a galleon, I wanted to write on the walls of the old garages that stood open in the alleys. I wanted to write in letters even bigger than I was. I wanted to write a song on those walls, boards weathered down to gray wood. I wanted to write words that made music played by trumpets and French horns and violins and deep vibrating cellos, and I didn't know how.

My bag for the hospital was packed. Lamyra, my best friend then, and I arranged that when the new baby started coming, I could call her. She would be to our house to take care of Rebecca.

Contractions started after midnight on the third day in May in the middle of a thunderstorm that broke an unseasonable heat wave. Through a wide window in the delivery room I watched the storm move toward us. Lightning bolts struck on the far side of town, flared across the darkness, so that for a moment the town's skyscape stood naked under harsh light. My doctor, the same woman who'd delivered Rebecca and who was our family doctor, had left Austria in 1938 and come to the United States. Her husband was a physicist and pacifist. They had six children. She was an early practitioner in America of natural childbirth. All her patients called her "Dr. Gertrude" or, simply, "Gertrude." She gave you your choice. Her white hair tucked under a funny old-fashioned cap around which a lace ruffle had been sewn, she sat on a stool at the end of the delivery table. We were alone, she and I. She didn't like nurses around until she needed them. I asked if she thought the storm would make the hospital power go out. "No," she said, and added, "You aren't going to take long. By the time the sun comes up, you will have your baby, I promise." She was seventy years old that year. She said I seemed very relaxed and asked if I minded if she took a little nap. I didn't. She let her head fall to her chest and began to snore.

The storm moved closer. Any minute I knew the world would change.

I winced and pressed down and grunted. Gertrude's eyes came open and she was all business. In a mirror set high above the delivery table, I watched the head, wet with dark hair, slide out.

I pushed again and Gertrude smiled, saying, "A girl. A big girl." Sarah howled. Lightning hit so near the hospital that canisters on a metal stand next to the delivery table rattled. Sarah howled louder. I heard nurses saying how good she looked, how strong, how healthy. I heard the rain start, hit against the wide window. I pushed again and delivered the placenta. From the corner of my eye I saw an aluminum basin, big as a dishpan, the shining florid placenta filling the pan and the umbilical cord curled atop. I asked to touch the cord. I did. Then the sunlight split through the clouds and streaked the sky all the colors you see in an old bruise. I was so calm.

You stayed in the hospital then for at least three days. Children were allowed in only for deathbed goodbyes, so Rebecca and I could not see each other. I hardly dared ask the friends and my husband who came to visit me and to see Sarah, "How is Rebecca?" Tender and empty, I was desperately in love with this new baby, who with her dark hair and dark eyes looked so entirely different from her sister. I felt guilty. I felt the way years earlier on a Christmas morning I had felt as I unwrapped a new doll and loved her fresh painted cheeks and clean clothes and the little white socks that matched and her dolly shoes that buttoned with cunning jet buttons. I thought of my old doll in the doll bed in my bedroom, of the days she'd sat with me through scarlet fever and measles when my grandmother said I'd go blind if I so much as looked out a window, and of all the afternoon boredoms when I was supposed to sleep and instead my old dolly helped me devise games. How could I give my heart over to this new shiny creature and leave my old baby with her matted hair and both her socks lost and her toes stubbed so that you saw through their ends the material from which she was made?

We brought Sarah home, Big Dog and Rebecca following up the stairs, and settled her into the bassinet. Rebecca peered in at the face that would be her sister, then turned and put up her bare round arms to me, her hands bean vines ready to catch hold. I sat in the rocker, pulled Rebecca up onto my restored lap, and nuzzled the halo of her wild hair, lifted the hair and admired and sniffed her white neck. We kissed and kissed and rocked and rocked. I hugged the big-ribbed barrel of her body. Big Dog thumped his tail hard and arrhythmically against the uncarpeted floor. He drooled.

Everyone we knew bought presents and hurried to our house to admire Sarah, to say whom she looked like and didn't, say how dark her hair was and how big her eyes, how brown. Everyone remembered to remember Rebecca.

Sarah was born with two teeth budded through her gums. When she suckled she suckled hard. From the first day she nursed as if she knew I would not offer enough. She nursed hastily, brutally, as if she suspected my body was a continent that any moment famine would overtake, where streams evaporated, locusts chittered, buzzards' shadows tarred barren hills. Sarah looked up at me from huge brown eyes set in a narrow baby face. Her gaze seemed skeptical. She seemed older than any baby should seem.

I loved her. When I went into the downstairs bathroom where all fall I'd thrown up, I'd smile at myself in the mirror.

Nursing didn't go well. Given Sarah's teeth, first two on the top and then two more, my breasts were always sore. Gertrude said, when Sarah was three months old, Switch her from breast to formula. Sarah seemed relieved.

So did Rebecca. How difficult it must have been for Rebecca, at fifteen months, from reigning in her mother's heart, being always the first thought, to waiting for the baby to nurse, for the baby's diaper to be changed, for the baby to be dazzled quiet with sleep. I don't think there's any doubt that for the first child, the second is paradise lost. Rebecca seemed hurt, but not unendingly. She tiptoed, she whispered, so the baby wouldn't wake. Big Dog the first few weeks seemed unhappier than Rebecca, drooping about behind me, wanting the old pats on his head and the old red balls tossed I had no time for. He slumped, a tragedy on four legs. While I took to the rocker or couch or my bed and nursed, Rebecca stood by or sat next to me, her mouth spilling the music of singular nouns a fifteen-month-old loves to hear: baby, dog, Big Dog, fish, Mama, doll, house, grass. While Sarah slept, Rebecca and I returned to our old games. Now, when we played or I read to her or we cuddled, I was always listening for her sister. We lived then on people's rather than animal's time. We were no longer only each other's.

Sarah liked her bottle. Food, she didn't like. Back then, you started your baby on Gerber's baby oatmeal at three months, you added applesauce and mashed banana at four, and strained veg-etables and mashed potatoes at six. Sarah didn't like the oatmeal, didn't like the applesauce. Six months, seven, eight, nine, she would eat almost nothing. Bring her silver spoon to her mouth, she clenched her small face, pressed her lips so hard her lips turned blue and wrinkled like lips of an old woman who smoked all her life. She gazed out at me from brown eyes that seemed to have lived other lives before hers. She screamed as the spoon came toward her. Her scream hurt my bones. I was afraid she hated me. I was afraid she would starve.

I wooed her with applesauce stewed from Golden Delicious picked from our tree. I romanced her with mashed pale slivers of poached Dolly Varden trout only hours from a high mountain stream, courted her with butterscotch pudding made from scratch and so tender a breath left it trembling. She frowned while she nibbled her toast strip abstemiously from my hand; when I walked away to answer a ringing telephone, she pitched it to the floor, where Big Dog worshipped at her high chair, fattening on what she tossed.

Gertrude checked and rechecked her. "She's fine," Gertrude

would tell me. And no, I wasn't giving her too much milk. Babies are all different, she'd remind me, just as adults are. She said "Bosh" to my worries and told me to mix Sarah's Gerber's baby oatmeal in the blender with banana and milk, pour this mixture in Sarah's bottle, poke a bigger hole in the nipple, and give her that for breakfast. "Then relax," she said, "relax."

I tried. All across town, I'd think, babies sit upright in their high chairs happily eating, mouths open, tongues awaiting the next delicious bite. Not at our house.

Sarah's refusal to eat left *me* feeling refused. I felt pushed away with each push away of the spoon. What was wrong was wrong with me. I was untasty to her, not the food. Hadn't—didn't Rebecca eat everything I offered? Was it because that second time I did not want to be pregnant? Had my terror and "Oh no" and the tears that followed stirred a bitterness deep in me that only Sarah could taste? At best, I would say to myself, she can only choke me down.

Rebecca had been a placid baby and outgoing. Sarah showed wary, sparing interest in others. Rebecca had been colicky, quick to catch colds, quick to whimper. Sarah went through her first year without a sniffle. She never spit up her milk. As Sarah's teeth broke through gums, she did not cry or even fuss. She was stoic, self-contained, courageous in the bathtub, where her sister at first had been frightened. She seemed almost feral, as if any moment she might revert to a life in the forest. You could imagine that nights, after we were all sleeping our dumb domestic sleep, she flew from her slatted crib out over fields outside town and hunted mice that ran between rows of corn.

I was afraid Sarah hated me, afraid that my troubled relationship with my mother would duplicate itself. Hadn't my mother disapproved of this second child, hadn't she said, "How can you take care of two?" with the emphasis on "you"?

When Sarah's father fed her, I was sure she ate more. When Lamyra fed her, I was sure she ate more. When they spooned mashed carrot or Gerber's peaches into her mouth, she seemed to open wider. She seemed not to scream as often. I sat nearby and watched avidly. My hurt must have shown.

She would come to me in dreams, in her baby clothes, turned to skeleton. I would see her gaunt. I would hear her bones clatter when she turned in bed. I would lift her from her bed and she would not weigh as much as a nickel, she would not weigh anything at all, she weighed so little that in my dream her Carter's two-piece pajamas, across which lambs played, were empty of her. She was down to all soul and no body.

I made the mistake of telling someone who was in his first year as a graduate student in clinical psych about my dream, and he, drinking coffee at my dining table, looked at me and said, "It's all wish fulfillment, your dream. You want her dead." He was only five years older than I, and I was so young that five years older seemed old enough to be wisdom. I did not feel anywhere in myself that I wanted her dead. I believed my feeling.

One Saturday at lunchtime, midway into her second summer, Sarah began to eat. I don't know why. I had made chili, the regular old American hamburger, tomato sauce, garlic, kidney-bean way. I offered her a bite and she took it. She took a second, third, fourth bite. I handed her a dill pickle slice. She ate that. She has been eating ever since, hugely, gratefully, as someone breathes deep who's been starved for air. Never fat, never even chubby, she still eats more than anyone at any table. She is a mother now. When Nick, her firstborn, was ready for solid food, he too evaded the spoon, twisted away his mouth, frowned, screamed. So I told Sarah this story.

MAKING MEMORIES

❦

MORE THAN THRIFT SPURRED ME SOME SUMMERS TO FILL JARS with pickles, fruit, and relishes. I was not the only one. You could walk down our alley and through open windows see bare-armed women sweating in kitchens, muscles popping up as they lifted hot jars out of the canning kettle, and you could smell the sharp vinegar and sweet fruit. These were women with whom I picked huckleberries along rivers and peaches in nearby orchards. We shared recipes for chow-chow and blueberry conserve and stood in each other's pantry gazing up at jars packed with dilled beans and Queen Anne cherries. We smiled and shyly touched each other's elbow with fingertips and said to each other about our canning what we said to each other about our children, "How pretty, how pretty."

Always high summer, canning season was. Noon heat all day. Sky molten blue. Early morning, you clipped the heavy laundry on the clothesline. Windless and the air so still (no wind flapping the big husband shirts or flowered little-girl skirts) you believed you could stand by the garden and hear the corn grow. The sound was a dry skimming swoosh like ballet slippers sliding across waxed floors. You admired the blooming potatoes and the carrots which were shoving up their feathery greens. You stopped to pluck a tenacious weed, then brushed aside humming flies and went inside, slamming the screen door as you liked to do, because you were a wife and a mother, this was your house. You walked barefoot across still-cool kitchen tiles. Watched the goldfish swim languidly in their warm water. Turned down the sound on the television, whose black-and-white screen Captain Kangaroo's face filled. You made potato salad studded with fat black olives and put it away for dinner and then daubed pink calamine on the children's mosquito bites.

You wanted to make something beautiful that would last. To retrieve something enduring from a hot day otherwise lost to children's ravenous need and many small failures. You wanted to save something. And it always seemed like magic, canning did. You packed hot sterilized jars with smaller-than-golf-ball purplish-red beets, added a bay leaf, onion rings, peeled garlic cloves, and poured in pickling syrup. Presto-chango, six months, nine months later, you opened the jar and spooned out the very same baby beets you popped into that jar the summer previous. Time—for the beets—had stopped.

It was easy, out of the chaos of meals (which took hours to prepare and minutes to eat), to feel that when you canned you were making art. Placing, as Wallace Stevens would have it, "a jar in Tennessee." Canned goods were to dinner what poetry was to prose, and pickled beets were one of the prettiest canning products. The bright red pigments, betanin and betaxanthin, that color the beet, bleed out a rich wine red into the pickling liquid. My jars of pickled beets had about them such a stained-glass-window ecclesiastic radiance that I used to say I wouldn't be surprised to find creatures from a crèche scene rise up, gather bundles, and walk out of the jar.

Canning (or "putting up," as our grandmothers called it) garden
and orchard produce is also a way of packing your own time cap-
sule. In summer you fill jars with peaches and nubby warted pickles and in winter when you open those jars, it all comes back.
There is the Saturday morning you set the plastic portable Zenith
in the niche of a tree trunk and teetered high on a ladder to reach
in among soft leaves for the peaches fuzzy as a newborn and
ruddy and golden. You cried while you sang along with Janis Jop-
lin singing "Little Girl Blue." There is the weekday afternoon
when the children went to the pool and your husband came
home early and you made love—then you got up from bed and
canned topless, sweat tickling down your spine into the small of
your back, the canning kettle steaming, the filled jars clattering in
bubbling water, and you wondering who you would be when you
turned thirty, wondering if you would live to get as old as forty
and have gray hair. You were not just making pickles or jam, you
were making a memory. You were canning days that otherwise
got lost. When winter's blossom-sized flakes drifted down on bare
trees and you put pickles out onto the table or spread peach jam
across a muffin, you were opening a photograph album. You were
eating memory.

I did turn forty. Making pickled peaches, now, provokes two
memories. One comes in snapshots of my maternal grandmother,
who first fed me pickled peaches and whom I watched make them,
and whose recipe I use.

The second memory shows up in my mind as a movie. The
pickled peaches aren't the movie's star; a dog is. Back when our
older daughter, Rebecca, was three, nothing would do but she
have a black miniature poodle. We got the poodle. Rebecca
named her Cher. Time passed. Cher produced several litters of
puppies, then hit dog middle age and began to run to fat. At her
heaviest, she weighed in at thirty-four pounds. Friends would

blame us for overfeeding her, and we'd point to our dachshund, who all his life remained as slim as the Duke of Windsor.

Every once in a while when I was looking for credit-card slips for the tax accountant or for the children's vaccination cards, I'd run across Cher's AKC papers. I'd stand by the rolltop desk and reread them, thinking each time that maybe there'd been an error, maybe she wasn't a miniature.

Three or four times a year we'd take Cher out to the vet— Larry—to get her toenails clipped and to be bathed and trimmed. Larry would always say, "Goddamn, that dog's going to drop dead any day." And he'd hand us another hectographed copy of his diet for dogs, and we'd read its purple type and go buy the cans of Campbell's beef and vegetable soup Larry prescribed.

And when we got Cher home, a topknot bobbing above her forehead, hair at the end of her stub tail shaped into a ball, and a ridge of her astrakhan-like fur encircling each ankle, it wasn't easy to keep from laughing. Her head was tiny and her muzzle delicate. Her trunk, of course, was massive. Inevitably one of us would say it: "She looks like a nail keg on legs." Cher would hang her head and slink off, tail down, to her basket, and we would feel, as we should have, ashamed.

The Campbell's soup diets never lasted long. All night Cher would be up and down. We'd hear her in the kitchen. She'd cry, the same pitiable whimpers that emerged when she delivered pups. After several years off and on of trying Larry's dog diet, we decided that these cutbacks only increased her appetite. The diets made her omnivorous. Anything available, she gobbled, whether she was hungry or not. A mother visited with her infant; Cher grabbed the baby's bottle, bit the nipple, lapped up the milk. When we hid the children's Easter eggs, if we didn't lock Cher in the house, she'd find every egg and eat it. In summer she'd wander out to the garden and pick off the ripe cherry tomatoes.

One of the first things you do when you can peaches is pour boiling water over the fruit to loosen the fuzzy peach skin and then plunge the fruit into cold water and slip the skin off one after another peach until the peaches are all naked. We—Rebecca and Sarah and I—used to end up with a plastic pail filled with peach skins, which one of us would carry out back to the mulch pile. Inevitably, Cher would stick her delicate muzzle right into that pile and gobble up the peach peelings, also the tomato skins, cucumber peels, the stem ends snapped off green beans.

Cher hung around the kitchen. Hot days she panted heavily, saliva dripping off her pink tongue. When we made pickled peaches, her corkscrew-curly black fur smelled for days of the sweet-sour, vinegar and sugar and clove and peach, that is distinctively the smell of pickled peaches. Those same days, the children would complain that they smelled like pickles, and that when we canned, their bangs were always sticky.

Cher was thirteen when she died (so much for Larry the vet's prophecy of early death!). It was a summer Sunday afternoon. I'd been playing ball toss with her out in the front yard while Rebecca filled the back seat of the Mazda with empty pop bottles she planned to return to the grocery store (she'd just gotten her license and was suddenly willing to do any chore that involved driving). I patted Cher's head, which by then had tufts of white hair, as did her muzzle, and went inside to start dinner. Rebecca telephoned a friend to ask if he'd like to go to Safeway with her; they talked awhile. Rebecca plucked the car keys off the dowel in the laundry room, kissed me, sailed out of the house. Seconds later, she screamed: a shriek pitched so high, conveying such grief, that it abraded the very air that carried it. Cher was in the car's back seat, dead. I think that the day Cher died marked for Rebecca the end of childhood.

Last fall I was visiting Rebecca. She led me to her pantry,

opened the door, and showed me shelves on which she'd lined up pickled beets (my recipe, taken from Adelle Davis's *Let's Cook It Right*), dilled green beans and dilled okra pods, mint pears and lime pears (from her grandfather's recipe), and peaches and black cherry preserves and apple butter. She toasted English muffins and we sat at her kitchen table and spread butter and the black cherry preserves onto the steaming muffins. The butter melted down into the bread's porous web and the dark cherries, surrounded by a pool of their own syrup, glimmered. The taste was that paradisal amalgam of salty butter, yeasty muffin, and sweet-tart cherry.

Out Rebecca's kitchen window we could see her German shepherd asleep under the weeping willow. We talked about Cher. We tried to remember what it was Rebecca used to say when Cher wagged her stub tail. "It was 'tut.'" Rebecca laughed. "I'd say, 'Cher is tutting her tail.'" I asked if she thought my feeling correct, that the day Cher died marked for her the end of childhood. She said, "Yes," and then her cheeks colored pink with embarrassment. She said, "Lots of things began to change about that time." And I knew she was blushing because she meant me. I changed.

At about that same time, the year Cher died, many women my age felt the world we'd made—children and gardens and kitchen—wearing thin, wearing out. The household arts appeared trivial to us, and we began to see grandmothers and mothers only as who they didn't become, what they didn't accomplish. We began to mourn what we felt were these women's unlived selves. We said, "If she hadn't spent all that time canning [or knitting or patching quilts or sewing our dresses] she might have been an engineer, a lawyer, a senator, an artist, a doctor." We lamented that she—they—had been only our mothers.

Mourning who these women did not become, we tended to

forget to celebrate who they were and what they did do. We forgot the back-yard gardens, rows and rows often scratched out of the poorest soils, that yielded meals which made us grow strong and bouquets which taught eyes and noses what beauty could be. We forgot the cunning thrift that turned scraps into rag rugs and quilts or gathered buckets of bruised windfall apples and stewed them down to jelly. Certainly we did not allow ourselves to consider that both the process of brining pickles and the jar of pickles itself might have given pleasure to our grandmothers and mothers.

For years, I gave up canning. I said I didn't have time. But most of all, canning (or sewing, raising vegetables, arranging flowers, knitting) in this new world of women engineers and doctors and bus drivers seemed to be a waste of my time. I told myself, I could be making money. Seeing Rebecca's jars made me want to pickle peaches again. I went to the hardware store and bought a canning kettle and a box of wide-mouthed Kerr canning jars and then to a farmers' market and chose firm peaches, one by one, until I had a basketful. Standing in my kitchen, feeling somehow shy and abashed, as if I were again a new bride, I dipped the fruit in hot water and slipped away the fuzzy peach skins. I was surprised how much my hands remembered.

POTLUCK SUPPER

❦

Doubt may give your dinner a funny taste,
but it's faith that goes out and kills.
—JOHN UPDIKE, Roger's Version

MRS. FREDERICK BROUGHT ONE OF TWO DISHES TO OUR CHURCH potluck. They were spoken of as "Mrs. Frederick's *famous* Swedish meatballs" and "Mrs. Frederick's *famous* sweet-and-sour pork-u-pines." The pork-u-pine's "quills" were the rice that Mrs. Frederick blended into ground pork. As the pork cooked and the fat melted, the pork shrank away, and the rice grains stuck out of the meatballs. For serving, Mrs. Frederick nestled her pork-u-pines shoulder-to-shoulder in baking pans, where the little meatballs looked, as Calvary Episcopal ladies were wont to say, "for all the world like baby porcupines."

Wooden lathing cross-hatched Calvary's new parish-hall windows, in a travesty of the mullioned windows for which Episcopal Church building committees go weak in the knees. Through the diamond panes, you could watch tall, bony Mr. Frederick, with his wind-burned cheeks, removing a baking dish from his bronze Coupe de Ville.

Mr. Frederick was just about the richest man in the county. He owned a vast hilly ranch that the river ran through, a river swimming with fat trout and hazed over in hot summer with mayfly hatches. According to our local newspaper, Mr. Frederick's bulls—"prize bulls"—provided sperm for herds all across the United States.

Mr. Frederick also owned the slaughterhouse whose cement-block buildings lay along the railroad tracks. Bawling cattle were unloaded from cattle cars at Mr. Frederick's before sunrise; refrigerated cars went out at night packed with silent beef. Outside the block buildings, the cattle, veiled by black flies, milled atop mountains of their own waste. Some dropped to their knees, capsized, and collapsed onto their sides. Other cattle stepped on them, climbed over, and walked across them. "Downers," Mr. Frederick's men called cattle who fell, "downers." But all the cattle, fallen or upright, roared as men in overalls prodded them through loading chutes to the killing floors. When we drove past, my children stopped their ears. "You can tell the cows are scared," they said in that overloud voice you get after you plug up your ears. They said, "I wish I could squeeze my nose closed, too."

The smell was terrible. When Indian summer hung on, inversion layers trapped air in the hollow our tiny town sank into. Then nothing kept out the slaughterhouse stench. Or the flies. An Egyptian plague of flesh-eating flies that tormented cattle also tormented us. "Close the screen door fast when you come in," I told the children, as flies darted into the kitchen, headed for the butter dish. I grabbed the fly swatter, slapped, and yelled, "Goddamn flies!" and hated myself for taking the Lord's name in vain, which I didn't want to do but did anyway. "It sticks a knife through God's side every time you say that," my grade-school Catholic girl friend Veronica had told me.

Mr. Frederick strode through Calvary's parking lot, bearing his wife's dish held high. Mrs. Frederick, almost as tall as Mr. and equally bony but, unlike him, unworldly pale, walked behind, teetering in high heels through parking-lot gravel. Alongside Mrs. Frederick walked Mary Bee Dillard, shoulders hunched to hide her big breasts. Mary Bee carried a picnic basket purchased in London in which Mrs. Frederick packed her silver, china, napkins, and Mr. Frederick's whiskey. Rule was, you brought a dish that fed four more people than your family, plus plates, napkins, drinking glasses, silver, and booze if you wanted it. Wine was provided, but it was cheap wine—jug Burgundy and Chablis—and we called it all "dago red."

Winter nights, Mrs. Frederick wore her mink. Snowflakes caught on her wispy faux-blond Mamie Eisenhower bangs and glittered on the mink's lapels. "A full-length ranch mink," Calvary ladies said when they mentioned the mink to a First Lutheran or Wesley Methodist lady. Our town was proud of Mr. Frederick's prize bulls; we Calvary gals took pride in Mrs. Frederick's mink.

Mrs. Frederick was big on wraps. Even on the sultriest, hottest summer evening on record, so without breeze that not a leaf lifted on the drooping cottonwoods, she wrapped a shawl around her shoulders. Ever since her hysterectomy, Mrs. Frederick said, she suffered "the torments of the damned from any chill."

The Fredericks, with Mary Bee, came late. "To make," said my cynical husband, whose family had produced four generations in the county, "an entrance." Before the Fredericks, car after car nosed into the parking lot, a few Cadillacs, many Plymouths, Chryslers, Dodges, Ford trucks, and several VW vans belonging to younger families eyed suspiciously as "hippie-ish," as "strange elements," but accepted because, as my mother-in-law said, "somebody has to help foot the parish bills."

Out of our 120-family parish, some fifty families, plus widows, widowers, bachelors, and maiden ladies, regularly attended the once-per-month Sunday-evening potluck. "Be careful now, don't tip it" or "Darling, don't spill," you could hear a wife warn her husband as he unloaded from a station wagon a bean pot oozing molasses, smelling deliciously of bacon and sugary navy beans.

As we ladies rushed through double doors into the parish hall, a vast high-ceilinged, half-timbered room, we kissed one another's flushed cheeks. "Oh, look at you, what an adorable dress," one might say, her hands on the dress's shoulders. "And you, too," the adorably dressed responded, "how pretty you look. I love your hair. Is Maggie still doing it?" We cupped cool ivory chins of each other's children, adding, "Rachel baby, I heard you were the star of Mrs. Blaisdell's piano recital!" and "Keith, how you've grown. Any day now you'll be taller than your father."

Men hurried to the three long tables on which the dinner dishes would be arranged and set down their burdens. They glanced about uneasily. No matter how many of these affairs they'd attended—and not a few men, like my husband, Jack, had come to these potlucks as children with their own parents—they appeared unsure of themselves, like teenaged boys at a formal dance. One after another, nodding hellos as they went, these men edged through the parish hall. Then out the door they strode, across the parking lot, and joined tight circles at the far end, where gravel petered out, next to the parish trash cans. Each can was lettered in black paint CALVARY EPISCOPAL; the lettering got touched up twice a year on parish workdays.

In spring or summer, when you looked out a triangular pane of mullioned window, you might see light flaring off silver flasks the men passed hand to hand. In winter, when snow covered the ground and next to the trash cans the limbs on spruces dipped low under their weight of wet snow and the men's breath blew out white clouds, you saw flashes of light as they lit matches or turned wheels on Zippo lighters. Cigarette ends glowed, cigar ends glowed bigger. If you happened to open the doors, you heard laughter and saw heads thrown back, and in winter you heard the men's feet stamping frozen ground, as they sought to keep warm. "Anything to stay out there and drink," my mother-in-law sighed, looking over my shoulder out the door.

Calvary Episcopal Church, in the town I call Coraville, was a hardship post. Priests came and went. Every few years the search committee geared up, riffling vitae and reading recommendations. My father-in-law, the search committee head, said, "It's a pain in the ass to hunt down one of these boys."

We didn't pay much, so we got men fresh out of seminary, not even thirty and still using acne medicine, or military chaplains ready for retirement. These old priests, with their weary, stand-offish wives (the Episcopal Church permits, even encourages, priests to marry), mumbled when they preached and wandered and lost the point they were making, and they rushed Holy Communion. People complained that they never got our names right and that if you wanted one of them, you discovered he'd taken off bass fishing or been gone to the nearest city for three days. As soon as their retirement day came, these older fellows packed up and moved, and we never heard from or about them again.

The old priest who'd been a Marine chaplain kept his head shaved shiny. He had a bulldog face and a thick neck that he didn't shave; white hairs stuck out from his pink ears and flesh rolls stacked above his tight clerical collar. He carried a belly ahead of him that his legs looked too puny to hold up.

He ended his homilies with war stories set, variously, in Saipan, Pork Chop Hill, or Quangtri. His sermon's hero was always a "raw recruit not old enough to grow whiskers" or a "big ol' colored boy from the South." The enemy always rushed the platoon. The boy always scrambled up from his foxhole and tossed grenades into a nest of "Japs," "Red Chinese," or "gooks." The grenades that blew Japs, Reds, or gooks to smithereens blew the boy to pieces. "He gave his life so his buddies might live," the priest said, pulling on his satin preaching stole. He'd lick his lips and look out at us looking up at him, us with our Sunday suits and dresses and shined shoes. He'd wait, holding our gaze, until we shifted in our pews.

He'd croon then, his rough cigarette basso ground down to whisper, "This young boy, he gave up his life just like Our Lord did. And probably not a one of those boys that was saved was as good a boy as that recruit (or colored boy), and for sure none of us is as good as Our Lord. But He gave Himself anyway."

Sermon over, we worked through Offertory, General Confession, Absolution, Comfortable Words, Sanctus, Prayer of Consecration, and finally said, "Lord, I am not worthy that Thou shouldst come under my roof, but speak the Word only and my soul shall be healed." Then the priest walked down to the altar rail, where we waited on our knees, palms up to receive the host. His cotton alb, which the altar-guild ladies kept white with Purex bleach, billowed around his big belly. He stood before you, Our Lord's body pinched between thumb and forefinger. His shoulders drooped, as if he'd been carrying something way too heavy for way too long. Under the alb, gas rumbled through his stomach, ending in explosions so loud that youngsters stifled laughter. Sulfurous intestinal gas drifted while he dropped the white wafer into your palm and said, "Body of Christ, Bread of Heaven."

But all this didn't matter so much. "These guys are just plumbers," my father-in-law said. "Their job's to keep pipes open between us and God. Besides, you gals run the goddamn church anyway."

He was correct about the gals. A cadre of six ladies ran our parish. To this cadre, a priest was no more than a hired hand, preferably handsome and well-bred, with an equivalently well-bred and docile wife. As long as he comforted the sick, counseled unhappy drunks who called people late at night, and didn't sermonize too much about the poor, the cadre remained politely indifferent to him.

When young priests arrived, they arranged on the church office shelves their encyclopedias of sermon aids and battered New Testament Greek dictionaries. They set end-to-end Buber's *I and Thou*, titles by Kierkegaard, Moltmann, Jaspers, Heidegger, Bultmann, Brunner, and martyred Bonhoeffer. They had Paul Tillich's sermons in tattered covers, and all three volumes of Tillich's *Systematic Theology*. They had titles by that peculiar misogynist C. S. Lewis. They had exegeses of St. Paul's Letters to the Romans and books by both Niebuhrs, Reinhold and H. Richard. You could often figure what seminary they'd attended by the titles. Priests from the School of the Pacific in Berkeley and Episcopal Theological Seminary in Cambridge had Heidegger's *Being and Time*. Berkeley graduates also owned Latin American liberation theologians, Allan Watts's Zen books, and Jung's popular titles. Men from General Theological Seminary owned Aquinas's *Summa*, Duns Scotus, Bonaventura, John Henry Newman's *Idea of a University Defined*, Dom Gregory Dix's *The Shape of the Liturgy*, and lighter books by Charles Williams, G. K. Chesterton, and Dorothy Sayers. Graduates of Virginia Theological Seminary, where professors were big on arts and existentialism, had Sartre's *No Exit*, Beckett's *Waiting for Godot*, or Eliot's *The Cocktail Party*. They had Auden's, Eliot's, and Gerard Manley Hopkins's poetry and Flannery O'Connor's terrifying stories. Even the most rigorously educated had Saint-Exupéry's *The Little Prince*.

I sometimes went into the office when it was empty and slipped books from the shelves. I sat in the armchair where parishioners sobbed out troubles or grumbled about each other, and searched for pages with sentence after sentence underlined, where "Yes, yes" was written next to a paragraph like this from Buber: "This is the exalted melancholy of our age, that every Thou in our world must become an It."

Sunday mornings, pale northern light filtered through stained-glass windows given in memory of wealthier Calvary dead. The windows' colors lay in slabs across the sanctuary floor, and caught these young men in a red-and-blue glow as they gripped the pulpit and searched out our faces and told stories about successful real-estate men with empty souls and lonely wives and children who were juvenile delinquents. They'd learned these stories in homiletics classes, where professors urged them to make the Bible relevant to the modern day. Others took to the pulpit as to a confessional and wheezed and blushed through allusions to "thorns in the flesh" and "dark nights of the soul." Young priests also brought liturgical innovation, guitar masses (for which the hippie-ish element played guitars, and sacred dance. In the last our junior-high Lolitas, led by big-breasted Mary Bee Dillard, dressed in white togas; they leaped and swayed and reached their skinny arms heavenward while we sang the Lord's Prayer to a tune that sounded as if the Carpenters had written it. "It makes me sick," my mother-in-law said, "to see them encourage Mary Bee to carry on like that." But Mrs. Frederick approved Mary Bee's leading the dancers. "It gets her out of herself," she said.

Three penitential years seemed the longest a priest could bear up under us. One shy blue-eyed blond bachelor who'd graduated from the seminary at Sewanee, in Tennessee, and who sang with an unbroken tenor and collected baseball cards, didn't last a month. My father-in-law said it was better the guy left, that he seemed "a little light in his loafers." When my older daughter asked what that meant, her grandfather tousled her hair and said, "That he might have been a queer, honey."

At potluck suppers, the old priests couldn't wait to get out in the parking lot for a slug of booze. The young priests stayed in the parish hall. They set up tables at which we'd eat and unfolded folding chairs and got the coffee urn going and hot water for people who wanted Sanka. They talked to parish teenagers about starting Saturday car-wash parties and a junior choir. If we didn't keep an eye on the teenagers, they slunk away into Sunday-school rooms, where they hunkered over on nap mats and smoked, usually cigarettes, but sometimes marijuana.

Part of what made Calvary a hardship post was that the valley in which Coraville rested was isolated. A dreamy late-1940s faded Technicolor-movie tenderness pervaded streets. You could easily believe Harry and Bess lived in the White House, North Korea had never crossed the 38th Parallel, and the *Saturday Evening Post* showed up in your mailbox every Friday morning.

The county's ruling, pioneer society was German, Welsh, Norwegian, Swede, dark-eyed Scotch-Irish, a few English. With the exception of the Scotch-Irish, faces were ruddy and fair, and eyes blue or green. Working out-of-doors, horseback riding, and golf turned skins leathery and cancer-spotted. Ruling families' names blessed downtown streets and county roads, but not streets winding through small neighborhoods built after the Second World War with GI Bill money; that was for newcomers, people who'd arrived in the 1930s and 1940s. These old families married their children and grandchildren to people with whom their parents and grandparents went to school. When they went away to college and wed what my mother-in-law spoke of as "fresh blood," the marriages often did not survive. Acceptance for newcomers, even those married to pioneer children, could take decades to earn.

Calvary had the most old families. Next came Wesley Methodist, which, together with the Unitarians, had the most members from the local teachers college. Unitarians were arty types who put up around town posters about peace and sold UNICEF Christmas cards. As for the college, my mother-in-law had graduated from it, but that was in the old days, and now the college harbored pinkos in poli sci and dope-smoking hippies and queers in art and theater. However, along with ranching and farming, the college provided the county's economic base. "So," my father-in-law said, "you got to put up with them."

Then came Presbyterians, who had the town undertaker, and then Lutherans. The latter had robust blond schoolteachers and registered nurses and a father-and-son chiropractor team. They had the family that delivered to your back door, before sunup, glass bottles of milk ringed from the bottles' shoulder up with yellow cream. Lutherans had the best food at their potlucks and lace tablecloths on their parish hall tables. But if this "best food" was mentioned, a Calvary lady, perhaps my mother-in-law or her friend Dottie, laughed and said, "But those Lutheran gals, my God, they're fat!"

After Lutherans came Baptists, Nazarenes, Assembly of God, a Mormon stake, and some conservative Lutherans who'd broken from the "downtown" Lutherans over a doctrinal point. Any number of small wooden frame churches came and went which my mother-in-law dismissed as churches for "white trash," "Holy Rollers," people who needed "emotional religion."

Roman Catholics had a good-sized parish in a modern structure near one of the postwar neighborhoods. RCs were of Italian, Polish, Lithuanian, Slovak descent, many of them children and grandchildren of the coal miners who had settled early in towns above the valley. Valley Protestants considered Catholics not quite American and spoke of them with humorous condescension as "mackerel snappers." Catholics went in for religious hocus-pocus, had too many babies, and were ruled by popes and Irish priests. Catholic priests' premarital counseling, my father-in-law liked to point out, "couldn't be worth shit." He'd get that look on his face of a lascivious monkey and say, "Would you want somebody who never played basketball to teach you to lob in the ball? Hell, you would."

Mormons also had too many babies and believed silly things, but worked hard and never "took welfare." Several Jewish professors taught at the teachers college; Jews drove eighty miles to a small city that had a Reform temple. "Jewed-down" was an expression with which local buyers and sellers felt comfortable. My father-in-law referred to a golfing buddy's wife as "a Jew woman," and my mother-in-law sternly corrected him. "Jew-ess," she'd say, "Jew-ess."

My in-laws were not the only people who believed and talked this way. For all that Coraville and the valley farms and ranches seemed set in an earlier, more innocent era, and that at church you could easily believe we'd all walked off a Norman Rockwell cover, we weren't so nice a bunch, or so happy. Husbands blacked wives' eyes, cracked teeth, pushed them down stairs, threw them out of speeding cars into country road ditches. A teenaged son beat his father almost to death with a bullwhip. My father-in-law and his brother got into a fistfight at a family reunion picnic; they broke each other's right arm.

It was common knowledge that Mary Bee's dad, the late Mayor Dillard, when Mary Bee was still in pigtails, began keeping her up half the night for company while he drank and wept about her mother. Mary Bee's mother disappeared before Mary Bee took her first steps and never ever so much as mailed a postcard to say hello.

"Girls in trouble," some as young as thirteen, were taken for abortions into that same small city that boasted the Reform temple. Several adolescent males shot or hanged themselves; one fourteen-year-old tightened a Venetian-blind cord around his throat, choking himself to death. Two Calvary teenagers, late one Friday night, were found in a storeroom at the back of Calvary's parish hall. Stark naked and high on cough medicine, surrounded by life-size Wise Men and Joseph and Mary from the crèche that at Christmas decorated Calvary's frozen front lawn, they fought the young priest who discovered them. He was so banged up my father-in-law feared he'd sue. But he didn't.

Pal Thayer, handsome drunkard husband of one of Calvary's cadre of six, went in and out of a clinic, trying to dry out. One sunless January afternoon Pal carried his Johnnie Walker Red Label out to the garage, slipped into his Chrysler, switched on the ignition and radio, and let carbon monoxide do its work. Pal's wife—Nan was her name, and she painted large pale watercolors—got home from Safeway, carrying fixings for dinner, and found him. "Nan pulled him right out there on the garage floor and gave him mouth-to-mouth, but he was already a goner," my father-in-law said, adding, with a faraway look on his face, "Old Pal loved that Chrysler." My practical mother-in-law noted that it was a good thing Nan had her own money, a modest trust whose funds grew out of real estate and blue chips. My mother-in-law and Nan had gone through school together from first grade on. Pal Thayer, as locals were wont to say, came "from somewhere else." Pal and Nan met during the war, but where was vague. As for what Pal did for a living, there'd been a sporting-goods store, a Western-wear emporium with a life-size papier-mâché horse at the entrance, a real-estate office, a radio station, all financed by Nan's money. The couple had two sons; both moved away to cities, one married and the other a "queer." After Pal Thayer's death people talked about why Pal "offed himself." The homosexual son—a ballet dancer in that Sodom that was San Francisco—was mentioned, as was Pal's "living off Nan" finally getting to him.

All California, except Disneyland, was Sodom. Sons of two pioneer families, while away at college, married "California girls." These women, both blond, for their California birth were considered sexual hotpots. Older men, when these women were mentioned, assumed roguish expressions. "Those California gals," they'd say, and lick their lips. About the California gal named Robyn, younger fellows sang, "Rockin' Robin, tweet, tweet, tweet," and essayed a few steps of the Twist.

As to why the ballet dancer was homosexual, one explanation

given was that "stock ran out." "Stock running out" was a common reason, locally, for troubles in otherwise good families. One way stock ran out was when good county pioneer blood was diluted through unwise unions. To mate with an outsider, an unknown like Pal Thayer or Mayor Dillard's wife, was to risk the taint of "bad blood." Male homosexuality, hermaphroditism, criminality, crossed and wall eyes, ugliness in women, religious mania, artiness, insanity, nymphomania: all could occur when "stock" ran out. As for lesbianism, that was easily explained: a lesbian was too homely to get a man, or her "plumbing" got messed up by childhood illness or "gland problems."

The young priests were buoyed by Christianity as theology. Only a few months before they stacked their books in Calvary's office, they had been arguing the ins and outs of eschatology: was the Kingdom of God a present but hidden reality, or was it to be expected only in the future? They had been grinding out in ball-point pen on their bluebook pages essay tests whose answers were to show whether Barth's distant *totaliter aliter*, wholly-holy Totally Other, or Tillich's nearer-at-hand cosmopolite Ground of All Being better described God.

These young priests came to Calvary in love with God. But God, particularly a seminarian's God, is easy to love. He may order up typhoons that kill thousands and let a baby die and let Himself be wrangled over by German theologians, but He isn't blowing bad breath into your face and yammering about altars or griping about how fast the organist takes recessional hymns. At Calvary, these young priests found themselves forced to try to love people. They'd expected we'd bring them intriguing crises of faith that could be met with those answers they'd written out in their blue-books. We didn't. We brought them ourselves.

When a new priest arrived, combatants in the battle over how the church should be run took him aside and tried to win him to their way of seeing things. Since the 1950s, when the new church had been built, occasional outbreaks of bad feeling had surfaced. The old church had been torn down when Safeway offered the parish a fortune for the midtown lot on which church, parish hall, and rectory then stood. Even to old-timers, Safeway's sum was attractive. So that the battle over the new church was never about having sold out to Safeway, moving across town, and rebuilding: it was about how that new church should look.

The way I heard the story, architectural differences were easily solved by compromise. The church itself was to be "modern." The result was a rounded low-lying brown-shingled heap that from the air looked like a fat hen, wings spread out into the parking lot— I saw Calvary from the air once when at the county fair I won a free plane ride above the town and floated there, for twenty minutes, like a creature out of a painting by Chagall. The attached parish hall was to be a one-story brick "traditional," in fact, a long, low-lying fifties ranch house onto which were pasted Tudor touches, like the mullioned windows.

The fracas came over altar placement. Some wanted the altar as it was in the old church, built against and facing the east wall, which meant that the priest celebrated the Eucharist, or Holy Communion, facing that wall. Others wanted a free-standing altar, which allowed the priest to go behind it and celebrate Holy Communion facing the people.

That altar placement could cause such a tiff is due to the division among Episcopalians between High Church and Low. Conservative High Churchers, spoken of as "Anglo-Catholics" or "spikes," want to conserve what the Episcopal Church lost four hundred years ago when Henry VIII split with Rome. Spikes refer to Holy Communion as "the Mass" and believe Christ to be bodily, literally, present in the wine and wafer. Evangelical Low

Churchers, or "Prots," as Anglo-Catholics disparagingly call them, speak of Holy Communion much as Methodists would; they say the "Lord's Supper," or "Communion." And as for the real presence of Christ in the elements, as far as Low Churchers are concerned, whether Christ is physically or only spiritually present it's to each his own.

High Churchers like incense, every-Sunday celebration of Holy Communion, psalms sung responsively, sometimes even a Mary chapel, individual confession, Stations of the Cross during Lent, and an altar against the wall. Low Churchers expect a Bible-based sermon, Holy Communion on one or, at most, two Sundays per month; they think the Prayer of General Confession a sufficiency, want no incense, no Romish carrying on about Mary, no oddball services like the Stations, no squawky plainsong; and on Sunday they want the whole shebang over fast, and they're all for freestanding altars. "Otherwise," my father-in-law said, "it gets too hocus-pocus. Why not just go be a mackerel snapper?"

A Low Church Calvary priest once told a confirmation class for parish adolescents that if he wanted he could turn grape Kool-Aid into Our Lord's Blood. "It's the thought that counts," he said. High Church parents demanded the fellow's dismissal but didn't get it.

Visitors to an Episcopal church anywhere can get some idea of who's High Church and who's Low. A High Church person, entering the sanctuary, will, unless he or she is crippled, genuflect when passing the altar. A Low Church person, at best, will nod. During recitation of the Nicene Creed, if, during the phrase "And was incarnate by the Holy Ghost of the Virgin Mary," the person genuflects deeply, he or she likely is High Church. The person who does nothing is Low Church.

Which church you attended and your position in that church's hierarchy were, social markers in the town. Within her church, a woman was expected to be "faithful." The faithful Calvary lady showed up on Sunday for church, children in tow and made to behave, went to her guild's monthly meetings, worked on the Christmas Bazaar, church cleanups, Bishop's Spring Tea, and contributed crafts and food to these projects.

Nan Thayer contributed paintings to the Christmas Bazaar. Her paintings, vases filled with pale flowers or landscapes dotted with faraway horses and cows, sold well. Just as we spoke of "Mrs. Frederick's *famous* sweet-and-sour pork-u-pines," so we all spoke of "Nan Thayer's famous watercolors." But after Pal died, she began producing paintings quite unlike her pre-Pal's-death oeuvre. In Nan's new paintings, red and black squiggles spiraled out at you off Nan's rough watercolor paper. They were so scary that you wanted to cover your heart when you looked. We propped these up on bazaar tables, and my mother-in-law's friend Dottie said, out of Nan's hearing, "These are about Nan getting Pal out of her system."

When you got a new desk calendar in December, by which time the ground was frozen and the trees leafless, you marked down third Thursday afternoons for guild and fourth Sunday for potlucks. You looked for Ash Wednesday and Easter week and Xed the Wednesday evenings between for Lenten Bible study. I'd begin thinking what I'd wear to Bishop's Tea, and what I'd knit and bake for next year's bazaar. I was proud my knit hats sold out the first morning and that older Calvary ladies praised my workmanship. I was proud that at potluck my pickled beets, made from beets in my garden, got eaten up, as did my beef pot pies and cheesecake topped with canned cherry pie filling, to which I added red food coloring to make it brighter red.

Nights when I couldn't sleep, I sometimes thought about what to cook next. I never expected to make my way into the cadre of six, but I wanted my husband to be proud of me. If Jack was awake, I'd crawl up close to him, breathe across his bare chest, and ask, "What do you think about my making for potluck that chocolate pound cake you like, except I'd bake it in the Bundt pan and drizzle it with mocha icing?" Whatever I suggested, he said, "If it's not too much trouble, sure."

All us younger women longed to produce a dish that would be spoken of as "Mrs. Weaver's famous apricot cinnamon rolls" or "Mrs. Delacorte's famous sweet potato–pineapple Hawaii luau bake." Fame wasn't easily come by and was made more complex by unspoken protocols. For instance, even though a twenty-five-pound roasted tom turkey, stuffed with cornbread and onion, or a baron of beef would have been ooohed over, and even though diners would have left not a bite, to bring either to the potluck would have been "flaunting." You would have been marked as a show-off. Dishes regarded as exotic or too foreign or too "gourmet" were "putting on the dog." And no one should even consider variants upon Mrs. Frederick's pork-u-pines or Mrs. Hopper's Tater Tot casserole.

Tater Tots are balls of chopped potato, browned and frozen. Package directions suggest either baking or frying. Preparing this casserole, Mrs. Hopper made meatballs from ground beef mixed with bread crumbs and several packages of dehydrated onion soup mix. She fried the meatballs, and then, without pouring away the gathered beef fat, added cans of cream of tomato soup and cream of mushroom soup. To this "gravy," she added sour cream, canned mushrooms, and garlic salt. In another skillet, she fried Tater Tots. Into a large baking dish, she poured the meatball-sauce mixture and then the Tater Tots. While baking, the meatballs sank to the bottom and the Tater Tots rose to the top.

The cadre who ran the parish were themselves ruled by Mrs. Frederick and Mrs. Hopper. Mrs. Hopper was wife to an eye-ear-nose-and-throat man looked up to by men and women for his virile holiness. (The Hopper vehicles, including the horse trailers in which Mrs. Hopper took horses to shows, had bumper stickers that read, *Even so, come Lord Jesus, Rev 22:20.*) Raised in the Episcopal Church, baptized and confirmed, Dr. Bud Hopper nonetheless put faith in Billy Graham. When Graham's crusade neared our state, Dr. Hopper canceled patients and took off. Night after night, Bud answered Graham's altar call, was saved and resaved. After his Graham conversions, Bud took people aside during coffee hour after church. He gripped your elbow and got his long nose close to your face. What he said to me on one of these occasions was "God really did something to my heart this time."

A physical opposite of pale Mrs. Frederick, Mrs. Hopper had a sturdy, waistless body. She wore Pendleton plaid suits in winter and sleeveless dresses that exposed her tanned, muscular arms in summer. A horsewoman, she cleaned her barn with help from a gangling retarded fellow with BO (a "simpleton," my father-in-law said, who ought to be "de-balled" before he raped some girl). Dallas, they called this fellow, after the city where Dr. Hopper found him at a Graham crusade. At church, Dallas knelt between the Hoppers; he babbled loudly and drooled when he prayed. At potlucks, he hunched between them and choked on his food, and vomited it onto his shirt and tie. The Hoppers smiled and dabbed away the mess and kept right on talking about horses or how good they thought the father's sermon had been that morning or how well the thirty-year-old Dallas was doing, learning his ABCs.

Our parish had two women's guilds, St. Anne's and St. Martha's. St. Anne is mother to the Virgin Mary. St. Martha is sister to Mary Magdalene. The tenth chapter of the Gospel of Luke has Mary Magdalene, seated at Jesus' feet, listening while He talks. Martha, scuttling about fixing dinner, turns to Jesus and says, "Lord, do you not care that my sister has left me to get on with the work by myself? Tell her to come and give me a hand." To which Jesus answers, "Martha, Martha, you are fretting and fussing about so many things; only one thing is necessary. Mary has chosen what is best; it shall not be taken away from her." Theologians call upon Martha and Mary to illustrate the argument between "faith" and "works." Martha represents the "active" life of "works" and Mary Magdalene the "contemplative" life of "faith." St. Anne's sponsored the annual Bishop's Spring Tea and Christmas Bazaar. St. Martha's sponsored spring and fall rummage sales. A third group of women, rather like independents in colleges that have sororities, belonged to neither guild and sponsored nothing.

All the cadre were St. Anne's ladies and, excepting Mary Bee Dillard, were married or widowed and connected, by birth or marriage or both, to old county families. You did not ask to join St. Anne's; you knew if you belonged. The only outsiders invited into St. Anne's were priest's wives.

Most St. Martha's gals worked. They were secretaries, CPAs, social workers, bank tellers, teachers, nurses, librarians, lab techs, travel agents. Non-working members were wives of forest service rangers, county employees, professors, schoolteachers, realtors, agricultural extension agents, small shop owners, and ranchers.

St. Anne's had no divorced members. Had you married into a proper family and been abandoned by your husband or left him after you couldn't take drunken beatings or his giving you VD, you drifted away from St. Anne's. You did not join St. Martha's. Nor, had you been a St. Martha's member and married into a leading family, could you join St. Anne's.

Sunday-evening potluck had its own ritual. Three long tables were set out for serving. Salads and vegetables and breads went on the first table, main dishes on the second, desserts and milk and Kool-Aid pitchers, half gallons of dago red and Chablis and coffee and tea urns on the third. Beyond these tables were tables that seated eight and four. These were where we ate, always with our own families. As soon as you deposited your dish at the proper long table, you chose the table where you'd eat and put out place mats and dishes and silver.

St. Anne's was responsible for arrangements. St. Martha's, after dinner, cleaned up. At meats and casseroles, you began with so-so dishes, prepared by ladies of small social consequence. Thus, the sixth-grade schoolteacher's Macaroni and Pimiento Cheese (elbow macaroni, white sauce, Velveeta chunks, and chopped pimiento, topped with bread crumbs) could go first, followed by the assistant city manager's wife's Turkey Tetrazzini (5 cups shredded turkey, 1 pound thin spaghetti, 2 cans sliced mushrooms, 3 cans cream of mushroom soup, topped with grated Parmesan cheese), followed by the grade-school librarian's Tuna and Potato Chip Loaf (½ pound crushed potato chips, 2 cans tuna fish, 2 cans cream of mushroom soup, 2 whole eggs, mixed together and baked in loaf pan). Several more dishes followed, perhaps a St. Martha member's Seafood Divan (cream of celery soup, canned shrimp and canned crab, canned mushrooms, pimientos, cooked cauliflowerets) and a tuna casserole gussied up with chopped green olives. After these, we laid out offerings prepared by more august ladies: thus, a lifelong St. Anne's gal's Tamale Bake and her daughter's Spaghetti Meat Pie would be given harbor next to Mrs. Frederick's pork-u-pines (for whose last-minute arrival we waited) and my mother-in-law's fried chicken.

My mother-in-law hated cooking. When I was first married to her son, she "fried" chicken by coating the bird pieces in Shake 'n Bake and then baking the chicken. During the early 1970s, Kentucky Fried Chicken announced they would open in our town. Unlike slow-growth liberals in big cities who fought the chains' arrivals, we, who had only Dairy Queen and A&W Root Beer, were thrilled. My mother-in-law, from KFC's opening day, brought the 30-piece KFC tub to potlucks. Had she not been one of the cadre of six, KFC would have been taboo. She, however, could get away with it and be praised.

In the parish kitchen, which we'd outfitted with two six-burner ranges and two new refrigerators from Christmas Bazaar sales, ladies tied aprons over "good" clothes and warmed Tahiti Sweet Potato Casserole (canned sweet potatoes, orange pulp, brown sugar, cooking sherry, marshmallow-whip topping) and Pigs-in-a-Blanket ("So cute," someone would say, touching pinky-sized sausages, around which were wrapped American cheese and refrigerated biscuit) in the oven. Another lady stirred Cheddar cheese soup for Broccoli Loaf, and next to her another woman, cheeks rosy from heat, kept her eye on simmering cream of shrimp soup that at the last minute she'd pour over Cauliflower-Broccoli Medley. Hungry, overexcited children, warned by their mothers to slow down and show some manners, to put back Lenten pamphlets they'd grabbed out of the rack in the narthex, chased each other across the parish hall and repeatedly had to be corraled. Somebody always had to go look for the teenagers.

Summer nights, gelatin salads puddled. So if you brought Golden Glow (chopped carrots, crushed pineapple, cream cheese molded in orange Jell-O) or Hawaiian Heaven (fruit cocktail, miniature marshmallows, banana slices, crushed pineapple, Cool Whip in lemon Jell-O), or Frosted Lime-Walnut (walnuts, celery, crushed pineapple, cream cheese in lime Jell-O), you set them in parish refrigerators until right before time to eat.

We took turns bringing older ladies who didn't drive to potlucks. These ladies specialized in buttermilk biscuits, yeast rolls, and corn sticks. They brought these, with homemade jam, in baskets covered with white linen tea towels. Older women also baked pies and cakes and, in summertime, fruit cobblers. When my husband was a boy, his paternal grandmother, long dead when we married, paid him to go up into the hills on his bicycle and pick blackberries and huckleberries for her cobblers.

While we admired each new dish as it arrived and determined placement, we kept an eye out for the Fredericks and Mrs. Frederick's Mary Bee. Whoever first sighted the Coupe de Ville called out, "Fredericks! The Fredericks are here!"

After her two daughters married and moved away from Coraville, Mrs. Frederick took Mary Bee under her wing. Mary Bee was in her late twenties then, and orphaned, a heart attack having toppled Mayor Dillard. Mary Bee's big brown eyes ("pinwheeling," my husband said, from the anti-psychotic drugs) stared out from a square, ruddy, horsy face, above which shimmered a corona of thin pale hair, teased and ratted to add fullness and height. After high school, Mary Bee volunteered in the town library. Every few years, beginning in junior high school, Mary Bee went "off her nut" (my father-in-law's expression) and quit bathing, talking, and eating. She'd refuse to crawl out of her bed even for the bathroom. An ambulance then drove up the circling road to the Dillards' house on top of the hill, next door to the Fredericks', and took Mary Bee in restraints to the clinic where Pal Thayer went to dry out. A month or two later, Mary Bee returned, apparently restored. (While she was gone, we offered her name in the list of prayers for special concerns.) Not long after the mayor's heart attack, Mrs. Frederick had her hysterectomy, an operation, she said, that "did her in." So Mrs. Frederick moved Mary Bee in with her. Next door, the house Mary Bee grew up in stood empty. Mary Bee wanted to save it, she said, for when she got married, which, my father-in-law said, nobody in his right mind would do except to get his hands on Old Man Dillard's money and Mary Bee's big boobs.

When the Coupe de Ville pulled into the parking lot, we hurried coatless out into the cold or, bare-armed, into heat. We carried in baking dishes and footed and filigreed real silver gratin dishes into which Mrs. Frederick fitted her baking pans. The progress from Coupe de Ville to parish hall was a matter of many trips. After the first, which bore Mrs. Frederick into the parish hall, Mary Bee lifted off Mrs. Frederick's mink and slipped it onto a wooden hanger. Or, if it was July, say, or even a warm, rainless May with the sky turning pale yellow to pink, Mary Bee tucked the shawl of the evening closer about Mrs. Frederick's shoulders.

In the last minutes we stacked paper cups next to the dago red, and Mrs. Hopper strode to the door. Hands around her mouth to form a bullhorn, she called, "Come on in, guys." The men turned laughing faces to her. "Okay, okay," they said, and ambled across the gravel, slapped each other's back, and guffawed. Only when they reached the parish hall did they lower their voices and shutter their faces into a pinched, pious look. Meanwhile, we who had children gathered them and stood at our table, holding the back of our folding chair.

The priest took his place in front of the long tables. Our noisy talking stopped. "Let us thank God for our blessings," the priest intoned into a silence broken only in summer by fans suspended in the ceiling. Husbands and wives and children and maiden ladies and widows, we closed our eyes and held hands and recited, "Thank you, God, who in Thy great glory has vouchsafed to feed us . . ."

We picked up our plates and formed a line, the priest and his wife and the Fredericks, with Mary Bee, at its head. Given that on a good night fifty families plus a dozen or more little old ladies and assorted singles came to potluck, you can imagine how many bowls and baking pans and baskets and platters lined these tables. We began at the relish trays, with salads, vegetables, and breads, and worked our way to meats and casseroles, where Mrs. Frederick's footed silver gratin dishes gleamed at the table's center and

her heavy silver monogrammed serving spoons stuck out jauntily
from pork-u-pines or Swedish meatballs.

Even those who for fifty years had attended these potlucks burst
out with "Oh my gosh, look at all this food!" And "I always look
forward to Mrs. Cummer's lovely pea and baby onion salad!" and
"I can't help wanting more than my share of Mrs. Gibbons's Cheddar biscuits!"

Rules, unspoken but strict, existed as to how one served oneself.
The first time a diner went through, he or she chose dabs from
at least every other dish, except items like creamed spinach, which
you either loved or hated. The second time through the line, after
everyone had served himself, you could take larger portions of the
dishes that remained. The Hoppers invited new people to share
their table, along with the priest and his wife. The Fredericks,
Mary Bee, and my in-laws and Nan Thayer sat together, with my
mother-in-law's best friend, Dottie Reynard, and Dottie's husband, Jack; the men at that table drank more from their bottles
than they ate, and they got loud right away. My husband liked to
eat with guys who fished and urged against getting stuck with
schoolteachers ("They bore the shit out of me"). If his fishing
buddies weren't there, he'd tell me to get a table with old ladies
who'd known his grandmother, because he liked their stories.

Looking down at the daubs of food on my plate, I knew who
had fixed what and in my mind's eye could see the woman and
her kitchen, the view from her kitchen window, her husband and
children. I thought of the work that skinny Aggie Milam, wife of
the big-bellied shoe-store owner (he cheated on her), put into her
tri-color gelatin salad (red, green, yellow). Saturday morning, while
the three Milam children screamed for breakfast, she had to oil
her turban mold and pour in the red gelatin and canned fruit
cocktail and then set the turban mold in the refrigerator and wait
for the red to jell; after the red jelled, Aggie poured in green

gelatin and miniature marshmallows, waited for that to set; then she poured in bright yellow gelatin and maraschino cherry halves, walnut bits and cream-cheese chunks. All Saturday and Sunday she had to keep her children and husband from opening the refrigerator door and sticking fingers into the yellow gelatin to pry out a walnut. Sunday evening, when Aggie brought the turban mold, white platter, and parsley to the parish hall, there came that terrible moment in the kitchen: Aggie upended her mold and prayed that the tri-color turban would slip out in one piece onto her platter. We all said "Yea, Aggie!" when the red-green-and-yellow-striped turban stood shimmering atop its parsley.

I didn't like the taste of much of this food, and it wasn't what I cooked at home. I don't think that many of us brought to potlucks what we regularly fed our families. (The only Campbell's soup I kept in the pantry was chicken noodle, because the children asked for it when they were sick.) Recipes for much of our potluck food came from the *Family Circles* and *Woman's Days* we picked up at the checkout counter at Safeway. These recipes ingeniously used products that came to market shelves after the Second World War. Potluck food, except for the older ladies' desserts, celebrated the postwar culinary democracy, the melting pot. It was public food, like "good" clothing, and when someone like Pal Thayer died, the food that you went in Nan's back door and left off on her kitchen counter, along with a note you wrote, saying, "Our prayers are with you in your time of bereavement."

When we ladies went back the second time, usually with a still-hungry child, for we pretended to delicate appetites, we checked how much was left of our Sloppy Joe Casserole topped with canned French-fried onion rings or our Almond Chicken Salad or our relish tray ringed round with radish roses, gherkins, peanut butter–stuffed celery curls, almond-studded black olives, home-made dilled okra, and salami twists in which you took a half slice of salami and rolled it around a chunk of cream cheese. A woman who'd tried, say, something curried that wasn't a hit had to keep smiling while she heard people at the serving tables praise the Frank-and-Three-Bean Bake and watched Dr. Hopper and my father-in-law spoon out a few more pork-u-pines.

Some dishes didn't go over. You'd see a wife whose beans, for instance, didn't soften up in baking whisper to her husband to please take a big helping so that her bean pot wouldn't stand there, still half full.

That "hippie-ish" element associated with the teachers college, which my mother-in-law tolerated for its pledges to the parish treasury, made casseroles with bulgur and brown rice and salads aquiver with alfalfa sprouts (which my father-in-law enjoyed saying, when he was in his cups, reminded him of pubic hair), dense heavy muffins, and cookies made with honey, all this in the era when anyone who ate yogurt was referred to as a "health-food nut." This group, busy forming organizations to save wetlands and build bicycle paths, spooned out helpings of their offerings. Everyone else, except the younger priests, avoided these dishes and spoke of them as "hippie food."

Desserts, we ate last. Desserts were Calvary's pride. Not only did older women bake from scratch their chocolate, angel-food, and lemon cakes, their butterscotch meringue and lemon meringue and rhubarb-strawberry pies, and their peach and berry cobblers and apple puddings, but several younger women who took cake-decorating classes in back of the downtown hardware store made sheet cakes and cut from them, say, a Mickey Mouse figure, with Mickey's big ears and sad round eyes, or a big duck iced with white frosting in feathery strokes on the duck's plump body and with shiny yellow frosting on its feet and bill. The children loved these cakes, as did my father-in-law, who pored over them, shaking his head, saying, "Well, I'll be damned." For holidays, these same women who took cake decorating made fancy cookies. For St. Patrick's they made shamrocks sprinkled with colored sugar green as bottle glass and, near Christmas, gingerbread men and women whose icing suits and dresses had buttons made from silver dragées.

People moseyed around the parish hall, balancing dessert plates and coffee mugs. The older men kept drinking and talking louder, about rents on downtown stores and good buys on car insurance and the cattle market and local football and basketball teams and frozen pipes and the lawn mowers they were buying. They got so boisterous that they woke toddlers asleep in their mothers' laps.

Ladies said how especially good the Turkey Tetrazzini tasted and how tender Mrs. Junken's pie crust was and wondered aloud how she cut her crust lattices. "With pinking shears," she told us, blowing smoke in our faces. Mrs. Junken was eighty-something, hopped about with a cane, painted her droopy eyelids with blue shadow, and had been smoking Chesterfield non-filters since the Second World War. If she wasn't hospitalized, Mary Bee Dillard, hand cupping Mrs. Frederick's elbow, led Mrs. Frederick from group to group. Mrs. Frederick complimented each of us on dress, children, potluck dish, or some task we'd completed, like touching up paint in the sacristy. Somebody always said to Mrs. Frederick that her sweet-and-sour pork-u-pines proved irresistible and Mrs. Frederick always smiled at Mary Bee and told us she'd helped and how she couldn't do without her.

Mr. Frederick, if he got you alone in the dimly lit hallway when you were coming from the women's room (where Christmas Bazaar money went to buy a pretty Oriental carpet and a full-length mirror), hugged you close to his bony chest and whispered in your ear and pinched some soft spot on you, a breast or chub at the waist. He might even nibble your earlobe and invite you to meet him at the Crossroads for a drink some afternoon before your children got home from school. His breath gave off bourbon and he said filthy things in your ear and pinched you again, harder, and then said, "I bet you'd like it like that, wouldn't you."

I never told my husband about Mr. Frederick, and I'd wager that nobody else told her husband either. Why I didn't say anything was that I knew, as we all knew, that Mr. Frederick's talk and touching me was how things were, and that to tell my husband would only make those things worse. Once I did say to my husband, though, that I bet Mr. Frederick chased after Mary Bee at night after Mrs. Frederick went to sleep, that he probably couldn't resist that bosom of hers. My husband said, "Maybe, maybe not."

One summer afternoon at a St. Anne's meeting on Mrs. Hopper's patio, the younger of us women were talking, and it slipped out that Mr. Frederick was somebody to stay away from. Mrs. Hopper, passing by with the teapot, heard us. She put her free hand on my shoulder and said, "The world, my dear, has got enough hurt without our adding to it."

By nine-thirty on potluck nights, women started collecting their empty bowls and platters, piling plates and silver into baskets or doubled-up Safeway sacks. Husbands carried sleeping children and lidded casseroles out to cars. Mary Bee Dillard got Mrs. Frederick's mink. But nobody left until whichever priest we had then went to the front of the hall and lifted his right hand and said, "The Blessing of God Almighty, the Father, the Son, and the Holy Ghost, be amongst you, and remain with you always. Amen." High Churchers crossed themselves and everybody began shaking hands and kissing cheeks and saying what fun we'd had and how much we looked forward to the next potluck. Any minute then, St. Martha's gals could begin swabbing down tables and taking trash out across the gravel parking lot to the cans lettered in black paint CALVARY EPISCOPAL.

TURKEY SEX

❦

OUR DOMESTICATED TURKEY HAD ITS BEGINNINGS IN A SLEEK, dark-meated bird, long of leg and neck, with iridescent bronze plumage. In the pre-Columbian era some ten million of these birds flew through forests from southern Canada down through Mexico. (The wild turkey could fly as far as a mile without stopping, at speeds of up to 55 mph.) Most North American Indian tribes only rarely hunted this turkey, and then for its lovely feathers rather than its drumsticks. (Some among these tribes judged the bird stupid and cowardly and eschewed its meat for fear of acquiring these traits.) But in Mexico the Aztecs domesticated the bird; Montezuma's chefs regularly prepared turkey dishes.

Spanish conquistadors carried the Aztec turkey (and New World gold) back to Europe in the 1500s. No edible bird that large— thirty-two to forty pounds—existed in Europe; among the wealthy, the turkey soon became a centerpiece for special occasions. Within a century, in England, Germany, Holland, and France, selective breeding had produced a flightless bird with white rather than dark breast meat. (Some found the new bird insufficiently flavorful. Waverly Root has written of how turkeys were killed in Alsace to make them less bland: "The turkey is kept without food or drink for a whole day. It is then driven all around the farmyard to anger it. When it has become furious and terrified, it is forced to drink salted ginger-flavored vinegar, and then strangled.")

Why turkey has white meat and dark is due primarily not to blood and blood's oxygen-carrying hemoglobin but to the oxygen-storing myoglobin. The latter is located in muscle cells and stores oxygen carried by blood until the muscle cells need it. Muscles that use more oxygen have a greater oxygen-storing capacity than muscles that use little oxygen, and therefore are darker red. Because oxygen use generally is related to activity level, muscles that are exercised frequently and strenuously need more oxygen. Once the turkey was domesticated and ceased flying for any distance its breast muscle of course became white.

In the 1600s the Aztecs' turkey, which had sailed to Europe with the conquistadors, returned to North America with English immigrants as a white-breasted, somewhat plumper creature, refined, one might conclude, rather like a Henry James heroine. Breeding of the bird, with selection for meatier breasts and thighs and the pretty tail feathers that were turned into feather dusters, continued over the next three centuries. By the mid-nineteenth century, turkey—domesticated and wild—had become the entrée of choice for Thanksgiving dinner. (Mark Twain, in his 1880 book *A Tramp Abroad*, writing about his homesickness in Europe for American food, lists "Roast turkey, Thanksgiving style. Cranberries, celery" among the dishes for which he longs.)

Before the Second World War, most of our domestic turkeys' breastbones rose in a high arch. On a twenty-five to thirty-pound turkey, this lofty Romanesque arch of bone tended to make the bird too large to fit modern ovens. Breeders set about developing a bird with a lower arch to its breast. At the same time, they also sought to produce an even heavier-breasted bird, to accommodate

Americans' preference for white meat over dark. By 1945 the apotheosis of turkey was considered to have been reached in the heavily fleshed Broad-Breasted Bronze, a turkey with a breast so wide that its legs (by then short and blocky) were not strong enough to permit easy walking. (This bronze-feathered turkey has since been replaced by white-feathered birds, thus eliminating problems with dark pin feathers.) Another result of this genetic tinkering was that the male turkey could no longer readily mount the female without damage to both birds. The male's frantic clawing tore at the hen's back. Attempting to solve this problem, turkey growers fitted the hens with canvas saddles that protected the female from goring by male turkey claws. But turkey producers soon gave up on the saddles and turned to artificial insemination.

I talked one morning, by telephone, with Dr. John Proudman, at the United States Department of Agriculture avian physiology laboratory in Beltsville, Maryland. Proudman has worked exclusively with turkeys for the past thirty years. Male turkeys, like most birds, he said, do not have penises. "The sperm issues from a small lymphoid ejaculatory organ, one-quarter to one-half inch in length, in the cloaca [the common cavity into which the intestinal, genital, and urinary tracts open in birds].

"Turkeys," said Proudman, "when they mate naturally, stand on the back of the female and lower this lymphoid organ onto the vagina. In response to this, the hen everts her vagina outward and the two organs come into contact. There is no actual penetration. The semen is put, very shallowly, right on the surface of the cloaca. A colleague of mine speaks of this as a 'cloacal kiss.' The semen is then deposited on the vagina, the male dismounts, and the hen draws the vagina back inside, bringing the sperm in."

Turkey-breeding farms employ insemination teams to "milk" sperm from the male and then place it in the female. To acquire turkey sperm takes two to three workers. "You set a male turkey in a holder to hold it still," said Proudman, "and begin to massage at the base of the tail and along the stomach. The ejaculatory organ everts and a little semen rolls down on it. It's a very small volume and it oozes rather than spurts. Then, using a straw, you aspirate, or suck, the sperm off the ejaculatory organ into a small vial. The objective is to get a clean, uncontaminated sample—uncontaminated, that is, with fecal matter."

Does the male turkey enjoy this?

"Oh yes, they become perfectly happy, after they go through a short training period. In fact, they are eager to get up there and be worked on."

Does the male turkey have an orgasm?

"I've not seen them with a smile on their face. But perhaps it does give them pleasure."

Turkey sperm, Proudman said, "is highly concentrated, more so than bird sperm in general and mammalian sperm. So, typically, before the hen is inseminated, the sperm will be diluted quite extensively in a saline solution." You can cover as many as thirty hens with semen from one tom. And your average hen will produce about ninety eggs in a reproductive lifetime of twenty-two to twenty-five weeks."

To inseminate the female, said Proudman, the "artificial insemination teams march the turkeys one at a time into an apparatus that holds them while the operator squeezes them in such a way that they evert the vagina just as they would were a tom on top of them. The ejaculate is in straws, and they either blow it in by mouth or aspirate it inward with a bulbed tube."

Ralph Ernst, a University of California at Davis Cooperative Extension poultry expert, has worked with turkeys for decades. In what Ernst spoke of as the "old days," the 1960s, breeders had not yet perfected methods of storage for turkey sperm. (Now turkey sperm can be stored for as long as twenty-four hours and retain motility.) "Back then," said Ernst, "the male would be milked for his sperm and then the sperm would be rushed to the hen. One person would sit down and put the head of the hen between his legs and hold her feet. From that position, you could push the oviduct and pop it up. The other person, the actual inseminator, would then take a slender four-inch tube filled with semen, insert it into the hen, and blow in the semen. It was hard work. These turkeys were big. But they didn't fight much. They get used to being handled."

How old does a hen have to be before she can be inseminated?

"You can push them to come into lay early, but it's not a good idea. If they are not big enough to lay eggs, you are likely to have a prolapse of the oviduct and the eggs are too small. Also, if you start them too soon, they end up by not laying as many eggs in a cycle. So you lose at the other end. In the old strains you waited until the hen was thirty-six, thirty-seven weeks old. Now it's about thirty-three weeks of age that you can inseminate. When they are in lay condition, you can put a little gentle pressure right around the cloaca and get them to evert, just pop right out."

When the tom is in what Ernst called "reproductive condition," at about thirty weeks of age, insemination teams will "pre-milk toms, because the semen isn't necessarily that good the first time. When the tom is ready, is in reproductive condition, and when he gets used to being milked on a regular basis, he will sometimes ejaculate prematurely, which can be a problem if you're not ready with a straw or an aspirator."

❦

Into the kitchen.

For the cook, the traditional Thanksgiving dinner can be an ordeal. I remember, in my first years as a housewife, getting up out of a warm bed while my husband and children slept. I pulled on my old blue chenille bathrobe over my flannel nightie and tiptoed across cold floors into the kitchen. Tossing the dachshund out the back door, I wrested the thawed turkey out of the refrigerator (one of whose shelves I would have had to remove to accommodate the huge bird). I undid the metal wire that bound the turkey's legs together at the ankle and spread apart the still-frosty legs; the cold flesh squeaked. I put my hand deep into the bird's chilly interior and pulled out the slimy paper bag that held the turkey's neck and heart, liver, and gizzard—the giblets. By that time, our two daughters likely would be out of bed, watching while I mixed stuffing in a big bowl, massaged salt and softened butter into the turkey's skin, and placed him or her, breast up, in the navy-blue enamel roaster. Then, by the time I lifted the heavy pan into the oven, my husband would have wandered in and filled a bowl with Grape Nuts and wandered back to our bed to read. Slightly nauseated from my contact with the turkey, I would bathe and dress. Soon the aroma of roasting turkey perfumed the house. I would begin the rest of dinner. By the time I'd managed three or four Thanksgivings, nothing about the dinner caused me worry except the giblet gravy. I worried about how ugly the giblets were and I worried that my gravy would have lumps.

Generally, gravy is made by thickening and seasoning juices that drip and ooze from cooking meat. Those juices are a gift, really, as in one of the *American Heritage*'s definitions for gravy, "payment or benefit in excess of what is experienced or required," and for the slang expression "gravy train," defined as "income that requires little effort while yielding considerable profit." One good way to describe that "benefit in excess" is a poem titled "Gravy," which Raymond Carver wrote not long before he died in 1988. Carver from the time he was a teenager had been a destructive drinker, and then in the mid-1970s, when a doctor told him he had to quit the bottle or die, he got sober. Ten years later, when another doctor told Carver he had lung cancer, he wrote "Gravy," in which he urged readers, "Don't weep for me . . . I'm a lucky man. I've had ten years longer than I or anyone expected. Pure gravy. And don't forget it."

THE NIGHT WE ATE
MIGHTY DOG

❧

IN THE LITTLE TOWN WHERE I LIVED SO UNHAPPILY AND HAPPILY for so many years, a day came when everyone "went gourmet." People had subscribed to *Gourmet* for years. The glossy magazine slid through slots in perhaps a dozen doors. Few of us who subscribed did much more than look at the photographs of hams glacéed with *chaud-froid* sauce or *tartes aux* this-and-that *fruits*—*pommes* or *figues* or *framboises*. The magazine intimidated us. Not only did the recipes demand unfamiliar techniques and ingredients, but the appointments—the china and porcelain, the silver, the august flower arrangements, crystal, napery—were beyond us. None of us owned tureens shaped as pheasants or tongs for sugar cubes (none of us had sugar cubes!) or Baccarat crystal. When luscious taffy-blond Mandy, one of the Tolliver girls (the Tollivers were among Coraville's oldest families), married Knox, whose father's father had founded Coraville's bank, they got so many wedding presents that packages had to be trucked in two moving vans from the church hall to their new house on the hill. Photographs of Knox, his father, grandfather, uncles, and great-uncles—showing rodentine teeth, slightly bucked, and retrograde chins—hung on the bank's walls. Anyway, Mandy *did* rather conspicuously own and use a Reed & Barton silver tea and coffee service, complete with sugar bowl and adorable round-bellied cream pitcher. We all wanted one. But you couldn't get it with Green Stamps, so I, at least, gave up longing.

I can't tell you precisely when we went gourmet. Certainly, by the bicentennial year of 1976 Mandy and my neighbor Marilyn, she of the dark eyebrows that grew almost together over her nose, had been taken up by a bachelor college professor who "cooked gourmet." But when—1974? 1975?—the professor began inroads into Mandy's and Marilyn's proud all-electric kitchens, I'm not sure. I do know that in 1976 a "gourmet" couple, driving a foreign car, moved to town from Boston and planted radicchio and arugula, neither of which we'd ever heard of or tasted. I know that on a hot August Saturday night in 1977, when poor bloated Elvis had been dead only a few days, culinary progress had been such that our set was eating a meal that tasted as much of the names of dishes—*à la* this and that—as of food itself.

But back before that—through the early to mid-1970s—calendars in our little town might as well have been flipped to 1952. In Coraville we were living lives the way lives were lived in the 1950s; we were still eating 1950s food.

Out beyond our valley, women read *Mastering the Art of French Cooking*; we enrolled in cake-decorating classes given in a room at the back of the more successful of the town's two hardware stores. We pumped out colored frostings onto vast sheet cakes made from Duncan Hines and Betty Crocker mixes. I could write pages describing sheet-cake landscapes, George Washington and Abe Lincoln portraits, the Easter Bunnies, Mickey and Minnie Mouses, Santas, and sleighs pulled by reindeer.

We clipped magazine recipes and reverently followed directions for meat loaf gussied up with Campbell's tomato soup and

Lipton's dehydrated onion soup mix. If we felt like gilding the old lily, we might concoct Poor Man's Beef Wellington. When the meat loaf was done, we'd take it from the oven, upend it onto a meat platter, and plaster the loaf—on top and along its steaming, fat-dripping sides—with rehydrated Ore-Ida instant mashed-potato flakes. Accoutered with bright green frozen peas, carrot coins, and gravy made with the meat-loaf drippings boosted with GravyMaster, this was an attractive weekday meal. Your kids and husband ate it, no complaints.

Our notion of a foreign meal was La Choy chicken chow mein. We thought canned black olives exotic; if almond slivers were poked into the olives' hollows, we'd likely say, "What will they think of next!" Garlicky food was exotic (with the exception of garlic bread), as were wines other than Gallo. Game hens were exotic. Eggs Benedict was exotic. And "exotic" was simply another way of saying "hifalutin" or "gilding the lily" or "making silk purses from sows' ears," all terms of opprobrium. And it wasn't that we weren't dazzled by what we saw when we turned *Gourmet*'s heavy pages, we just never wanted to be seen as taking on airs.

We gave dinner parties. These parties tended to have themes. Terrilyn Jo, a stocky bottle blonde with piggy blue eyes and a heart of gold, one year went all out with a dinner that celebrated the opening of the football season. For place cards she bought toy footballs. She took toothpicks, construction paper, and Elmer's glue and made tiny pennants on which she wrote our names and stuck the pennants into the toy footballs. Terrilyn Jo's husband, Nate Jr., a wide-shouldered ex–college lineman and our up-and-coming real-estate magnate, mixed drinks at his four-stool bar, complete with refrigerator and sink, the whole set-up ordered all the way from High Point, North Carolina. To go with drinks, Terrilyn Jo whirred up cream and Cheddar cheeses in her Waring

Blender (we were nuts over blenders). She shaped the cheeses into a life-size football and coated the football with paprika for color. Dessert was devil's-food sheet cake frosted green for grass and white for yard lines. Toothpicks made goal posts.

Food focused on a grand piece of meat—a baron of beef, canned hams stuck with pineapple rings and cloves, a bronzed turkey tufted round with parsley sprigs. Fancy desserts were standard. A favorite was Black Forest Cherry Cake—a three-layer chocolate-pudding cake cemented with canned cherry pie filling and frosted over with chocolate and stemmed maraschino cherries.

These dinners gave us ladies the opportunity to wear party dress. We didn't have many chances to show off our décolletage or creamy shoulders and pale arms with their oval vaccination scars or the watered silks and brocades and beaded velvet dresses we bought, usually on sale, in the nearest city. We made our men wear suits, and sometimes we got together and ordered them boutonnieres.

Maybe little romantic affairs took place. Certainly, at these parties, gazes across tables were sought out and met. Footsie was played. Marilyn said these events reminded her of Saturday nights at all-girl summer camp, when boys from the boys' camp came across the glittering lake to dances. "I used to kiss a kid nicknamed Snap," she whispered, "until my teeth ached."

In my mind's eye I can still see Nate Jr. grasping the fragile wrist of the wife of the owner of the hardware store where we took our cake-decorating classes. The store owner's name was John, and he was a plain-faced, tall and stooped, soft-spoken, hardworking fellow with whom my husband, Jack, had fished since they were boys. John's wife, Sally, was tiny and anorectic. The biggest thing on her was her big brown eyes. We knew, because she told us, that she hated fat on anybody's arms or legs, and that when she ate too much she put her finger down her throat. Even though

she was thirty and had two children, she didn't look older than
twelve. I remember seeing her naked in the dressing room at the
pool and being shocked that she had pubic hair, and such a wide
flowering bush at that.

Now, looking back to the evening when Nate Jr., off the backs
of whose hands vigorous black hairs grew, grasped Sally's pencil
wrist, I guess that it wasn't the first time he had touched her. I
guess, now, they'd already made love, probably when Jack and
John were out on the river. I guess that Nate had lifted up Sally's
childlike legs to go deeper in her, that he'd kissed her belly with
the same avidity that overcame him when he chewed rare roast
beef and juices rolled down through the cleft in his strong chin.

After dinner, the host turned on the stereo (because the hostess
sent her children to spend the night with grandparents or children
of another guest, we didn't worry about waking babies). We
stacked the turntable with the Stones' *Beggars Banquet* and *Sticky
Fingers* and James Brown's "Get Up I Feel Like Being a Sex
Machine" and prepubescent Michael Jackson crooning "Ben."
Carole King's *Tapestry* went on, as did Marvin Gaye's "Too Busy
Thinking about My Baby," Simon and Garfunkel, Sam Cooke,
Creedence Clearwater Revival, the Doors, and always Elvis singing "Heartbreak Hotel" and "Poke Salad Annie" and, for slow-
dancing, "Love Me Tender."

Among the men, my husband, Jack, was the best dancer. Put
on the Doors' "Light My Fire" or the Stones' "Honky Tonk
Woman" or anything by James Brown, and his wide size-eight feet
enacted intricate tattoos and his arms pumped fast as a busy oil
rig. Pelvis pushed up against his partner, he danced oozingly slow
to the likes of the Sam Cooke tune "You Send Me." He mouthed
Sam's "You-ooo-oo." His big popping frog eyes closed, as if in
sleep, and his hand wandered soothingly along the knob on his
partner's spine.

Winter, when temperatures fell below zero, we kept windows shut. What with this food and dancing, the men tended to let gas. We pretended we didn't smell what we smelled. Marilyn said, "That's just life, isn't it? Farting."

Marilyn was what, then, you called a "big drink of water." Five-ten and built big—big breasts, wide hips, long legs—when Marilyn got a few drinks in her she got to doing what she described as the "boogaloo" and the rest of us called "the dirty boogie," an arrhythmic bump-and-grind of such athletic quality that you expected to hear her tendons whine. Sweat poured down her rapt face. Some nights Marilyn got so hot she pulled off whatever beaded or sequined or velvet garment was gripping her body and danced in nothing but her half-slip and the industrial-strength bra whose straps cut her shoulders. Jack, who'd gone through school from kindergarten on with Marilyn, had at least minor hots for her. You could tell by the way they danced to Marilyn's favorite, the Creedence Clearwater doing "Proud Mary." Jack's buggy frog eyes fastened onto Marilyn's gold-flecked irises. Their mouths slackened, tongue tips flickered. Their pelvises enacted ravenous intercourse. Jack thrust toward Marilyn for a few bars, Marilyn taking each thrust as if it were a boxer's blow to the gut. Then they reversed, and Marilyn thrust toward Jack, and Jack, lids demurely fluttering, mouth puckered, appeared to take Marilyn's thrusts deep into his bowels. In those 1970s Coraville living rooms, carpets rolled against walls, overstuffed couches pushed back, Marilyn and Jack—who was a good three, four inches shorter than she—put on quite a little show. I recall that during the Watergate hearings, when Jack was drunk on vodka that Terrilyn Jo chilled in her deep freeze, in mid-dance he stopped, grabbed Marilyn's naked shoulders, dug his face into the deep pool between Marilyn's breasts, and lapped up her sweat.

I wasn't amused, and you'd have thought Marilyn's husband,

Bennett, a shy anesthesiologist, would have put a stop to Marilyn's antics. If he had any responses to her dancing, his long, horsy face didn't betray them. He never danced, except on one unforgettable evening. Bennett was immune to music, dull beyond conversational burnishing. He leaned against walls along with the rolled-up carpets, nursed a drink, and inveigled men into conversations about furniture refinishing. Jack, who had gone to school with Bennett, too, said that Bennett at thirty was precisely as he had been in first grade. But Bennett wasn't unkind and he asked us ladies about our children, and when we said, "Well, Sarah fell off her bike and banged up her knees," he inclined his head in a listening posture. Next time you saw him, he'd ask, "How're Sarah's knees?"

The night Bennett *did* dance was the night of one of our annual Halloween parties when he came dressed in Marilyn's spaghetti-strapped silver lamé sheath, a flamingo-pink feather boa, wobbly overrun high-heeled pumps (spray-painted silver by Bennett), and a wig of loose blond curls that he and Marilyn had bought, used, at a Goodwill in the nearest city. Marilyn had made up Bennett's face, even gluing on black false eyelashes along his upper *and* lower lids. No way did he make a plausible woman. Thick, rough black chest hair rose out of the silver sheath. Muscles bulged along his arms, and a blue tattooed anchor from Bennett's Navy days was fading along his right bicep. Not even the lashes, crimson lipstick, turquoise eye shadow could transform his long face and strong chin into feminine mien. But while most straight men of Bennett's type made fun of themselves when they wore women's clothing, Bennett was grave, solemn, almost respectful about his gender change. He walked gracefully from living to dining room, carefully took his seat at the dinner table. He picked at the Halloween carrot-and-raisin salad. He chatted quietly with the women.

Marilyn came as a dance-hall girl—fishnet stockings, red satin miniskirt, black bustier. Mandy and Knox came as Gainsborough's *Blue Boy* and *Pinky*. Mandy sewed the outfits for weeks. She got the idea from her playing cards, the backs of which had Old Master paintings. Sally was Peter Pan, a perfect green-suited replica of the peanut-butter-jar label's Peter Pan; Sally's husband, John, came in a tall black hat and old black suit and said he was a chimney sweep, a service he was thinking of adding to the hardware store. Nate was his usual cowboy, holstered with real guns, and Terrilyn Jo was a cowgirl. Jack and I wore bunny outfits— long johns, big tail made from yarn and long ears Jack constructed by bending wire and stretching white flannel over the wire. We attached the ears to flannel hats I sewed up. We tied the hats under our chins and we marked black whiskers on our cheeks with eyebrow pencil.

When the three-layer chocolate cake with orange frosting overlaid with a white-icing spiderweb was eaten and the rugs were rolled back and Diana Ross put on, needle dropped onto "Ain't No Mountain High Enough," Bennett walked right up to Jack, put out his big hand, and, looking down into Jack's bunny face, huskily asked, "Shall we dance?" Jack acceded with an obvious blush. Diana wasn't even into "to keep me from getting to you" before you could see Bennett had learned something from Marilyn. He stood his ground and pumped his pelvis. Jack, bunny ears askew, pumped right back.

I hurried into the kitchen. So did Marilyn and Terrilyn Jo. Even with the dishwasher surging, you heard Diana. Marilyn and Terrilyn Jo and I stood next to the stacked dirty dessert plates, Marilyn's big breasts pushed up out of black satin and me in my bunny suit. "I just don't know what gets into Bennett." Marilyn sighed and dabbed her finger into orange frosting left on the cake stand. Terrilyn Jo, who from where she stood could see Sally, in her

Peter Pan outfit, wrapped up in Nate Jr.'s cowboy arms, added, not unpleasantly, "Men."

I loved the dancing. I remember one winter evening shuffling pelvis-to-pelvis on a four-tile spot in my dark kitchen with Nate Jr., to Elvis ululating through "Crying in the Chapel." The moonlight outside struck white snow heaped along the side yard. I rested my cheek against Nate Jr.'s wash-and-wear shirt and pressed against his flinty erection while Elvis sang that his tears were tears of joy, he knew the meaning of contentment now, he was happy with the Lord. The evening's dances had broken through Nate Jr.'s deodorant and left him smelling like chicken-noodle soup smells in school cafeterias, and I figured Terrilyn Jo was watching from somewhere in the dining room with a broken heart. I didn't care.

Our set tried enlarging itself by inviting new couples. Most of these couples came to town when the husband got a job at our local state college. Housed in a cluster of turn-of-the-century white-pillared brick buildings at Coraville's north edge, the college had started out in the late 1800s as a female seminary. During the 1910s, after Coraville's great destructive fire, the state turned the seminary into a teachers' training school. Only after the Second World War, when the GI Bill began filling classrooms, did it offer a full liberal-arts curriculum. The college, alas, attracted only students and teachers wanted by no other institutions. It brought to town a series of academic waifs and strays, misfits, malcontents, and miscreants. Among the professors, some were dumbly grateful for the job and others resented their stay with us.

We began including a sculptor and his wife from California. They were among the grateful and almost at once bought, near the college, a clapboard house that needed paint. The sculptor, Brett, taught art education. His wife, Evangeline, wrote poetry. They were new parents, and Brett, I remember, modeled a series of clay heads of his owl-faced baby son. They were a quiet, kindly couple. She wore no makeup; he dressed in work shirts and jeans and had a clean-shaven open face. Brett and Evangeline came to several Saturday-night dinners before offering to host their own.

The moment Brett opened the door, which he'd painted red, I sensed trouble. The overwhelming aroma was that of garlic and a meaty hot wind of what I took, correctly, to be lamb. From a stereo unfamiliar music played. Brett smiled. "From *Zorba the Greek*, the bouzouki."

Dark hair flying behind her, Evangeline offered *dolmas,* a heap of wrinkled brown olives, feta, and round loaves of still-warm bread. I venture that none of us had ever seen a *dolma.* A terrible silence fell, making louder the frenetic bouzouki player's efforts. Jack, who always said that having grown up on his mother's cooking there was no food that frightened him, popped a *dolma* into his mouth and urged Bennett and John to try one. So we got through the drinks hour, eating the salty olives and the salty harsh cheese, sipping the retsina, which tasted, Marilyn whispered, "like roofing tar smells."

Evangeline led us through dinner. *Avgolemono*—lemony-scented chicken soup adrift with rice; Greek salad with lettuce, red onion rings, cucumbers, more feta, and more wrinkled brown olives; and the entrée—two Pyrex baking dishes of moussaka. "Eggplant," Evangeline said, when asked what was in the moussaka, and "ground lamb and cinnamon and garlic." Not one of us could so much as pronounce "moussaka," and as I looked fearfully around the dining table, lengthened by adding card tables, I noted that our set—faces still unlined, hairs ungray, marriages intact, affairs few—seemed baffled.

Evangeline served baklava for dessert and ouzo and dark bitter coffee. The needle went back again on the bouzouki tunes.

Even before we sat down to dinner, I had seen the bookshelves stacked with poetry volumes. I was thrilled, because I read poetry but never dared say so. At most, women in our set read new novels, Book-of-the-Month Club offerings, bestsellers like *Deliverance* or *Love Story*, although I cannot recall once, among our crowd, any discussion of any book. So while I ate moussaka and forked in lemony spinach, I imagined winter afternoons when Evangeline and I would eviscerate Lowell's "Skunk Hour," line by line. I returned to my fantasy of the silver tea service, saw my fingers reach out for the teapot's silver handle. After dinner, while Evangeline moodily wrapped herself in a flowered challis shawl, I said that I too read poetry. Evangeline looked me over. I saw myself as she must have seen me—fingernails bitten to the quick and feta cheese dribbled on my taffeta skirt. So I didn't, as I'd intended, invite her to bring her baby for an afternoon.

Not long after the fall of Saigon, a dark-bearded bachelor philosophy professor scuttled about town tacking up hand-lettered signs: GOURMET COOKING CLASS! WOMEN ONLY! Pierre, his name was, and he claimed to be French. "But Huguenot, Huguenot, *not* Catholic," Pierre said, placing his damp white palm in yours, then tossing back his head of dark oily hair and giggling. Sweat dribbled down his high forehead and spit flew when he talked. He had grown up in South Carolina, but to hear him speak, his accents reminiscent of public-television British, you'd never know he'd lived a day in the Old Confederacy. When he wasn't chattering, he stood alone at rooms' far reaches; he drew down his mouth into a dreary, sour expression and watched us.

I often saw Pierre evenings when I did my grocery shopping. He bounded about Safeway, polished licorice-black oxfords tapping. The black wool Johnny Cash–like coat, which he wore well into June, flapped and flew behind him. Pierre stopped by meat counters, almost empty by evening of hamburger, pork chops, picnic hams, T-bones and chuck roasts, and chicken. He rang the bell for the butcher, a Missouri Synod Lutheran who'd lost his left index finger while dressing out an elk. Typically, Pierre asked the digitless Lutheran for brains, livers, testicles, and gizzards of lambs, calves, and chickens. One night the Lutheran asked me, "Is that guy queer?" I said I didn't know. Then the Lutheran rolled his toothpick between his lips, said, "He sure makes himself overfamiliar with the box boys, is all I know."

Charitable folk said Pierre was a lost soul. Not me. I said to Jack that Pierre was a pretentious jerk. He sensed I didn't like him. At a party, one of the New Year's Eve gatherings to which everyone was invited, he stood so near I felt his breathing in and breathing out and smelled his musty body and the bergamot he used to oil his hair. He whispered, "You're a burnt-out case, aren't you?" Then he walked away.

I wasn't all that happy. But I was getting by.

Marilyn and Mandy kept waiting for someone else to join Pierre's cooking class, but no one did. Pierre agreed to teach them anyway. Pierre soon insinuated himself into our monthly dinner parties. And on evenings when Mandy or Marilyn was hostess, Pierre planned the dinners, shopped with them for the groceries, even had them drive him (he didn't drive) to the nearest large town to acquire wines and cheeses.

By the Bicentennial year, when town fathers ordered the planting out along Main Street of red and white petunias bedded with blue ageratum, Pierre had entirely commandeered Marilyn's and Mandy's dinners. During cocktail hour, Pierre supervised serving hard breads that he baked and antipasti. "The *anti*," Pierre hissed as he proffered platters arranged with pickled cauliflower, white beans, marinated asparagus, salami and pepperoni, and cheeses, "is from Italian for 'before' and the '*pasto*,' from Latin *pastus*, past participle of *pascere*, to feed." Also served before dinner were Pierre's pâtés, aged in tea towels drenched with ports and brandies. Pierre's bread was rock-hard and looked, my husband said, "like roofing tiles." I never tasted the pâtés, so fearful was I of getting sick.

Pierre favored Italian. He guided Marilyn and Mandy in preparation of pastas and gummy risottos. We had sauces littered with bitter artichoke and unfamiliar, dangerous-looking mushrooms and rabbit. These rabbits were aged, Pierre told us, by hanging in his back bedroom. American meats, he said, lacked sufficient aging to soften muscle and acquire flavor.

As Marilyn or Mandy brought dishes to the table, Pierre ascended from his chair, lifted his wineglass, and, spittle airborne as he spoke, screeched, *"Pièce de résistance! Salut* to our chef! *Salut! Salut!"*

Strange new wines showed up. Pierre lectured. "An abstemious little white," he'd say, pursing his lips. Or: "So robust, round, full-hipped this red is." I was reminded of the occasional program at the city library to which I took Rebecca and Sarah. Our local travel agent turned the library lights low and showed films of foreign countries and spoke, from notes, about "Chartres, Gothic Glory" or "Wild Alaska, Our Forty-ninth State." Not even we ladies were interested in Pierre's discourses, and the men sat glumly silent, longing, I suspect, for bloody beef, canned ham, tom turkey, and talk of real estate and fishing.

Pierre passed demitasses. "Espresso!" he warned us, "not eXpresso." The espresso was made in a hissing, temperamental contraption that the hostess's husband had lugged from Pierre's house to his. Bennett didn't mind, but Mandy's husband, Knox, sucking on his rattish teeth, grumbled about having to load up "this little fairy's Mr. Coffee."

The oddest of these Pierre-influenced dinners was the meal Pierre hosted at his boxy rental. The night was chilly late-spring weather when you laid out old sheets over sprouting lettuces.

Pierre greeted us, dressed in his customary black vest over white shirt. Fine sprays of blood crisscrossed the filthy white apron he'd tied around him. I've got quite a sniffer—my nose detects distant gas leaks, grass fires, a woman's perfume on a male lapel, a hard-boiled egg that's been in the refrigerator too long. My nose went nuts when Jack and I walked through Pierre's front door. The most intense smells were those of lavender, lamb, and garlic. Pierre's oven held two legs of lamb, marinated, he told us, in wine, garlic, and lavender, the latter acquired from Provence, where lavender, he assured us, was a crop hovered over by elderly crones.

Before our meal Pierre served his roof-tile bread and rank pâté and treated us to Callas singing *"Un bel dì vedremo"* and the terrifying *Turandot* aria *"In questa reggia."* Pierre let the record play all evening.

I sought out his bathroom. I wanted to be alone. To get to the bathroom, I had to pass through a lightless, bedless bedroom. At the room's far end I saw a rack of the type pushed through New York's garment district. From that rack hung three small bodies which I recognized as rabbit, a ham from which slices had been cut, and a half-dozen long sausages. Exercise mats covered the floor, and atop the mats I saw barbells and a jockstrap.

Roll around in your mouth, if you will, English Lavender after-shave and meat more mutton than lamb, and you'll guess why I didn't easily fork in Pierre's lamb. I sat stiffly and swigged red wine so sour my sinuses ached. I don't recall dessert. Next day I kept an icebag on my forehead and huddled in bed. I wept to Jack that I'd never go back to Pierre's house, and I never did. I said I was sick of this gourmet carrying-on, and I was.

But in fact our gourmet revolution had only begun. During that Bicentennial year, the aforementioned couple from Boston—Carter and Belva—moved to town. They came because Belva accepted a job in our college's anthropology department. In no time, they bought a house near the college and had a hot tub built where the back porch had been. They hacked out the evergreen foundation plantings and planted decorative kale. They installed a gas stove. They ordered from back East something they called "recycling bins" and showed us how they separated out cans and bottles and newspapers, each into its own container.

Belva was as tall as Marilyn and pounds thinner, her figure rubber-band stretchy and small-breasted. She pinned her fiery auburn hair atop her head with tortoiseshell chopsticks. Not only was she the family breadwinner, but she did the yard work and could be seen that Bicentennial summer, skin pale in skimpy halter and shorts, stacking a wood-sided trailer bed with branches she lopped from trees.

Carter, tall and slender too, with long sandy-blond hair caught up in a rawhide tie, didn't work. "Never," he said pleasantly, "have I worked. At least not at a job. I am more interested in becoming than in doing." Carter did shopping, cooking, washing and ironing, and what he called "child care" and we called "baby-sitting." When you saw Carter at the store, the couple's two redheaded sons were with him. He kissed and petted them as if they were girls and he were their mother.

Carter read books that we did not yet know to describe as "New Age" (he touted a book titled *Living Simply Through the Day*), he meditated before a burning white candle, and he wrote daily in what he called a "spiritual journal." An Egyptian ankh on a heavy silver chain dangled in his chest hair. Carter played no sports, knew nothing about football, and expressed horror at our husbands' tales of hooking bass and winging mallards. Rather than the faded blue jeans our husbands wore about the house, Carter dressed in dashikis and muslin smocks that hung over baggy shorts or, in cold weather, woolen army trousers (although he'd not served in any armed force). On his feet he wore Earth shoes or

Swedish clogs. He eschewed underwear, noting that Jockey shorts lowered the sperm count.

Carter and Belva's mutual passion, "other," they said, "than sex," was gastronomy. In no time, Pierre was practically living at Carter and Belva's house and their sons were calling him "Uncle Pierre."

So socially ascendant did Carter and Belva prove themselves that they instantly became a seventh couple in our six-plus-Pierre. Seated tailor-fashion on our carpets, they sighed at the loss of Boston and said how happy they were to have found us. They led the conversation to recycling and ecology, Tantric yoga, European youth hostels, and open marriage, which, they assured us, their marriage was. They tsk-tsked us for using insecticides on our gardens and power lawn mowers for cutting grass.

Belva exerted her charms on Bennett, leaning forward to listen to his drawled tales of oils used for rubbing down old tables. She took Jack out on the dance floor and outdid his pelvic thrustings. Carter turned to us women; he praised our glittering dresses and our skin. He asked what sign we were and read our palms. He ran his hands through Terrilyn Jo's stiff peroxided hair and had the gall to say, "You're far more attractive than Sally. You're so *womanly*." When we danced, Carter closed his eyes and swayed and rubbed his body with his fingertips. "First," he cooed, "you have to love yourself."

Carter and Belva sent out invitations to our dozen. "Casual dress," they wrote. So we wore jeans and stretch pants on that first Saturday after Elvis had died and already been buried, next to Gladys, his mother. When Carter—in a white smock over white shorts and his hair out of its rawhide and hanging about his shoulders—greeted us at the door, he said, "We ask guests to remove shoes."

Nate Jr. frowned, flopped down on one of the plump pillows

arrayed on the waxed living-room floor, and grunted as he tugged at his cowboy boots. Knox snarled but complied. Jack, pulling off his tennis shoes, grumped, "My feet will stink you right out of here."

"No matter, no matter," Carter assured.

"What's that?" Jack asked, indicating the drone emerging from tall KLH speakers.

"Ravi Shankar," Carter replied. "Sitar. Ragas. My meditation music."

Belva wore a poppy-printed sundress. "Marimekko," she said when we complimented her. She touched her long fingers to the tops of her lightly freckled and bra-less pale breasts and tilted her head demurely to the side. She kissed us, one by one, first one cheek, then the other.

Swathed in a clean apron and holding aloft a long-handled wooden spoon, Pierre bustled from the kitchen to add his embraces. "Welcome," he burbled, "to our happy home."

Carter, Belva, and Pierre set us down on the fat pillows. "Marimekko," Carter said when Margaret admired the pillows' print covers.

Belva and Pierre bore trays from the kitchen. "*Apéritif* time," Carter said, although I'd guess none of us knew the word *apéritif*. And with the *apéritif*, white wine, we were offered *crudités*—baby carrots, assorted radishes, anise sticks, cauliflowerets—and urged to dip them in the *aioli* prepared by Carter from what we were assured was "special garlic."

The trio directed us to the table and placed us in our chairs. Then, as if we were fat little goslings near-naked under our first down, the trio, like huge hissing geese, herded us through soup, fish, entrée, sherbet palate freshener, roast and *entremets*, salad, cheeses, dessert, and demitasse. I don't recall what we ate. I remember the soup was an algal green topped with fiddlehead fern.

I remember that Belva and Pierre had organized the menu and that Carter praised their "analytic palates." His palate, he said, drawing a long face, "lacked acuity."

Carter, Belva, and Pierre, enunciating carefully, instructed us as to the name of each dish, translating French to English. I recall many *à la* this's and an *en papillote* that. We received instruction from Pierre on the tying of a proper *bouquet garni* and from Belva, who spoke, without pause, in paragraphs, on the reduction of sauces. Bennett choked on a fish bone and threw up a gobbet of fish into his plate. Nate Jr. and tiny, starving Sally pouted beautifully because they weren't allowed to smoke. Studying our faces, Carter and Belva and Pierre spoke vivaciously of each dish's provenance and steps of preparation. Mandy and Marilyn nodded newly educated assent to all this.

An extraordinary number of wines were poured. I grew dizzy with drink while Pierre and Belva discussed various valleys from where the wine came, talked exuberantly of oaken kegs and natural tannins, and Belva spouted a phrase I shan't ever forget— "the masturbatory eroticism of a true Merlot."

If there was talk of Elvis and his funeral, I do not remember it. I know the night was hot, that Nate Jr. and Sally went outside to smoke and didn't come back for ages. I remember thinking that Marilyn was getting so deep into this gourmet crap that I could hardly stand being with her anymore. I remember that a mosquito bit me and left a nasty red swelling on my arm and that there was no dancing *and* that the next morning Jack and I played our old Elvis albums and I felt I'd died and gone to hell.

All that winter, spring, and summer the brown UPS truck stopped at doors. The deliveryman teetered up front sidewalks; poor fellow was loaded down under boxes packed with sauté pans, salmon poachers, vegetable mills, asparagus steamers, *tarte* pans, whisks, garlic presses, stockpots, mortars and pestles, demitasse cups. Mandy had her electric stove pulled out and gas put in. ("That Tolliver money," my mother-in-law clucked, "watch it go down the drain.") *Mastering the Art of French Cooking*, the *Larousse Gastronomique*, the two hefty maroon-bound volumes of the *Gourmet* cookbook, and Richard Olney's lovely *The French Menu Cookbook* and various Elizabeth David titles were delivered from the nearest big city's bookstore.

Our dinners continued, month by month turning more "gourmet" and more frequent, with at least one meal each month at Belva and Carter's long table. Belva, Carter, and Pierre's gastronomic zealotry took what I felt was an hysteric pitch. As we bit into *aux* this and *à la* that, the trio watched us without reserve. They studied our expressions. They queried us closely as to our responses. I felt like a farm animal on whom ag college grad students were experimenting. With our crowd serving as chorus, the trio, through long evenings, tsk-tsked over unforgivable treatments of eggplant or strategies toward chicken so unthinking as to be almost wicked. So I also came to feel indoctrinated, an ignorant catechumen under instruction on the secret rites of a cult. I felt like screaming and throwing my plate.

Dinner-party talk rarely strayed from food. Bennett reported improvements in his *béarnaise* and subtleties imparted by various vinegars he whisked into it. Elizabeth David on basil was discussed. Margaret was deep into puff pastries and showing a tendency, which Pierre disapproved, to encase "every bird and beast in *chou* paste." Mandy bought a pasta maker; her kitchen was hung with so many drying strands that she had to lock her Siamese cats in the garage. Jack purchased the KitchenAid attachment for sausage-making. Even Nate Jr. produced opinions on cuisine— "Adding dill to the court bouillon for the salmon seemed a bit of a cliché." Only little Sally, bony and big-eyed as ever, remained immune.

And whereas in the old days parties finished with us dancing together in drunken bear hugs, now evenings ended with Belva and Pierre's demands that we contribute to a kitty for an upcoming meal; the money went for the likes of white truffle oil, candied angelica, wheels of Brie, and sourdough starter sold by a gentleman in Vermont.

Pudding cakes were long gone, as were Philadelphia cream-cheese footballs. Dancing ended, as did dressing up. Late at night when Jack and I stretched out under covers and talked in the dark, I complained that Carter and Belva dealt with us as missionaries deal with primitive tribes. I said that the unspoken question in Carter and Belva's prattle seemed to be "What did you do all these years without us?" I said that it wasn't just the talk about food, food, food and the extraordinary culinary competition that had begun to make couples within our crowd testy with one another. I said I also sensed all kinds of funny business in Carter and Belva's hot tub, whose glass enclosure glowed with candlelight far into the night like a tiny Taj Mahal. Bennett spent entire evenings with Carter and Belva, I told Jack. Marilyn confessed that he had demanded they "open" their marriage and "share" with Carter and Belva. Knox, meanwhile, was buzzing her with faintly dirty phone calls from the bank, and she and Mandy, who'd been tying up her taffy-blond hair and meditating, early mornings, with Carter, were hardly speaking.

Jack, who'd lived in Coraville all his life, said, "It's just a phase. It'll pass," and went off to sleep.

There is a coda to this. At Carter, Belva, and Pierre's urging, our crowd began once a month to have Friday-afternoon salons. The notion was that we'd have wine-tastings and hors d'oeuvres. Each couple was to bring two dishes. Carter, Belva, and Pierre chose and purchased the wines, for which effort and expense we reimbursed them. We took turns hosting the salon, which began at five-thirty. As the months progressed, the salon grew in size and the dishes in complexity.

That year Reginald, an old friend of mine, was spending a lot of time around our house. In mid-afternoon, he would bring over fresh crabs and crack them. Then he'd put two Revere Ware pans on the stove, a pan for him and a pan for me, and melt us each a quarter pound of butter. We'd stand there and dip crab legs in hot butter and eat crab and talk. He thought Coraville gourmet madness funny and always wanted to hear about the latest dishes. One day one of us said to the other that if you gave it a French name, people happily would eat dog food. No sooner was this thought spoken than Reginald and I were throwing on coats and heading to Safeway. As we took can after can of dog food off the shelves and dropped them into our cart, we admired the beagles and poodles and Labradors on the labels. We laughed so hard we had to push our cart to the back of the store where the bathrooms were. We bought onions, garlic, thick-sliced bacon, shelled pistachios, bread crumbs, and parsley. We rushed home and fixed dinner for Jack and the girls. After dinner we asked Jack if he thought dog food would make anyone sick and he said he didn't. Once the girls got to sleep, Reginald and I opened the dog foods and sniffed. Immediately we realized that some smelled too strong. The most acceptable, for texture and odor, were Mighty Dog and a Safeway house brand. Reginald set me to chopping onion and mincing parsley and pressing garlic, while in the big mixing bowl he, by hand, mushed bread crumbs, pistachios, instant potato flakes, and a bit of oatmeal to stiffen up the dog food. We tossed in the onion, parsley, and garlic. Reginald lined two meat-loaf pans with bacon and pressed in our mixture. We slid the pans into the oven. By midnight the pâté—or *pet-té*, as we were calling it—felt firm. The kitchen smelled not disagreeably of bacon and Mighty Dog. We agreed we'd let the *"pet-té"* cool and next day, a Thursday, check it for odor. It smelled fine.

Friday afternoon, Reginald and Jack and I showed up at the salon, held that day at Knox and Mandy's house on the hill. We carried in our platter. The pâtés, swathed in bacon and arrayed round with fresh watercress and cornichons, looked pretty.

Right up to the last minute I felt torn. I loved Marilyn and Bennett, Terrilyn Jo and little Sally and John, and wasn't unfond of Nate Jr. Any moment I could have said, "No, let's not put the pâté out on the buffet table." I said nothing.

Not a soul, other than Sally, didn't spread thick smudges of Mighty Dog on the fresh bread we'd brought. Not a soul, including our trio of gastronomic leaders, didn't compliment Mighty Dog's richness and the just-rightness of pistachios.

The more Mighty Dog my old friends ate, the dirtier a betraying Judas I felt. As I watched them chew, I noted that we were looking older, sadder, our flesh slacker, our hair beginning to take on gray. So I felt even worse a sinner.

Almost twenty years down the road now, I still feel bad that I did this and wish I hadn't. I wish we were still thirty, that Elvis were alive and singing in Vegas. I wish I could shuffle around my kitchen with my nose in Nate Jr.'s smelly wash-and-wear shirt while Elvis sings that the tears he cries are tears of joy.

ADULTERY

❦

I DON'T THINK I EVER BETTER GOT THE FEEL FOR THAT COM-
plicated business of insinuating cold butter into flour and thence
into a high-pitched oven (500 degrees for the first five–ten
minutes!) that produces *mille-feuilles* pastry, don't think I ever
stirred, sniffed, and tasted my way to a more provocative lime-
ginger-garlic-soy-molasses marinade for duck than during the year
I went out on my husband. Our daily menus, already intriguing,
grew more complex. I dared myself beyond the great American
mamas, Fannie Farmer and Irma Rombauer and Irma's daughter
Marion Rombauer Becker, beyond rib roasts and sweating pork
butts and pineapple-and-clove-stuck hams, beyond mashed potatoes pouring out lavas of fat-gilded gravy. I acquired soufflé dishes.
I bought a mandoline. I bought whisks. I learned to scrape ginger
root. I turned the aforementioned *mille-feuilles* into elephant ears;
into a delicate casing for baked apple cored out and filled with
rum-soaked raisins; into tidy squares with custard between them,
the flaky squares drizzled with a translucent strawberry sauce.

Nights, I studied Elizabeth David's *Summer Cooking*, with its
advice on scattering chopped basil across *ratatouille en salade* and

suggestions for hors d'oeuvres of mushrooms marinated in olive oil. I read the *Larousse Gastronomique* and marveled at all the things you could do with eggplant, and went ahead and did them, even eggplant soufflé. The latter puffed up past the white collar I'd wound around the soufflé dish, and once on the tongue, the eggy fluff released the purple eggplant's sharp, dolorous smoke.

During the adultery year my husband, Jack, gained eighteen pounds. The younger of our two daughters, who ate heedlessly, without cost to her figure, said, "I'm having to watch it, Mom, at the old trough." Nights when we gave dinner parties, our belly-heavy company crawled from the dining-room table. Their lips glistened with lamb fat and Elizabeth David's mint butter ("Pound," she writes, the fresh mint leaves and butter "to a smooth *ointment*"). Raspberry purée dribbled down shirtfronts, *crème caramel* freckled bosoms. Our friends threw themselves down into the living-room couches and sighed among the poppy-printed pillows.

"Such is the way of an adulterous woman; she eateth, and wipeth her mouth, and saith, I have done no wickedness." (Proverbs 30:20) Let me assure you, I do think I did "wickedness." Let me assure you, I didn't go unpunished. The adultery ended up in a godawful mess, that I'll tell you right now.

The affair, circumstantially, began in cooking. Summers, I put up pickles, preserves, salsas, chutneys, jellies, jams, fruit. The September noon that I ran into the gentleman who became my partner, my adultery angel, adultery demon, love of my life, also destroyer, the temperature was in the mid-seventies. The sky offered that visibility-unlimited cloudless blue that makes you tilt your head backward. You look up and think how illimitable, how without measure and sempiternal the world is, and how happily mortal you are; a medium-range contentment puts a wriggle in your walk that flips the hem on your faded blue denim wrap skirt

and raises your chest beneath your favorite Liberty of London
print blouse. Breezes floated down off surrounding hills and carried cidery scents off pear and apple orchards that soldiered down
the green hills. When I looked out those windows bosomy hills
made you feel sleepy; I could have rested on their softness. The
mountains that rose behind the hills *didn't* look soft. They seemed
ill-tempered and dangerous, and were; almost every year somebody slipped down into a crevasse and died before the whirring
Life Flight helicopter could rope him up to safety. I used to wonder what it was like, to lie curled up, crushed between black basalt,
breathing raspily with a broken rib poked into your lung, thinking
about your wife, your baby, your mother, how you'd done no good
in your life; then maybe, when your head rolls backward, you see
a vulture ride the air above you.

When you flew above Coraville in a light plane, as I had, and
looked down, you saw church steeples and college bell tower,
parks' viridescing squares, trim ribbons of streets, the two super-
markets' asphalt parking lots, the water tower graffitied by that
year's Coraville High graduating class, the two-story stucco Elks
Lodge atop Cora Hill, the aforementioned orchards, and beyond
them, farms and ranches and plotted fields, fences, and along the
fences the yellow wild mustard and shelterbelts of wind-twisted
trees. Easily, you could pick out your own house, your evergreens
and quivering aspen and weeping willow, and your friends' houses,
your children's schools. I recall that the afternoon I went up in
the plane, I could see my back-yard garden and count eight rows
of Country Gentleman corn. I couldn't see the pole beans that I
planted between corn rows to let the cornstalks serve as supports,
but I wanted to.

The supermarket lot where I parked wasn't crowded in the way
city people imagine crowds. Maybe twenty cars and pickup trucks,

keys dangling from ignitions, nosed between the white lines on the asphalt lot.

Glancing neither left, right, nor forward, Peter floated out through the store's whiny automatic doors, his hands fidgeting open a sack of pipe tobacco. I rushed toward the same doors. What I had in mind was twenty pounds of sugar, rings for my old mason jars, and, if any were left, two maple-frosted doughnuts for whose pleasure I'd forgone a hunk of Oregon Gold Cheddar and the bowl of leftover black-bean soup that awaited Jack when he bicycled the six blocks from his office for lunch and nap. I intended to eat the doughnuts after I stowed the sugar and jar rings in the passenger seat and while I drove up in the hills to Potts's orchard to collect three flats of Bartlett pears for preserves and chutney (green and red bell peppers chopped fine, grated fresh ginger root, raisins, mustard seed, pear chunks) and the fourteen quarts of mint pears I put up every year. I was dreaming of those frosted-with-maple doughnuts and how the cool scratchless icing would melt across my tongue and down the walls of my cheeks, and Peter was fiddling with the tobacco packet.

We were each as happy then as people need to be and didn't know it.

We bumped. I was gazing into his tie, an ugly non-silk item striped brown and gold. I remember thinking what a viciously ugly tie it was and that you rarely saw a pretty tie in Coraville like the pretty ties in *The New Yorker*. At the time I *didn't* think the following, although I had before and since: that in Coraville men who *did* wear suits, ties, white shirts regarded the tie as a sign of the step up from manual labor to authority over other, lesser men and women. As in any area dependent upon agriculture, Coraville's outskirts convulsed with fattening hogs, breeding rabbits, sheep, mad bulls, dairy cows, alfalfa, potato, corn, and dryland wheat. The men and women who guided this brute vigor to market came to town in rusty mud-splattered pickups. Cow manure and straw stuck to their boots. The Coraville men tied into their ties from J. C. Penney's and the Sears catalogue sat at desks in city and county offices, stood behind counters in banks and stores, and lorded it over those country folk. These city men, too, over lunches at The Alcazar and Papa's Steakhouse, told jokes that featured bulls and rams and roosters. This fecund blood-dangerous world was always threatening to invade the tiny town, break into churches and hardware emporiums; the seed of farm children, likewise, threatened the virginal beds of city daughters. Nobody wanted his daughter to marry a farmer. A rancher, maybe, but not a farmer. Ranchers, often, were rich.

We literally bumped into each other. He stepped right down on my navy-blue Ked. We were both standing on the sensored flooring, so Safeway's door stayed open while we apologized, Peter doing most of the apology, since I was the principally injured. Peter, his six-foot five-inch Ichabod Crane frame bowed at the waist, addressed me with old-fashioned formality. He bit down on his pipe stem, studied me.

Aware we were keeping the door open and straining Safeway's air-conditioned chill, I touched Peter's jacketed arm with my fingertips, said, "Well, nice to have seen you," and turned to go into the store.

Peter grabbed my elbow, turned me around, and propelled me a few feet into the parking lot. "Have you seen my new car?" He pointed toward a navy-blue Alfa-Romeo. "It's used, but it's new to me."

Before I knew it, I had agreed to forgo my pears and climb into his Alfa-Romeo and lean back into the leather seat and drive to the river, to play, as he put it, smiling down on me as if he were sunshine itself, "a little hooky on a lovely afternoon."

When I said, "Okay, why not?" he grinned and pitched his keys in the air and caught them with a jingle, and then smiled at me again and put one of his long skinny arms around my shoulders and squeezed.

We'd talked at Friday-afternoon town-gown parties whose stated goal was getting faculty from the teachers college and town burghers together (and whose unstated purpose was booze and mild dalliance). I had chatted with him and his handsome wife at Democratic precinct meetings. I'd never given him a second thought. My only memory of him before the ride in the Alfa-Romeo was thinking he looked like Abraham Lincoln with blond hair and that he had a charming way of leaning over from his great height to talk with me.

Certainly, I never thought he was interested in me sexually. First, he was a serious and voluble churchman and nature preservation do-gooder (that's what Coravilleans called preservationists, "do-gooders"). Second, he was fifteen years my senior. Third, I never imagined men as interested in me sexually. I was always shocked when men did flirt; they would have to come right out and say it straightforwardly so that I could not but believe it.

He pushed the top down on the car. The drive from town to river took us past cornfields. Black crows flew up from the corn's stiff, stubborn rows and then settled, on their wide, tarry wings, onto air currents. Ten minutes brought us to the river. The water twisted below us. The water shone. Peter talked jubilantly of the new car, how much he liked his job, the good grades his three children still at home made, and his daughter's marriage. He even exulted over a line of poplars he'd planted in his back yard two years earlier, which had grown, he said, four feet.

I asked, teasingly, "Isn't there *anything* wrong with your life?"

Had I not asked that, I swear nothing would have happened.

He slowed the car. He took his glance from the winding uphill road to look at me. His eyes were the blue color you see in old marbles. "I have a terrible need for affection." I still remember how that sounded, said by him in a low tone with a quick vibrato, as if said by a talking cello. I know this is cornball and in bad taste, but there's that moment during Handel's *Messiah* where the chorus sings, "And the heavens were rent." That's what that moment felt like when Peter said, "I have a terrible need for affection." The heavens were rent, as if God had reached in under His big flowing white God robes and took out from one of His secret pockets a buck knife and just reached down and ripped a mile-long slash across that cloudless blue sky.

You can't believe what a homey person I was then. I always seemed to smell of the starch I sprayed on my husband's shirts when I ironed them and the bread I baked every day, big high loaves that rose and rose. I baked every kind of bread, and cinnamon rolls, and soft, eggy brioche, and French bread in long narrow tins; for the French bread, I'd put a bowl of water in the oven to make steam and whip egg whites and take my pastry brush and paint the loaves with the egg whites to make the loaves shiny.

He slowed, steered into a graveled turnoff, and stopped. He said, "Let's get out and walk." I nodded a yes and he took out his key, which jangled on a ring filled with keys, grabbed a tan poplin jacket folded behind his seat. I pulled myself up out of the car, which felt tinny when I shut its door. I brushed down the back of my wrap skirt, which had wrinkled sweatily under me. He offered me his hand, which was dry and cool, and we walked uphill, away from the turnoff, our feet crunching on the gravel. The ascent put him out of breath.

I can't remember what we said. I remember only the rattling in his chest, his rapid indrawn breaths. I knew enough about men his age not to ask if he wanted to rest. At some point he stopped. He asked, "Is it all right if I hold your hand?" I nodded a yes. I couldn't see why not. We reached a rise that looked down over the olive-green river that ran from mountains, down into the valley along Coraville's edge. We meandered down a few feet onto a patch of grass under droopy cottonwoods. We'd not had much rain that year. The grass was brown. We looked onto the catarrhal rush of quick water through basalt canyons.

Did I know we were going to kiss? No.

His mouth tasted of metal. My heart sank. I'd gone this far, I figured I had to keep on. My tongue found rough fillings, bridge-work, the ridged plastic of a partial plate. When I pulled away from his embrace as if to catch my breath, he asked, "What's wrong?"

"Nothing," I said.

He bowed his head against the shoulder of my blouse. I looked down. I could see pink scalp between his graying hairs as he kissed the skin that lay bare in the V of my shirt. Over his shoulder I watched rust-colored ants crawl out of a rotted log.

After it was all over, cottonwood leaf clung to his prim beard and his hair had the tousle of someone risen from a night of fever. He said, "Thank you," and nodded, his thank you as formal as if I'd passed him a crystal bowl heaped with pastel after-dinner butter mints. He patted my bare arm the way you'd pat a child who'd behaved well while the doctor gave her a polio shot. And, believe me, I felt rather that way, like a child dragged to the doctor who'd squinched her eyes and swallowed her medicine.

He asked, "Do you mind if I have a pipe?" and when I said I didn't, he said, "My wife and my boys don't like the pipe."

The river gurgled, breezes lifted the branches on scrub trees, he pulled on his pipe. I fussed with the space where he'd spread out his jacket, straightening the poplin sleeves as I would tidy rumpled doilies on an easy chair's arms. I pulled a leaf and a blade of dead grass from his hair. I didn't know what else to do with my hands. I was thirsty but didn't say so.

He began running his hand up and down my legs. He said, "You don't have varicose veins."

"Why would I?"

"My wife," he said, "has varicose veins."

Driving home, the navy-blue car spiraling down through the hills, I asked, "Do you do this often?"

He didn't, he said, frowning. He had, he added, never done it. And asked me, rather prissily, "You?"

"No."

He asked when he could see me again, and I didn't know what to answer. So he said, "Well, how about tomorrow?"

"Okay," I said, waved a silly little wave, got back into my car, and drove winding roads up into the hills to get my pears. I was worried Mr. Potts might have sold them to someone else, but he hadn't.

That night I lay awake while Jack slept. That I'd committed adultery, and with a man I knew only to speak with in the most banal social manner, did not then seem so outlandish as in fact it was. Peter felt familiar, not as if I'd known him since childhood, but rather as if all these years I'd been expecting him, that he had been promised to me, and so I was not so much surprised, perhaps, as relieved that the promise had been fulfilled. He for whom I waited had arrived.

After that first afternoon we contrived to meet or talk on the telephone almost every day.

We didn't, mind you, start saying "I love you" right away. We didn't say that at all, not for months. We flirted. We played hard to get. We turned moody on each other. But never, for more than a day, did we turn away or try to turn back. It was as if after that first coupling, which was not in any way "lovemaking" but rather what an animal might have done and no more pleasurable for me than the rooster's entry for the hen, we had caught a disease, a fever, that made it impossible for us not to see each other.

I wasn't unhappy with my husband. Jack was dainty and beautiful, built small, low to the ground. We could have lived in houses with six-foot ceilings and jumped up and down and still never bumped our heads. He had perfect little hands, size-eight feet with well-formed toes whose nails more than once when I was feeling silly he permitted me to polish bright red. He rescued me from my miserable childhood and I rescued him, he said, from coming home and marrying someone he sat next to in first grade.

For a novice to adultery, I proved remarkably apt at fitting into my life Peter's and my meetings. I was well organized and thrifty. My ability to knit complicated Aran Isle patterns while reading, my petit bourgeois shrewdness at stretching a roast loin of pork (baked with prunes that I'd soaked in burgundy) to a second meal of ersatz-Chinese sweet-and-sour pork served me well in arranging Peter into an otherwise ordinary domestic life.

Fall rains began. The air turned cold. Soon we could no longer go to the river. Peter was too tall for lovemaking in my old Volvo or his Alfa-Romeo. No way we could use the town's two motels. The hotel had burned down years earlier. The entire downtown had burned down twice.

I found a place to meet, an A-frame far out in the country that belonged to a gay male friend. He used the house—"the chalet," he called it—in summer and on weekends. The chalet's original owner had built the two-story structure as a hideaway, and hide it did, off the county road, down an unmarked driveway that twisted a half mile through scrub timber and blackberry bushes grown wild. "No more than a sheep path," Peter would sometimes say, and add, wincing, that the ruts were hard on his car's under-carriage. The chalet rested in a deep hollow. Trees, distance, and the hollow hid its high-peaked blue roof from the road.

Sometimes I met Peter at the chalet. But more often he drove into our alley, parked, walked through the roofed patio to our back door, and knocked, as if he were any friend of the family. I'd always be ready and somewhat anxious at having him hang about at the back of the house, in the laundry room, pantry, and kitchen. When our affair began, I offered to meet him. He said no, that would be "cheap." He said that unless something came up that made it impossible for him to pick me up at my house and deliver me back, that is what we would do. He said, "Gentlemen call for ladies." He said, "You start acting guilty, people start wondering what you're guilty of."

Peter didn't think we were guilty of anything. "We're enhancing each other's life," he said. And later, he said, "We bring each other joy."

I came from that generation of women who believe men know best. Peter said, "Don't worry." I always ended up believing Peter. That, and I didn't want to stop. I wanted to go on forever, seeing him.

In no time, we had our routine. Peter's job was such that he could disappear for several hours without question. Given that my children were in high school and that my husband came home for lunch, ate, and then napped and returned to his office, we began to meet two–three times per week at a few minutes after one.

A fifteen-minute drive brought us to the chalet. We drove quickly past city limits onto a two-lane county blacktop and past the abandoned one-room schoolhouse my father-in-law had attended, the first spot where we could safely lean across the gear-shift and kiss. Then we passed barns and silos, passed a high, blinking radio antenna in a deserted field, a stinking slaughter-house, more barns, then sheep and cattle and horses munching pasture, then cornfields dotted in fall with crows. Once in one of these cornfields we saw a hawk soar down and plunk a mouse out from between the rows and ascend with the mouse wriggling in its beak.

At the chalet, Peter took the key from me and unlocked the door. If my friend's fat Siamese glowered at us from his filthy

cushion in the living room, Peter grabbed the cat by the loose skin
on the back of his neck, carried him through the kitchen, opened
the back door, and tossed him out. If I'd brought Peter's lunch,
I'd set it on a table that looked out onto pasture. Peter washed
his hands. "To get the cat off," he'd say, and then take his Swiss
Army knife from his pocket and uncork the wine he'd brought,
wrapped in brown paper. I walked to the cupboard and took down
glasses.

We made love, sometimes on the double bed upstairs, with a
beach towel stretched across the plaid coverlet, or downstairs on
the couch or floor. What I liked with him was that what I thought
of as "love" seemed to be the impetus for, the precursor of, the
"sex." He didn't seem simply horny and hankering.

But what do I know? Maybe it was that he was older. I'd come
out of a generation of women who worked at sexual proficiency,
took pride in orgasm. To know how to do what I thought of as
"sex tricks" pasted a big shining star in one's crown. The more
daring, the more athletically challenging; the dirtier, the better.
But for Peter sex was won, earned even, by romance. He didn't
try fancy positions or ask me to wear garter belts.

As September, then October and November passed, things between us grew increasingly serious. With each step up or step
down, depending on how you want to look at this, one of us, for
a day or two, turned bitter toward the other. We didn't want to
be in love.

Back then, though, I believed I couldn't help myself. I believed
love was weather, what insurance adjusters call an "act of God,"
a tornado or cyclone, and that the best you could do was curl up
in a culvert or run down into a storm cellar until the big wind
passed over. Now I don't think that. But now isn't then.

One problem adulterers face is explaining where they've been
during the hours they're busy with adultery. In my case, nobody

asked. My husband was at work until five or five-thirty. The girls got home at four.

Another problem adulterers face is that they become liars, if nothing else, by omission. I lied daily, constantly, by omission. Worse yet in its comment on me is that I *wanted* to tell my husband, but for the wrong reason. I wanted to tell him because he was, or had been, my best friend. I wanted to tell him how happy I was.

All that fall and winter, when I should have looked more and more harried, because I was a liar, a cheat, and because the housekeeping, cooking, and gardening I normally did in the afternoon had to get done in the morning, all I did was bloom. I have a photograph of myself taken shortly before Christmas. I am standing on our front porch. Snow covers the flower beds and hummocks of straw I'd spread, that fall, over the lily beds. I had cinched my black velveteen trench coat tightly at the waist. My face is pale but lovely and my eyes are open wide. I don't guess I ever looked prettier than I did then. Everyone said so, even my daughters, even Jack.

I think there are women, and I was one of them, who lose their virginity, bear babies, suffer deaths of those close to them, *and* are not yet women but still girls. They are, and I was, still innocent. Their experience, for whatever reason, has not yet cut deeply into them. They might well be sixth-graders in pigtails; all the pubic moss and sweat and menstrual fluids are mummery that masks a child.

It's easy to say that I was restless, nearing forty, that I was foolish, that I was flattered by the attention Peter paid me. That my children were getting ready to leave home, that I was frightened about who I would be, what I would do, when they left. All that's true. But I don't think any of the psychological explanations entirely serve. Even now, when I look back on that year, with horror at what I did and the pain I caused, all I can tell you is that I loved him. The hours with Peter, bit by bit, became my real life. As that happened, the light changed on the other hours. Every staple item of life appeared transformed, transubstantiated even, newly lit, radiant.

Somebody might suggest I cooked that year the most superb dinners of my housewifely life because I was trying to atone for my adultery. I wish I could say that was true. The fact is, I cooked so lavishly because I was so happy. The eggplant soufflés, the baked apples filled with rum-soaked raisins, the translucent strawberry sauce were overruns of my happiness.

I became something of a Luddite. Previous to adultery, I had given over the chopping, shredding, blending chores to the Cuisinart. Jack had given me the powerful professional model for Christmas several years before. He wrapped the huge box in shiny bells-and-holly paper, and then on Christmas Eve day, before the stores closed, he collected green and red cabbages, carrots, onions, apples, hunks of Cheddar and chocolate, and a quart of cream from the dairy for me to chop and dice and shred and thicken. That Christmas morning, once we'd eaten our cranberry muffins, pork sausages, eggs-over-easy and been to church, where, even singing my favorite, "Break forth, O beauteous heav'nly light, and usher in the morning; / Ye shepherds, shrink not with affright, / But hear the angel's warning," I couldn't keep my mind off what I'd chop with the Cuisinart.

After that hour under the drooping cottonwoods, I used the Cuisinart less and less. When, for instance, I made coleslaw, I couldn't bring myself to abandon the veined cabbage head to the Cuisinart blade. I took out my knife and shredded. Before adultery, I hurried through garden and kitchen tasks. After, I took pains. I felt engaged in something beyond myself, something sacramental. Martin Buber makes the distinction between "I and It" and "I and Thou." Beets and baking hens and butter lettuces, Dungeness crabs, plums—all turned to Thous, to numinous, hallowed visible forms bestowing invisible grace. Recipes began to hint at ritual formula, as in John Peale Bishop's "The ceremony must be found / that will wed Desdemona to the huge Moor."

Holidays aren't easy for adulterers. That Christmas my friend was ensconced in his chalet, Peter and I had family and social obligations. We saw each other briefly, at parties, from several days before Christmas until almost a week after New Year's Day. Peter called from pay phones. He said, "I miss you." He said "I'm counting the days."

The first afternoon that we were able to meet again, we almost forgot to make love because we held on to each other and said, again and again, "I missed you so much." Before this, we'd never said, "I love you." Now we did. I cried. Peter cried, big tears dribbled down his cheeks. "What's wrong," Peter said, "is we've fallen in love." His hands shook when he lit his pipe.

Hardly a thought was given to how things looked. We did whatever it took, no matter how foolish or dangerous, to see one another. The phrases "crazy in love" and "fool of his senses" come to mind. As do the judgments "immoral," "selfish to the core." In present-day courts, you perhaps could even make a case for our suffering "diminished capacity."

No sooner did my husband leave for work and the children for school than Peter would pull into the alley and rush through the back gate, back yard, across the uneven brick patio to the back door, and grab me and kiss me. We'd make love on the couch, the stairs, anywhere but my husband's and my bed. We'd sit afterward at the small round kitchen table where I read cookbooks and made grocery lists and fed my husband his lunch and the children did their homework. We'd drink coffee and chat, for all the world as if we were a blissful married couple in our own home.

Sometimes we talked about what life would have been like if we'd met in our twenties and married. "Do you think we'd have been happy?" I asked.

"We would have," he said.

Afternoons when we drove out to the chalet, we sometimes stayed so late that Peter would call someone with whom he had an appointment and say he was stuck somewhere. We got out my friend's Barbra Streisand records and danced, slowly, over the carpets. Peter, one afternoon, took my face between his cool palms. "I adore you," he said. "I live on the idea of you."

So we went from winter's end, through spring and summer. Off and on, we seemed to come to our senses and use some caution. But we could never stay away from each other for long. I think we tried. I really do.

At Jack's and my house, we had company for days at a time, all summer, picnics out on the lawn and floats down the river. My friend was spending a month of vacation in his chalet. I had trouble getting away to see Peter. We talked on the telephone, we wrote each other notes and sent them through the mail. I made Elizabeth David's rice salads. I concocted sandwiches from pork loin and slices of apple sautéed in butter. Early mornings, I baked chickens I'd marinated all night in lemon juice and garlic. I contrived huge composed salads from the garden, with red-jacketed new potatoes, with green beans, yellow crookneck squash, white pattypan squash, cherry tomatoes, and Japanese eggplant. I made apricot ice cream and herb sherbets and blackberry cobbler and raspberry shortcake and strawberry cream pies. Everyone ooh'ed and ah'ed and asked, "May I have just one more, please?"

I grew more ambitious with my canning. The Big Boys put out so many and such heavy red fruit that August that I even tried catsup. I sat at the little kitchen table with my bare feet on the chair where Peter had sat. You name it—say, for instance, a pear—and I pulled one after another cookbook from the kitchen shelf and read recipes that called for pears. I read these recipes as if my waiting Bartletts, Anjous, Boscs, Comices, or Seckels were heroes or heroines, eager to star in the complex narrative twists of a great novel. I wanted the plot of chutney, grainy rough butter, or a pale honeyed preserve buoying up pear chunks. I wanted a cast of characters that would engage these Boscs or Bartletts in action thick with subtextual and mythic underpinnings. For pears, I wanted happy endings, I wanted weddings where bridesmaids wore wreaths wound from white daisy and blue harebell, I wanted dancing.

I considered the nameless ebon-skinned plums from my father-in-law's trees. For years, these plums had called for a chutney deeper, more tragic, than any I'd been able to concoct. The plums' flesh, dark as aged beef, demanded some catastrophe from which they would emerge, solemn and serious, ready to be wedded to duck breasts or a dry Virginia ham. I steeped them in a few spoons of Burgundy and added onion, mustard seed, brown sugar, malt vinegar, cloves, cinnamon, allspice, golden raisins, green and red bell peppers, raisins, grated ginger, walnuts. I put the plum chutney up in wide-mouth half-pint jars. First, I thought I'd give some for Christmas. Then I thought, No, I can't bear to.

Of course this all had to end, and end badly, and it did. It was that time of year when company quit coming and we put away the picnic gear and the rafts and oars and put the storm windows back up. It was that time of year, too, when we ordered cords of orchard woods for the fireplace, and in late afternoon the girls and I stacked apple and cherry and pear tree trimmings. Nights began to turn cold. The garden got puny, the squash leaves yellow. Pole beans were long gone, the second planting of bush beans, too. I dug up the glad corms and dahlia tubers. I piled hay on the lily beds. Any morning you could expect to walk out into the garden and find tomato vines blackened. The girls were back in school. I was thinking about airing winter clothes on the back-yard line, to get out the mothball smell. And Peter and I, we'd whisper to each other, were still in love.

You can bet that many nights, many long days, I've looked back and asked myself if I sensed what was coming. I didn't. The day came and I didn't even guess at it. The day was watery, windy, not raining yet, but it would. Early morning after Jack left for work and Rebecca and Sarah for school, I'd picked out the dewy garden a fat warted Hubbard squash, leaving its frayed umbilical vine attached. I'd been watching it for months. I carried it into the kitchen. The vine scratched my arm. The squash must have weighed six pounds.

I've had a lot of time to go back over that day.

All morning I was in and out of back yard and kitchen. Clouds gradually deepened. Hornets whirred up under the eaves of the patio roof, and I told myself to remember to get Jack to use a hornet bomb on them that weekend.

I made up a batch of whole-wheat bread—three cups white flour, three cups whole wheat. I'd rubbed down four game hens with olive oil and garlic. I stood one of the fat little hens on its end, where its head had been chopped off. Sunlight from the kitchen windows slanted down and illuminated the hen's interior. The ribs curved to meet like cathedral arches in a matchstick miniature Rouens. James Taylor's brother Livingston was singing "Please Come to Boston" on the record player while I melted butter in the big iron skillet. I chopped the hens' gizzards and livers, and when the butter pooled in the skillet, I tossed in the innards and sautéed them with diced onion and garlic. Into my big stoneware mixing bowl I tore up the last of the sourdough French bread I'd baked earlier in the week. I chopped dried apricots and added them, along with a handful of white raisins, to the bread.

I got dressed. I would guess I sucked in my stomach and looked at myself in the mirror. I was wearing a new dress, a red stamp-size plaid buttoned down the front with tiny jet buttons. I liked the dress a lot. I closed all the upstairs windows against the coming rain. I had a new raincoat and, at the last minute, grabbed it.

One-thirty, on the dot, the little car scattered alley gravel as Peter nosed its hood in under the garage canopy.

"That's just a very pretty dress," he said.

At the chalet, we heard thunder roll across the valley. The chalet living room darkened. Peter's fingers were cool.

Our drive back into town was uneventful except that Peter drove faster than he normally would. He saw me glance at the speedometer. "I've got an appointment at four," he said. It was already ten to four. We made plans for the next day, to meet. In my alley I jumped out, raincoat over my shoulders. I pushed open the back gate, walked across the patio bricks, stopping to lean over and pluck dead heads from the French marigolds. The rain spit against the patio roof.

I went into the kitchen and lifted the towel off the bread dough I'd left rising. I drew in a long breath of the yeast aroma. I poked a finger into the puffed-up dough, which was soft as a new baby. My fingertip dimpled the dough. I remember, distinctly, how happy I was, all the places we'd kissed each other, what a good time we'd had.

Nobody was home. I ran upstairs and changed into my jeans. Back down in the kitchen, I sifted flour out onto the marble slab. I gathered the sticky web from the bowl and plopped it onto the field of flour, dipped my hands into the flour, and began kneading. I made bread a little wet, with not quite as much flour as recipes called for. My husband and daughters didn't like what they derided as "health bread." They liked their bread soft. So I cheated some on the flour.

I buttered the tins, put in the dough. I broke an egg, its yolk with the red spot in it indicating the egg had been fertilized by some antic rooster. I whipped the egg white with my whisk and with the pastry brush painted the beaten white over the top of the loaf. As the loaves baked the egg whites would make them shine. I put the bread on the middle rack in the warm oven, set at 375 degrees. The heat radiated onto my face.

The wind lifted the curtains off the sills. Fruit flies circled above ripening tomatoes stacked in the windowsill above the sink. I was singing, along with Livingston Taylor, about Boston in the springtime.

The phone rang. I answered. It was Peter. I thought he'd called because he wanted to say how wonderful the afternoon had been. I could hear people talking. I asked, "Where are you?"

"Phone booth. Out by the freeway." He spoke roughly. He said, "We're busted."

Peter, a few days later, was permitted to resign and left town. After I confessed to Jack, he forgave me. But I had broken the bond between us, and it never mended. My daughters were embarrassed, wounded, disappointed, repelled. Even my father was disgusted with me. He said, "No man is going to want you after what you've done." Eventually I packed up and left home. Years passed before I cooked much of anything again.

About adultery, I don't recommend it. I also have to confess that for that year I was happier than I'd ever been before or have been since.

DUSK

❦

AS THE SUN SLIDES DOWN, HEARTS SINK WITH IT. BETWEEN FIVE and eight in the evening, away from the equator, the sun sets at an angle to the horizon. The sun's light, reflected by the earth's atmosphere, lingers—orange, violet, cerulean blue, purple—long after the sun itself disappears. During these hours public life concludes, personal begins. Birds seek out nests. Diurnal beasts return to burrows. Twilight is for gathering in, for getting ready to sleep spoon-fashion. The loss of tribe catches up with the lost. Exile is sharp.

Those to whom no hours seem dearer kiss at the door, a door varnished in faded dream shades of blue. They hug children not yet blemished by adolescence. Say "Here, kitty" to a sizable tortoiseshell tabby, stoop to tighten the flea collar on a dog. The dog, wagging a docked tail, answers to a sonorous name. There may be a small fire in the fireplace. Because their dinner requires ingredients, the garlic, green onions, butter lettuce, shrimp in shells, parsley, basil, yellow noodles heaped up, the blue Hero olive oil can displaying a bare-chested Greek youth, the Parmesan wedge, the china cream pitcher form a circle on white tiles.

To those men and women, what I point to is only a bad

memory, an on-again off-again anxiety for the future. When one of them, putting out the cat, catches a glimpse of the solitary stranger now far down the hill, sunset gliding over his receding shoulders, they remember they were once the stranger and don't want to remember. The solitary walker will not be invited in. But then he doesn't want to be. To walk past the blue door and sit back among pillows on the ivory couch? To listen to the crackle of applewood catch, the splinters flame up? He would drown in what he doesn't have. She would choke, coughing politely, on who she isn't. Life is not literature. No "lust, betrayal, and murder" rage and holler. Dusk serves no distractions, only memory distorted by sunset's tricks of light. At twilight the mind frets with its own emptiness, dwells on absence, distances between, regrets, on what-is-not, raises its fear of fear to frenzy. One hears tires on asphalt, feet on pavement, going home. To stop off in the dark bar, to order a drink and stare past bottles into the black mirror, is stalling. No matter what the sun sets across, a man or woman who goes home alone quits playing for matchsticks. It is the time of day when he or she must rest upon what grandmothers called "inner resources."

The supermarket's pneumatic door wheezes. What does one person eat? Wednesday food columns wheedle: "Dining alone? Don't stint your best friend! Set a place with your most delicate china." What happens is that one pushes the cart down aisles, reads about chili on the Hormel can, chicken divan in the freezer case, and because to eat this food elicits more hope than can come true, one grabs bread, cheese, and pressed ham, gets a can of chicken noodle just in case.

The lines of solitaries, pulled up to the nine-item checkouts, would appear to agree. In one basket: a six-pack diet Coke, one can water-packed tuna, two bottles Miller Lite, a frozen chicken pot pie, an orange, an apple. In another: Campbell's cream of asparagus soup, a box that holds twelve individual packs of Fritos corn chips, two grapefruit marked with green X's, three splotched bananas, iceberg lettuce vaporizing in a plastic bag, one carton Kools.

Downcast eyes reconnoiter other eyes. If the eyes meet, they widen with pretense of heavily populated thought. Elbows lean on cart handles, shoulders droop, stomachs let go the broad muscle band. In one pocket a hand buffs its own fingertips. There is always the embittered ex-husband. This one is draped in a too-large brown suit. He rubs the back of his neck, where a fresh haircut left rash along pale skin. His eyes follow the plaid-shirted father tut-tutting an infant strapped to his chest. Should the ex-husband kill this man whose presence mocks him? Or the wife who six months ago loaded his belongings into the hall? He is ready to strangle someone. He hates the papoosed father, and he despises the self-satisfied young man leaning on a crutch one line over, Levi's hacked to accommodate his plastered foot, dangling a bottle of vanilla from relaxed fingers. The ex-husband remembers just such evenings when he was sent out for the one last thing. Vanilla would have been for her White Mountain frosting that gleamed on birthday cakes. Later tonight, as he talks long-distance with his four-year-old, who tells him she has a baby-sitter and Mama is out, he will burn the rib-eye steak he waits here to buy.

A saturnine brunette holds Judith Rossner's paperback *August*. Her rib cage lifts as, turning the page, she takes a sudden breath. She is taking home peanut butter marbled with grape jelly, whole-wheat bread, an orange box of canary treats. She will fall asleep on the couch at nine-thirty, this book in one hand. The heavy-hipped blonde in blue buys Fritos for brown bag lunches and a hank of purple yarn. By ten tonight she will have eaten, idly, four of the packages, aware they are empty when her molars, crunching down, startle her. While she crochets squares for a granny afghan, she will pray for the telephone's buzz, will lift the receiver off its cradle and check for a dial tone. No one will call. If someone does, it will make no difference.

Standing alone in the express line, almost none of these men or women do not feel diminished by the couples inching past with dangerously loaded carts. Even the most content of the single householders the census counts begins at six-thirty to doubt his bachelor lightness, to malign her independent pleasures. Among those duos watched, silently, by the singles are husbands and wives whose prime emotions for one another are terror and spite. They harden and moisten by commandeering images of rock stars and pinups, by holding hostage imaginary women at the office or men from the past. Their children's noisy and expensive existence mocks their futures, harnesses them in double jeopardy. But if the looks of the single men and women standing by could kill, bodies would pile up in the aisles.

Far away from you, your lover dozes on the tweed davenport in the house he shares with his wife. The lamp with the ruffled shade tied in a maroon bow is turned on. He says she hates sex. You do not know if this is true. Actually, he does not know. She has her own buried life. She suspects about you, suspected others before you. He takes your face in his hands and says, "I adore you." When the sun goes down he says to his wife, "So, how was your day, honey?" and she pecks him on the cheek.

As you wait to cross the street, the light rainfall softens your grocery sack. The green in the trees leaches out and the trees turn to charcoal sketches. Any minute now, streetlights will twinkle in the puddle. Everything dear Abby says is true.

LONG TRAIN RIDE

❦

ELEVEN A.M. AND WE SHIVER OUTSIDE THE OAKLAND, CALIFORnia, Amtrak depot. Outside, because the depot, built in 1912, has been closed for repairs since the earthquake in late October. Fifty, sixty of us range along the tracks' edge, awaiting the *California Zephyr*.

Ticketed into a roomette for New Orleans via Chicago, three nights' journey, Jack and I lean against a shopping bag and duffels in which we've stacked clothes, books, tapes, cassette player, lunch. We are under the spell of departure; we stare down empty track to the point at which parallel lines appear to meet.

Since the summer we've titillated each other with this journey. Our talk has been by telephone—we live states apart. We've reminded one another of how, so many nights in the bed we'd shared, we had heard long-drawn-out train whistles moan at the town's edge. There came a time when the railroad threatened to bypass our red-brick depot. We do not mention that I said, apparently teasing, "I intend to get out before the train doesn't stop here anymore." Nor do we talk about the early morning when, without goodbyes, I drove to the depot, left the keys in my car, got on the train going west, and never came back. Six months later the railroad dropped our town from its roster of stops. We recall, instead, a summer hike when dizzily, terrifyingly lost, we looked down below us and saw rails curve—shining—out of mountains and knew where we were.

A man hunched under a backpack asks where we're headed (he's from West Berlin). "New Orleans," we say. Our answer is and isn't true: the train itself is our destination; we are our destination; we're riding just to ride.

Zephyr due in ten minutes, we pace. Jack bumps up next to a couple who speak in tense, low voices. We are drawn to watch them. His tweed jacket and her trench coat, their bookbags, indicate recent student life. They lean on each other, holding hands; both wear wedding rings. She looks uncannily like Sylvia Plath at twenty-five—long in the waist, blond, pale. Her cheeks flush; her eyelids are puffy as if she might have been crying. She rises on tiptoe in her scuffed brown boots and whispers in his ear. He frowns, brushes back his dark forelock, squeezes her hand. She winces. Rubs one scuffed toe over the other. We quickly look away, down the tracks. The snub-nosed diesel-and-steam-powered Amtrak engine zooms toward us, pulling silver cars painted with Amtrak's red-white-and-blue logo, its vibrations rising up through our feet, our knees, our chests.

Weighted under duffels and our shopping bag heavy with wine and meatball sandwiches, we heave up the car's high steps and search down the narrow hall for our roomette. On both sides of the passageway, compartments face one another. We glimpse through sliding glass doors our fellow passengers arranging luggage, settling in.

We find it. Tuck into a room fitted out with facing seats and, between the seats, a fold-out table and a wide window. Outside, porters smoke and people wave passengers goodbye. We stow our duffels on the overhead rack, set out our lunch.

The train lurches, rolls. Henry introduces himself, our porter until Chicago. A high hefty belly fills out Henry's Amtrak sweater. Gray-flecked burr tops his perfectly round head, his big eyes bulge, and although he speaks to us hospitably, even merrily, he looks near tears. First call for dinner, he tells us, we'll hear at five-thirty. Tucking behind our heads those flat white pillows that serve as pillows for all transportation, Henry says that when we're ready for bed, he'll make up our bunks.

Henry gazes from one to the other of us, as a baby-sitter might study potentially unruly charges, then reaches up across Jack, briefly obscuring Jack's face, and presses a button in a panel of buttons. An electrified *ding-dong* sounds from down the hall. "That's my call, in my room. Anything you need, push this button and I'll be here soon as I can. Okay?" We nod. Okay.

We unpack our cassette player, tapes, uncork a Gewurtztraminer, offer a toast. "To us."

I ride backward, Jack forward. Our roomette feels playhouse cozy, a niche, a nest already feathered with bread crumbs. Between the two walls, the glass door (we've pulled the brown drape), the wide window, and us there's easy continuity: this room fits us like skin. We stretch our feet, touch toes, grin.

The *California Zephyr*, a pamphlet informs us, was named for Zephyrus, god of the West Wind. "Aboard the Zephyr, you'll travel from ocean to mountain range to prairie." Over the next 2,422 miles we're promised "three mountain ranges, three major rivers and two deserts."

We're almost to Martinez—thirty miles in forty-five minutes—before we begin, truly, to study what's outside the window. Deep draws and gullies sprout the waste vegetation that takes over when bulldozers have cleared land. Jack giggles. "Lots of good places around here to leave off body parts." I laugh. He frowns, ashamed, and then I am ashamed, and then in the muddle of our shame we are redeemed by the sight of a white horse, tail held high, who picks his way through rusted wrecks stacked inside a junkyard.

Some dozen passengers wait at the tiny Martinez depot. A gray-haired man, followed by a gray-haired woman, leans on a walker, unsteadily stumps the platform. The left side of his face droops, eye unfocused. Soon after, we hear footsteps and an excited female voice in the passageway. I peer out our curtain and see the man lurch unsteadily, the woman—surely his wife—gripping him by his belt from behind. They enter the roomette across from ours.

Milky fog rises off Suisin Bay. A suspension bridge materializes out of haze; then a mothball fleet—ships from World War II, Korea, Vietnam—offers itself as sharp lines etched in fog. The train advances north, the ships emerge in sharper detail: eight rows and ten–twelve ships in each row, rusted gray hulls fretted abovedeck with cranes and booms.

Our window frames the outside world. From our seats, noses near cool glass, we see images zip by serially. We are the camera eye; for a moment anything out there is ours: settling ponds bubbling green scum, green-headed mallards and tweedy coots scudding the eddies, rough-legged hawks soaring into updraft.

The hawk, Jack assures me, is searching out a meal of warm mice. I ask, How does a hawk kill a mouse? "By grasping it with its talons, and squeezing. At least," Jack hesitates, "that's what I think happens. I do know an owl will swoop down, grasp the mouse in its talons, and fly into the air a bit and squeeze the mouse, and the mouse will squeak—*eek*—and then, frequently, the owl will drop the mouse and go to the ground and pick it up in its mouth and eat it.

"I've seen owls simply kill mice for fun—not to eat them. One of the summers in high school when I worked as an irrigator a great horned owl would follow me over the fields. That owl would dive down repeatedly, and in the course of a morning might kill several hundred mice."

Suckers for scenery, gullible to the natural world, our eyes feast.

"Ah," says Jack, "white heron!" The car gently rocks, maternal under us. A second hawk dives down into waving grasses, another white heron floats through mid-air, then iridescent green mallard heads shine atop the marsh. Starlings rise into blue sky. Wheels click on the track, the train grinds on the slight grade to Suisin–Fairfield. At this moment what we'd talked about for weeks comes true: the train whistle sounds. Across our compartment we call "Whooee whooee," and do not mind how silly, how high on what's happening we are.

Sacramento Delta presents us with quilt scraps of varied greens. Light fog hangs low along the river, the banks marked by drooping cottonwoods, eucalyptus windbreaks. This is Joan Didion country; she grew up near here. We have both read her first novel, *Run River*, whose background is the Sacramento city and river. *Run River*, I tell Jack, furnishes almost my sole knowledge of land we're passing, "and because of the novel, I think of this land as perennially hot, 104 degrees, and believe Didion's heroine, Lily, and Lily's husband, Everett, are always here. Everett's always just gotten the hops down, Everett and Lily are always drinking from the bottle of bourbon Everett keeps by the bed." Watching the state capitol's golden dome pass by, and admiring beside the tracks a concrete-block building on which blue letters announce CALIFORNIA ALMOND GROWERS EXCHANGE, I don't add, but think that Lily, after they've made love, is perpetually crying out, "Keep me, baby, please keep me," and Everett hasn't kept her, he has not. He lost her, and she was away in some San Francisco hotel and he was here somewhere, not far from this train window, drinking as if it did not matter what happened to Lily. Which was not true: it did matter to Everett.

Past Sacramento, hopper car after hopper car stacked with coal blocks our view. Where before we had multimillion greens and

high-flying birds, where our eyes felt satisfaction, talked talk between mind and landscape, now there is hollow, chasm. I make
myself look away from the window, look into my lap, look at my
hands, at anything but these innumerable, uncountable coal cars,
but I can't. Then, as suddenly as the coal cars arrived before us,
they're gone—we're gone.

Jack points out high-school bleachers, wooden risers, where
"bindlestiffs used to sit, watching," Jack says, "a baseball game
that doesn't exist."

Looking behind me, I count thirty–forty people on the risers
and then passing in front of our window a park. A campfire flares,
flames soar up transparent in mid-afternoon light. A dozen people,
indistinguishable by sex under heavy clothing, huddle around the
fire.

We leave the valley and wind up the Sierra foothills, over whose
lower reaches snow has settled. The Amtrak pamphlet: "Between
Sacramento and Reno the Zephyr climbs to Donner Lake and
skirts along the 2,000-foot drop of the American River Canyon,
crosses the Sierra Nevadas, climbing to 7,000 feet." Grinding upgrade, the train groans.

Is it the unaccustomed early-afternoon wine, is it what's been (is
still) between Jack and me, is it distance lengthening between me
and what's now my home that's unsettling, saddening me? Who
can say why I left, why he did not come for me. He does not
know the answer to the first question, nor I the answer to the
second.

Tracks edge the Truckee River, and Jack enthuses over mistle-
toe hanging from leafless trees, coots lighting down on rocks along
a river's edge. How odd to see all this and to hear, smell, none of
it. "I wish we could hear rivers gurgle," I say. "Do you remember

when you taught me to lie down by the riverbank with my ear
turned toward water so I could listen for the undercurrent?"

Our feet touch under the table. Jack rubs my toes with his toes.

❧

Four-thirty, axles and couplings creaking and singing, our engine
draws us to 3,500 feet. Twilight stripes the sky red, rose, pink,
turns the snow blue and, in hollows, lilac and plum. A mule deer,
doe, huge delicate ears popped up, noses her way down to a
stream on whose riffle falling sun flashes. "She seems entirely un-
aware of the train," says Jack.

Over the intercom, the club-car steward: "Complimentary
strawberry margaritas will be served." We glower. "In cans," he
adds.

Five o'clock, dark mountains, and inside, yellowish light envel-
ops us. Jack's feet rest on my seat, and my feet rest on his. We're
warm as hens setting nests in a brood house. Our mutual odor—
my perfume, Jack's aftershave, leavings from his meatball sandwich, the wine, and now the coffee I'd rung Henry's bell for—
steepens. Across the hall, the elderly duo has left their roomette
door open. We learn that they are headed for Chicago to visit a
daughter. The husband is recovering from a "massive stroke," and
the wife, who talks with Henry, leaning against the doorjamb, says
about her husband, "He's in my care and doesn't like it. He
doesn't like me at all." The husband coughs: a hacking throat-
mangling agonized cough.

When we hear "First call for dinner," we go, praying no one
will sit with us. Opening the door to the diner I am struck first
by an aquarium light flooding down over two rows of tables for
four. I listen. Something's missing. This is what it is: Amtrak uses
plastic tableware; one no longer hears cutlery rattle in the swaying
car.

No luck on dinner alone. Hair dyed field-mouse brown, rhinestone butterfly glasses astride long nose, mouth red and wide, she—Pam, maybe sixty—boasts a firm body and under her beige sweater an impressively high bust. Just retired, she tells us, voice nasal. Twenty years as a sandwich maker in a Bay Area junior high school. Army husband died four years after he retired. Five children. Oldest daughter never married—a real pill—still at home. Eyebrows rise, raising nose, raising sparkly glasses. Daughter has big problems.

Born in Pennsylvania. Going back for Christmas. Going to hit all the malls. "So, where you off to? Malls," she continues, without giving us a chance to answer, "Pennsylvania's got great malls."

Waiter, black and tall, apprises us of specials. He's pushing pork kebabs. Pam engages him in talk about how this and that dish are prepared. He emits rapid tongue clicks, then, leaning down over her scintillating glasses, says, "Baked, lady, the chicken is baked in an oven."

We order halibut. She orders chicken. Says the daughter who lives with her goes to a headshrinker, it's that bad. She's got to get away from her daughter. Some children. Are heartbreak.

Enough to say the Amtrak coffee's not swell but not bad. Same with the food. Edible. Instant mashed potatoes. Enough, too, to say that while we eat we pass Donner Lake, without seeing it, site of the Donner Party debacle, the very spot where starving pioneers boiled hides and straps from wagons and then ate one another. Enough.

We don't finish our fish or eat the potatoes, and Pam scolds. "It's all my years in that lunchroom," she explains.

At the table across from us the young couple whom we'd watched outside the Oakland depot, the Sylvia Plath–like blonde and her mate, pick at halibut, gulp wine. (I am already calling her "Sylvia.") She has changed out of boots into flats; her eyes are no longer tear-stained. He lifts forkfuls of white fish and broccoli florets to his mouth and surreptitiously turns his eyes to her while he chews.

The waiter clears away the two plates from Sylvia and husband's table. Sylvia reaches across the table, touches her husband's hand, which he clenches and unclenches. Her wrist bears violet bruises.

The train has wound slowly down from the Donner Pass to Reno. We've dragged our cassette player out in our roomette. Mighty Clouds of Joy harmonize—"I can fly higher than an eagle, you are the wind beneath my wings"—when Reno blazons out of the night in neon: Harrah's, Bally's. We roll away, back into the dark. I press my brow against the glass: if you don't look through the window, what you see is your reflection and you're stuck looking at you.

Jack, preparing for tomorrow's landscape, studies his worn copy of McPhee's *Basin and Range.* The Great Basin, through which we are passing now and will go on passing tomorrow, is "big desolate land, dry washes everywhere," says Jack—between the Sierra Nevada and the Rockies, covering much of Nevada, western Utah, and the far edge of eastern California. "The Great Basin," Jack reads to me, "is the largest sinkhole in the U.S. The mountains, trending north to south that pitch abruptly up in the middle of the Great Basin trap enough moisture to generate small streams, and in turn these streams produce, among other rivers, the Humboldt. What little bit of water actually falls on the Great Basin flows toward its center. None flows out. So what rivers there are— the Humboldt, for instance—flow for short distances and end up as salty lakes."

Jack looks up from his book, asks if I want to visit the club car, "I do, I do," I answer. The walk between hurtling cars takes daring, and I grip Jack's arm as the couplings shudder and in unsteady rhythm cars part and join and part.

The coaches' overhead lights have been dimmed. Some passengers read. Some stare straight ahead, others through windows. Many are plugged into cassette players, thrum fingers in time to music, mouth words. Some sleep, heads slumped, skin sheened with sweat, arms and legs akimbo, postures one sees in photographs of soldiers in bunkers under siege. To observe strangers undefended in sleep seems trespass, transgression.

The club car clamor startles us. Lights are low, and at almost every one of a dozen tables and benches and swivel chairs facing windows passengers drink beer and talk loudly, flirt. The car reminds Jack of vinyl-booth-and-plastic-fern suburban mall bars. He had hoped for a glamorous club car from 1940s films and feels on the verge of sulk.

Jack juggles ice-filled plastic glasses, Scotch, almonds. Tosses all onto the table we share with two men in their early thirties. Both tell us they take trains because they fear flying (we would hear this again and again from fellow passengers). Doug, a Sears appliance salesman in Davis, lost a niece on the Pan Am flight that blew up over Lockerbie.

Blond Sylvia's mate slips a hand under her turtleneck collar, massages her neck. Sylvia scowls, turns toward the dark window, which shows back her face as a livid oval. He smiles, his teeth small, even, white. The bruises on Sylvia's wrist are finger-size.

This couple reminds us (we say this, out loud) of how, years earlier, we fought, struggled. I would advance, he would retreat, then he would advance, I retreat. We lived together for years, then have not lived together. Neither of us goes into detail as to how we live now. We discuss our daughters, long gone from home, the taxes we pay jointly, property, old friends. We do and do not miss one another. We have passed the fever point, survived sickness's desperate hours. Sitting at this table, grasping a glass when the train sways, I ask Jack if he agrees with this assessment. He says he would not have put it so, but he agrees.

That our compartment felt playhouse cozy I have already noted.

But we did not guess, until we slid open our door and saw Henry had made up our bunks, plumped pillows, turned down our light to a burnt gold, caramel gloom, how fantasy rich this tiny space might be. Curtain pulled across the glass door and while outside the window dark Nevada streams by, our roomette becomes the space which, in childhood, could turn into jungle or igloo or medieval castle enough to house any plot. We undress, lifting arms and legs to slip out of jeans and shirts. I change into a nightgown and Jack, who's never owned nightwear, wriggles into navy-blue cotton pajamas he bought yesterday at Goodwill—"dead man's pajamas," he's sure.

A web belt hooked to the upper bunk keeps the bunk's occupant from being thrown out. Jack belts himself in and soon I hear his snore. From the stroke victim's roomette across the way, coughing, gagging, and choking attain operatic intensity, then subside into gurgles. I prop my head on a pillow on the lower bunk and pick out the small lights of small towns' glimmering in the darkness, hurtling by. The train picks up speed, and motion under me, rocking, rocks me to sleep. At four o'clock Jack clambers down; we cuddle spoon-fashion while the half-moon drops low over the desert.

We meant to be awake in Salt Lake City, but we slept, never saw the city. By the time we come back from the bathroom down the hall where we brushed our teeth and showered, by the time Henry makes up our bunks and restores them to seats, the train is climbing the Wasatch Range. Our car pitches, tosses.

Jagged cliffs shadow profound gulches and on distant snow-white hills, shining roads wind mysteriously upward. Jack goes for breakfast, Henry brings coffee, wishes me good morning. Through a gap in the drape I see the gray-haired woman on her knees before her husband, his stockinged foot in her hand. She rubs the foot and he moans.

Nine-thirty, Mountain Time, when Jack, who comfortably eats breakfast with strangers, returns (aroma of bacon in his hair and flannel shirt) and reports that in the diner most tables were taken, the chatter sounded "moody, murmurous, morning-after." He ate "old-fashioned French toast, thick bread slices, eggy and moist, sluiced with maple syrup. Three slices of bacon." Our dinner companion of the night before sat at the table behind him, telling again the story of her daughter. Sylvia and husband, he says, in answer to my question, weren't at breakfast, no.

Nearing 7,200 feet. The half-moon—bleach white—curves in a cloudless blue sky, the blue a pastel summer color. Hoar frost sparkles on alders, aspens, willows' bare branches. Frost stipples bushes, sagebrush, and high coarse grasses. Alongside the tracks rise thirty-foot inclines. Jack estimates the snow as six inches deep. "Not much for this elevation."

Animal tracks crisscross snowbanks. "Elk, deer, maybe some coyote, rabbit for sure live out here," says Jack.

Three rosy beige mule deer gaze at the passing train from the cover of leafless trees. One turns his back toward us, tail lifted up exposing the flag, the tail's underside, lighter in color than his body.

Crossing over Soldier Summit at 7,200 feet, the very top of the Wasatch Plateau, we watch eleven silver passenger cars emblazoned with Amtrak's red-and-blue logo unwind behind us, and then we descend into a canyon. "This," says Jack, "is what a major river canyon looks like from inside. Eons ago the river was here and rock rose up and the river just kept cutting in at the same level. New young rivers are quite straight, but a river like this that existed before the mountains lifted up has kept its meanders."

Price River turns its gray tongue of water toward the tracks. "I'd expected a little bit more out of the Price than this," says Jack, "but it must race down through here in springtime, I see washes every quarter mile or so along here. The land's all been eroded out by the river."

Greenish-tinged leaden gray vistas spread out far from the tracks, scruffy with sagebrush and bunchgrass, on which rests here and there a deserted frame shack, more hut than home. "Failed homesteads," Jack sighs, adding, "I guess there was nothing much to do here but wait for God, huh?" I cheer up again only when a black crow, the first bird we've seen in an age, lights atop a cottonwood.

Eleven-thirty, wanting people, we head for the club car. Between lurching cars (pitching now that we go downhill) we stop, breathe cold air. Above us the sky has maintained its utterly pure blameless blue. Not a cloud.

At six tables in the car's rear, you may light up. Two white-haired men in cowboy shirts drink beer at the table farthest back. Across the aisle from them two women sip coffee. One, a bottle redhead who's teased her fiery hair high into a corona, wears a sweatshirt whose sequins spell out RENO. Dora her name is. Second is our friend Pam. The near-noontime sun is hard on their faces.

Dora says to Pam, "Don't care what you smoke or what you drink or what you eat, you're gonna die of somethin'. I don't drink. Never liked it. Don't party. If I don't smoke my Carletons, what have I got?"

Guy across the aisle fingers the cowboy hat on his knee, leers at her. "If you quit smoking, you might take up partyin'. Way I'm feelin' now, all shut up in this train, I wouldn't be all against that."

Dora nods, garnering the compliment as her due. "Somethin's goin' to kill you. My mother, she lived clean all her life, died of a ruptured navel. So you never know."

You don't know. What's gonna get you. All agree.

An elderly woman, white hair uncombed, fits her gargantuan

frame draped in a white-and-black print dress onto the chair opposite us. Sour odor rises off her. Her large loose mouth is bereft
of teeth. she has bought a ham sandwich, which she gums, and
noisily sucks Coke from a can. She's traveling to Denver with her
little sister. They've come from Reno, sitting up all night in coach.
"Like this," she says, showing how she gripped the pillow across
her lap and let her head fall on the pillow's top. She mimes snores.
On the backs of her hands the skin, stretched tight over delicately
articulated tendons, is clear and fresh as a young woman's.

Doors hang between cars, rails click, we talk, our table partner
gums and sucks, we catch snatches from Dora and Pam's conversation, and we watch as out the window the folds and dramatic
rises go by, colored in iron-ore reds, and above, jagged crests, sky
cold blue, remote.

Pam says to Dora: "My youngest girl, the one I was telling you
about, she has an eating disorder. Her self-esteem went down and
down." Tears pop into the corners of Pam's eyes, she wipes at her
face, looks pleadingly at Dora. "What do you suppose causes her
to do this?" Dora shakes her head, pats Pam's hand. "I've aged
five years in one year. She is trapped in self-destruction. You don't
know what it is to watch somebody kill themselves right before
your eyes."

Dora says to Pam: "Our son—the older one—God, he was trouble. Bad checks. He was brave enough to come to his dad and ask
for help. His wife was on dope, still is. Which was why bad
checks."

Pam's been widowed so long she doesn't know if she'd want a
man anymore. "My husband was just getting his life together, getting his retirement plans to come true, when he got MS—multiple
sclerosis. It ate him up. He finally went from esophageal cancer.
Sometimes you just don't know, huh?"

The woman across from us wipes drooled mayonnaise from her

mouth, says when she was young she listened to old women talk about dead husbands and didn't think there was much to it until she lost her own. "Then I knew. He and I, we used to sit in the parlor, and he'd read in his chair and I'd sit on the couch and crochet. Now I never crochet, naw."

Dora lights another Carleton. "Bad things always happen in the winter, at least to me. "My husband got diagnosed with vascular hypertension in '81. Late '83 he got so plugged up he had to have his leg off below the knee. So, '83, he had his leg off and then that same year our son-in-law was out in Wyoming living in a camper in our back yard. He had a butane heater in there and he was getting ready to make himself his breakfast coffee and the butane went up and he got blowed out of there. It was bad. We took him to Laramie to the burn center there, he had third-degree burns on his face, his chest, down right near his privates. Doctors at the burn center said he wasn't burned bad enough for the burn center. Our second son, the one that's a bull rider in the rodeo, he got himself in a fight with some black guy and he got shot right in his ball sack. That was fall '83, too."

Pam: "God, but you been through it, haven't you?"

Woman across from us laughs, says, as much to herself as to us, "My God, I wish that gal'd shut up. Hell, wish my sister was in here, she'd go for that talk." Toothless, fat, sour-smelling, wild white hair, she nevertheless looks lovely. She uses her hands as a well-loved woman might, caresses her freckled arms as if her hands remembered for her how her husband had touched her. I think, He is loving her still. I think, When I am old, I would like my life to have made me able to touch myself like this. I think, There are lessons in life I would rather not learn.

Peevish voice over intercom: "Toilets are stopped up. Please do not put disposable diapers in toilets. Please."

One p.m., back in our compartment, we've crossed into Colo-

rado, at DuBuque, pass the Colorado River, emerald green and
sparkling with ice. "Nice easy canoeing water, a desert river," says
Jack, "not even any cottonwoods along the banks, sagebrush comes
right down to where it's been scoured. It must flood quite heavily
in the spring and then drop rapidly, leaving no moist land where
seedlings could survive."

Between Rifle and Silt, ice chunks ride the Colorado. A ten-
foot-wide ice floe turns and spins midstream; green-headed mallards and brown hens light along the banks. We pass a burned-out
area, limbs charred, trees blackened. Then, so close we look into
its eye, a raven spirals down past our window, carrion chunk
clamped in its beak.

Three p.m. Snow crowns Glenwood Springs' brown sandstone
tower-and-turret Victorian-era structures. On the platform, Sylvia,
mate behind her lugging suitcases, rushes toward a rangy gray-
haired woman, who in turn runs toward her. The woman—surely
Sylvia's mother—pats Sylvia's cheeks with green mittens, kisses
her once, twice, on the mouth. Sylvia's husband sets down the
suitcases, puts out a bare hand, which the mother shakes. Backs
vanish into the depot.

"Hard to figure," says Jack, "what was going on with those two,
isn't it?"

Ten minutes later we're grinding upgrade. The train groans and
creaks, rises through narrow crevasses and, as far as I can see,
brown rock. Only domestic touch: found-wood fences, cottonwood
saplings on which strands of barbed wire stretch. The train brushes
the rock outcrops almost intimately, and creeps between them,
ascending, up and up.

A Western movie from our childhood is what the landscape
becomes. The plot turns on vice and virtue, black hats and white,
a brunette dancehall vixen and a blond rancher's daughter. I am
not sure, am never sure, that virtue will triumph, am always afraid

that somewhere deep behind the prospect before me, in a cold dark, I will hear the heart break with the crack of a pistol shot.

Five-thirty p.m. The falling sun colors curdled clouds violent red while we share dinner with a retired schoolteacher from Santa Cruz. She wears a burgundy knit vest, a plaid shirt, white hair in a girlish bob. At the moment of the earthquake she was "tooling uphill in my ancient VW," and when it hit she thought her tires had gone flat. She orders vegetarian lasagna. She takes the train twice every year to Chicago, where her brother lives. She's been eating the vegetarian lasagna for three years. "Sometimes"—she smiles—"it's broccoli, sometimes it's zucchini squash." She suggests we order the New York steak, and we do.

In the coaches, as we make our way back from the diner, the smell hits us of garbage ripeness, as oranges and apples and lunchmeat sandwiches, two days in overheated cars, spoil. There are as well the unwashed armpits and crotches and feet, food digesting in upper and lower intestines, the sour eructations arising out of mouths from all that digestion, booze seeping sweetish ketones out from pores.

Two hours later the conductor announces we are ready to cross the Continental Divide, at 9,200 feet. "Will be downhill all the way from here to Denver," he says.

Almost midnight before we leave Denver. I roll against the wall and sleep. Snow drifts through my dreams, and I wake in the morning in Nebraska. Sitting in my lower bunk, blanket wrapped around my shoulders, Jack snoring lightly above, I peer out the window. Snow drifts in around the corn stubble, and at the edge of the cornfield a coyote stands in full point. From the intercom, the conductor's voice proclaims Omaha, "where the temperature—brrr—is minus 4 degrees." Red-faced guys alongside pickup trucks parked next to Magda's Cafe watch the train pass by from under their billed caps. Nobody waves.

Jack wakes up, hurriedly dresses to get to breakfast. I wander our car's hallway, visit with the wife of the stroke victim. Her husband wasn't able to sleep all night and dozed off just at dawn. Is it the train? I ask. "No," she answers, her hand chilly on my arm, "it's this way at home, too."

In our compartment Henry, round face filmed in sweat, gathers sheets, blankets. I ask how long he's worked on trains.

"Twenty-three years. Started out with Burlington-Northern."

Does he like his work?

"Don't like it anymore."

How long since he liked it?

"Liked it the first seventeen years. When it went Amtrak, didn't like it anymore. Once Reagan broke PATCO, it hasn't been ever the same since then. It ain't fun no more. Ain't no fun," says Henry wearily, "ever since Reagan."

Was he surprised Reagan was elected the second time?

"No, I was surprised he was elected the first time. By the second time it weren't no surprise to me. Nothin' about politics is. A. Philip Randolph would turn over in his grave if he could see what's going on now. Sleeping Car Porters idn't anymore a union, in fact. It's in bed with management. Day of the workin' man is over. Nobody cares about us no more. Believe me." Henry, sweating heavily now, turns from folding the mattress onto the top bunk, rolls back his eyes, pins me with them. "Nobody."

Late morning, we tune our radio into Council Bluff's classical music station. After a Haydn symphony, the news broadcast: marijuana is the most used drug in Iowa, cocaine second.

The snow blows down curving streets dotted with brick two-story houses; snow covers cattle, barns, fields, trees, fences. Jack and I, silent, stare out onto white landscapes through Iowa into Illinois. Hypnotized by snow, we fall as deep in ourselves as the snow is falling around fence posts and fields.

Lunch we share with a bulky-muscled geologist in a purple T-shirt and a long-haired anthropologist in plaid flannel. The geologist "prospects gold, freelance." The anthropologist is a land developer. They roomed together in college, in Colorado, ten years ago, and are on their way to Chicago to meet friends. "Gonna party."

Four p.m., outside Galesburg, the train begins intermittently to lose electrical power. No lights. We stop, sit on tracks, snow blowing past windows. "Weather," conductor announces, "going to make us late into Chicago." He sticks his head in our compartment, tells us we're likely to miss our New Orleans train.

Twenty miles from Chicago, four hours late, speed ten miles an hour, we drag past bright-lit, empty commuter stops. We accept, now, a night and day in Chicago, imagine beige bedspreads, stained carpet, and framed rural landscapes in the Quality Inn (where Amtrak, we're told, puts you up).

Conductor peers into our compartment, tells us *City of New Orleans* waits on Track 26, we may catch it if we hurry. Goodbye, Quality Inn; goodbye, going to sleep under factory-painted green field, red barn, brown cow.

Shaky-legged, we tumble off the *Zephyr*, whose rocking metal mothered us since Oakland, into the cold's sharp teeth. I am stunned. Can't move. Pushed from behind, I start, one light-soled pump in front of the other, and march.

Talk about surprises. We're ushered into a brown doom of a car—high-backed seats, almost every one boasting shoulders and a head, eyes staring imploringly forward. Heat rises in visible waves. Car stinks like a roadside zoo: steaming carnivore bodies, potato chips and hot dogs and booze, and armpits and urine.

Seven-thirty p.m. Should have pulled out two hours ago. White-haired conductor says no sleeping cars left, forget it, he's got twelve more passengers than he's got seats.

Our eyes sort out of the sepia ruin the families and lone riders from Detroit and Chicago: Poles, Germans, fair-skinned, dark-haired Scotch-Irish who must have come north from Appalachia, and blacks protecting their hairdos under plastic shower caps.

Jack takes an aisle seat at the head of the car; I get an aisle seat behind him. Wayne's my seatmate. "Why-ine," he says it. Born in East Texas fifty-five, maybe sixty years ago, Why-ine's football-guard big. Looks like, smells like an old-fashioned smokehouse ham. Brother works as a machinist in a textile mill. Goin' to visit him. Wayne's drinking beer. Two empty Jax cans are already stashed in a paper sack by his huge feet.

"Twelve degrees out there," Wayne tells me, pointing out the window, where yawning porters, exhaling spumes of white breath, lean against empty baggage wagons. He nods toward the front of the car, says, "The toilets are frozen up, So's the water for the drinking fountain. Hell of a thing."

These cars, he explains, were made in 1953, not a goddamn thing done since, except "reupholstery and slapping on paint."

Why didn't Wayne fly? "Fear of flying. I'm scared."

"Toilet don't work, water don't work. What kinda train's this?" The speaker, paper cup cone in hand, rocks back and forth by the water fountain. Five-eight or so—runty—hair dark and piled and oiled long on the sides, spiked on top, dark clipped mustache above a thin tight mouth, a navy-blue sweatshirt on which is spelled out in white letters

DETROIT
WHERE THE WEAK ARE KILLED AND EATEN

Creases are pressed into his jeans, the hard crease you see put in prison denims, and the fabric hugs his buttocks and bandy legs, flares above polished black boots.

"Guy's a nut," Wayne confides. "High on somethin' and peakin'."

For sure, when this guy turns and looks down the length of the car, his eyes burn us down. He fakes a right jab, left, another quicker right to empty air, shrugs, heads down into the next car. "He'll be trouble," Wayne predicts, "before the night's over."

The train lurches forward, wiggles side-to-side through dark Chicago train yards. Here as before, when we arrived, gas fires flare at switches and the wind twists the flames skyward and the snow drifts, blows skids. We pick up speed, iron rims grind on iron track, rattle through the yard out into downtown. Wayne points out to me the Sears Tower, whose illuminated windows light the snow driving slantwise down through the dark.

The conductor punches tickets. I ask again about our roomette. "See for yourself, lady, I got too many on this train now." Spit flies from his mouth. A huge black woman, three hundred pounds, shower cap pulled down over her hair, turns sideways to push past him. Her hip bumps him. He wheels to face her. "Didn't you ever learn excuse me?"

"He hates us," Wayne says, and offers me a warm beer, which I refuse.

Jack makes friends with his seatmate. He, with his wife and their three-year-old son seated across the aisle, took the train from Detroit to Chicago and are going on to New Orleans; his wife, he tells Jack, has "airplane phobia." The wife sits to the side, on one hip, pale clean-washed face turned up to the over-head light. Her brown hair is long. Her son, on her lap, sucks at the foot of a large gold cross on a chain around her neck. His flesh phosphoresces. He has beetling violent blue eyes. He digs his tiny fingernails into his mother's soft upper arm. She winces. She turns, head hanging in the aisle, says to me, about him, "He's hyperactive."

Behind us black Southern voices discuss the snow, how cold it is, about what folks will do and who they will hang out with in Memphis, in Jackson, in McComb, in New Orleans.

Car's too goddamned hot, is what Wayne says, and Wayne's right. I'm sweating. Wayne is polished in sweat and smells commandingly of ham hocks. To see out the grimy window, dirtier than that window left behind in Chicago, I must gaze across Wayne's vast plaid-and-brown Sansabelt-trousered belly.

Jack turns around, head hanging in the aisle, gravity loosening the flesh at his jowls, suggests the club car. "We haven't had dinner, remember?" I'm up and have his hand, which is hot as on nights when he'd been ill with something he'd caught from the children and would reach for me out of fevered sleep. Between cars the fierce wind blows snow, and we spot moment to moment through one-after-another tenement windows women at stoves, men and women bent over kitchen tables. We see half-buried cars, neon signs. We smell snow, or think we do. We kiss each other's cold lips.

Only two of the twenty orange-topped tables in the club car are empty. His hand on my elbow, Jack sits me down, and then heads to the counter, where three waiters sell drinks and sandwiches. In this club car the tables are not fastened to the floor and roll with the train. Jack returns with paper boxes stacked with tuna-fish salad packed into croissants and two packages of Granma's oatmeal cookies, two Scotches, two small bottles of white wine, and coffee and cigarettes. "Which are not our brand, because there are only two brands for sale." I unwrap a cookie, dip its edge into the will-less coffee, and am not dissatisfied with the comforting nursery taste. I drink one glass of wine, immediately, then two.

My stocking's torn—when did that happen?—at the ankle. My skirt is irreparably rumpled. And now I tell Jack, "I've spilled wet cookie on my sweater."

Jack's eyes deepen into their sockets. He takes his Scotch like cough medicine. Shudders.

Two young men huddle over the table behind us, and at the table in front of us three blondes ogle them. Near the snack bar four black women wearing bright sweatsuits flirt with the waiters.

The guy in the Detroit sweatshirt strolls past, a butt-pumping jailhouse walk. I'm convinced he's an ex-con. Carries two Buds to a table across from us, sits with legs spread, back straight, leather gloves tucked in loops on his army field jacket. Slips out of the coat, loosens the sweatshirt from his jeans and wide, studded black belt, slowly strips off the shirt one arm at a time. Down to olive-drab undershirt. Arms bare. Lifts one arm, shows trimmed black underarm hair, flexes muscles, flexes forearms, pops tattoos running down both his arms to the tops of his hands. Nobody isn't watching. He lights a Camel straight and grins and exhales.

Ten p.m. More Scotch. More wine. Detroit sweatshirt-stripper, two more Buds. He leans over his table, ears plugged with earphones jacked into a Sony radio. I ask Jack if we can talk to him and Jack says, "Why not?" and we pick up Jack's Scotch, my wine, cigarettes, stand at the guy's table. He pulls out phones. We ask, "Mind if we sit?" and he stands, says, "Welcome," says his name's Pete, asks ours.

Pete and Jack shake hands. "You her old man, Jack?"

"Yup."

Pete tells us he's forty-two, been living in Detroit, grew up in Connecticut, his father was a cement worker and he was also. He went to Vietnam as a Marine—"landed in DaNang in January 1965, left in February 1966. Now"—Pete frowns—"I'm a drunk."

The tattoos look like sheaves of grain. "That's what they are," says Pete, spreading his arms onto the table. "Mussolini's symbol. Mussolini said, 'A bundle is stronger than a single branch.' The sheaf on one arm looks so different from the sheaf on the other because two different tattoo artists did them. First in 'Nam, second in Philly."

He reads Nietzsche, Schopenhauer, Hegel, listens to Wagner. Nazism was influenced by Hegel's dialectic, so he's tried to read Hegel's *Phenomenology of Mind.* "Tried once to go to college, went to Wayne State for a few months, but intellectuals are almost all Jews, and Jews are patronizing, they live far from the real world, they look down upon the proletariat, on guys like me, cement workers' sons. They rub our noses in the fact we're workingmen."

He's headed back to New Orleans. Going to a Number Six Motel to dry out for two days before he goes to his friend EZ's house. "EZ is a fag. Fag hairdresser. Lives with his mother, EZ does. We have a relationship, EZ and I, but not what you'd think. I'm no hairdresser, no ass-licking interior decorator, no fucking florist, no nurse, no nurse's aide. No baby, I ain't."

Beer on Pete's breath and a stronger smell, welding-torch acetylene, reaches me. Pete searches my eyes, asserts his glance into my half-drunk gaze. Flag-salute reverence in his voice, he declaims: "You goin' to read about me in the newspapers one morning, I'm gonna be that loner white guy what's had all he can take. It's gonna happen. I'm gonna happen. I'm gonna walk into one of those French Quarter fag bars, I'm gonna kill me some queers."

The train smashes through Illinois over deepening snow, wheels clacking under us. The white-haired conductor and his assistant chew sandwiches, the black girls sing in three-part harmony "Georgia on My Mind." The wine comes home. I begin to like Pete.

"Goin' to New Orleans, huh? You gonna love New Orleans. I go to some great right-wing meetings in New Orleans. David Duke, the guy the news media's sayin' is a Klansman, he's my man—debonair, de, de, de, de-bo-fuckin'-nair my man Duke is.

Do you think Duke's crazy? I think he's great. Says he isn't a Kluxer, isn't Nazi, but I know that what he is is a fascist." Pete puts back his head, mouth open wide, and crazy freakish baboon laughter pours out.

Pete expects a gargantuan economic depression. "I bought survival food." He pins Jack with his eyes. "You know survival food?" Jack nods assent. Pete has on board with him, in checked baggage, 934 pounds of survival food, a survival food cookbook, and a bazooka—no ordnance.

Eleven p.m. People return to cars, leaving all but our table—Pete's Camel smoldering in a filthy ashtray—empty. I drink which glass of wine? and my seatmate, Wayne, pushes through the door, pulls a chair to our table, sits. His shirtfront and armpits are sweat-dark. "Fuckin' hot in there, man, fuckin' hot."

Pete tells Wayne about survival food, the bazooka. Wayne rubs his brow with an Amtrak napkin. Pete says that one night in Detroit when he'd smoked too much crack—"You guys know crack?" he asks, and we nod obediently—he had to go to an emergency room for intubation. "Was, you get it, choking to death. Had an AK-47 with me. Wrapped in a towel and stuck in a paper shopping bag. In the hospital they took the shopping bag, never even looked in it, I know, because in the morning when I got ready to leave, they give me back the sack. So I left the hospital, got back out on the street, ran into these three Negroes who said they were wanting to smoke some with me but really wanted to rob me, I knew it, and so I unwrapped the ol' AK-47, and put it to their Negro noses."

"Bet they stood back," says Wayne.

"You bet they did, Wayne." Pete pulls himself to his feet. "Wayne baby, you goin' to read about me in the papers. I'm that loner white guy who's had all he going to take. I tell you, Wayne, I'm happenin'. I'm gonna walk into one of those French Corner fag bars." Pete goes into a crouch that tightens his jeans at legs and crotch. He mimes shooting all of us. "Rat-a-tat-a-tat." Jack strokes his forehead. Wayne grins big. Pete retakes his seat, tells again he's got 934 pounds of survival food and cookbook and bazooka. "But no ordnance, want to keep it legal, Wayne."

Wayne says, "Shee-it, if we had ordnance, Pete, we could blow a hole right through the goddamn car, get cool air in here."

After chitchat about the heat, about where we're headed, more talk about survival food, cookbook, Pete yells, "I fuckin' hate cats."

Jack moans, whispers, "I was a kid, we used to shoot cats."

Pete touches Jack's arm. ".22s?"

"Shotguns. Didn't have to stop the car that way. Sometimes we didn't even use a gun. Just clubbed them to death."

Pete leans forward. "Clubbed 'em. You're my man."

"Shotgun"—Jack's spittle flies—"just blows a cat apart."

To get back to our seats, we all stumble through four unlit, pitching, clattering coaches from whose high-backed seats asleep white and brown faces glow and gleam. Open mouths, flared nostrils, heaving chests, pour out snoring, watery gurgles, coughing, groans, and sighing. Cars heave, our hips and arms hit elbows and shoulders and legs that slump toward the aisle; these limbs do not recoil when we bump them. Between the cars, snowy Illinois below-zero air stabs my chest. My fingers on my bare throat are numb.

Wayne rests his cheek against the window, eyes closed. His seat is let back as far as it will go and his unshod feet are on the footrest. I lean over to adjust my footrest similarly, and when I'm not immediately successful, Wayne reaches across my lap for the lever and brings down the rest. "So fuckin' hot in here," he says. And I agree.

Drunk. Hot. I peer out across Wayne's plaid belly as we pass a two-story house on a hill, its peaked roof snow-covered. One upstairs window is lighted and behind curtains a figure moves. The train rumbles under me. My head thrown back on the high seat, I slide deep into stuporous sleep and dream myself turning in a rustle of cool sheets, window open by me. Wayne's hand is on my stockinged knee, he is with two fingers tracing a small circle above my kneecap.

I pull myself up, pull down my skirt, whisper, "Knock it off."

"You know you want it," says Wayne. "You know," and grabs my face in his hands, against my closed mouth, presses wet lips, pushes huge teeth.

I don't know what I want.

I head to the women's bathroom. I do not have the heart to waken Jack, and why should I, who have for so long now lived alone, managed on my own (Why did he not come for me?). What could he, would he, do? And what does it matter, this Wayne? In the bathroom I read my watch: 3 a.m. Neither of the metal sinks will drain. Someone vomited in one. The toilet compartment door swings back and forth with the train's swaying, and hits—*bang, bang, bang*—against the wall. The toilet hours ago ceased to flush. Urine puddles flow back and forth across the floor. Unwrapped, used sanitary napkins and disposable diapers are stuffed into the wastebasket. I look in the mirror. My lower lip is bleeding.

Bivouacked against the wall on a built-in orange vinyl-covered bench, I smoke cigarettes and from time to time get up, turn on the spigot in the cleaner of the two sinks, fill my palm with water, and sip. The car rocks under me, sways. Maybe I doze. I don't know.

When first light gilds the dark car's dark interior, women visit the stinking bathroom. No one doesn't mutter disgust, or kick aside toilet-paper wads stuck into the enlarging urine pool. Bloody napkins, feces pile up in the stopped toilet. Three black women, on their way home to Louisiana from Chicago, stand before the mirror and with bright-colored plastic picks comb out tight curls. No one pays me any mind, and I am happy among bosoms and hips and soft susurrant Southern voices talking about how they slept (poorly, because of the heat). They pass around skin cream; rose scent for a moment overcomes the stench. A young white woman, blond high-blown hair caught in a gold-tone butterfly barrette, edges into a space before the mirror, and the black women cease their talk, fade back from the smeared glass.

Between rattling cars, I peer in the window to our coach. Jack's still asleep, Wayne's asleep. Legs weak, arms weak, and hands trembling, I head for the club car through three more coaches in whose seats sleeping faces, features racked askew as in Cubist paintings, prop against pillows and windows. I sit at the same table we sat at last night. Pete's butts and ours still overflow the ashtray. The sky eastward is striped blood red and burgundies and deep orchid, and the west is gray. I'm hungover. Stone Age pterodactyls stroll through dank ferns. A peroxided-blond mother opens her blouse and nurses her baby. With her free hand the mother points at her second child, a boy perhaps three, with a plastic gun. She says to him, "I'm goin' to blow yew away! Whaddya make a that?"

Overnight, we traveled 600 miles south. Frost tops grasses, cat-tails, but in deeper spots where moisture gathers, green grows. Near Memphis we slow, pass through a suburb in which trimmed emerald lawns slope from colonnaded one- and two-story brick houses. Sun lusters grass, deepens green, stiff breeze shifts grass blades forward. From a shuttered white house a woman of my age, pink chenille bathrobe flying behind her, blond cocker spaniel leaping at her side, leans over and picks up a rolled newspaper, smiles.

I think back to three days ago, Oakland's green hills, wrecked depot. Almost nothing turns out as you think it will.

Wayne, hair wet-combed up off his hambone forehead, enters

the car, sees me see him, stops, looks at me. His tongue comes out and he licks his thick pink lips and hikes up his Sansabelts and walks past me to the head of the car. I won't be routed out by him and stay, buy coffee when the snack bar opens at six. Out the window Tennessee goes by, scrubby pines and tar-paper shacks and turned-over fields that await cropping, and then among more pines, I spot two whitetail does, frames far more delicate than the mule deer our train spooked high up in the Utah mountains. Motionless, demure, they stare at the train. I know I won't tell Jack how I spent the night and don't know why I won't, and I am not sure our being together will ever be all right, even if we could go back to a time before that morning I left, and start again, because I cannot put my finger on what was wrong—with me, with him, more with me than with him—and it would, I am trembling, only go wrong a second time. Which does not mean that it isn't in its own way "love, baby."

Eight-thirty a.m. We're into Mississippi before Jack awakens. Holding hands, we huddle in my seat, which even with Wayne making camp in the club car exudes Wayne's ham-hock reek. We press thighs and knees, and clutching, our hands sweat. Jack has not shaved, and vague occluded pre-noon light strikes the reddish hairs on his cheeks and chin. "I'd kiss you, babe," he says, "but I haven't brushed my teeth." I lean over to comfort him; my head swims.

The train dawdles through planted forests of mixed deciduous trees. We go back over hangovers from the past. Worst we recall is a fifth of July. We watched wrestlers on our black-and-white set, pale lucent bodies ceaselessly slipping in and out of one another's grasp while bluebottle flies buzzed, settling around us on the night-before's party.

Ten minutes later we pull into Batesville, on whose town-square prewar storefronts I read: *Ebony Skin Care, Dress For Less, Elsie's*

Flowers and Gifts. Fashion Gallery, McAdams' Seeds, Feeds and Groceries, Stubbs' Grocery, Clyde's Fish and Bait. Fifteen minutes more, we're in Duck Hill, then Winonia Hill.

We stop at Hammond, Louisiana. A tumble of passengers falls into the arms of parents, grandparents. Blonde who nursed her baby and pointed the plastic gun at her son in the club car early this morning, hobbles stiffly toward a woman who must be her sister. The sister takes the baby in her arms, opens the blanket, and looks at its tiny face, and over the sister's mouth a smile spreads slowly.

Five miles from New Orleans. Slumped over at the back of our car, Pete is sleeping. We are glad. Our talk with him the evening before is one of those non-gravity-respecting antics you performed back when you took drugs, which you can't believe the next day you actually did, or, Jack suggests, like those moments when adrenaline suddenly gifts you with unnatural strength so that you lift a car off a child stuck under it when before and after you could scarcely pick up a bag of groceries. "You know what I mean?"

I nod, but I'm not sure I do know. I want a bath, sleep, a hot meal, in that order. We admit, all we care about is getting off the train.

APPLEBUTTER

❦

COOKING IS ABOUT MORE THAN FOOD (AND SO IS EATING!). AN
unopened pint jar of applebutter (actually, pear-and-apple butter)
sits on my desk. The taste of the applebutter—honeyish in color,
not much darker than applesauce, a simple mix of four cups of
fruit, two teaspoons of cinnamon, a teaspoon of cloves, a few
dashes of nutmeg, one-fourth cup white sugar and one-fourth cup
brown, vinegar, and lemon juice—comes to my mouth as readily
as the words to any song I like. Next to the pint jar I have a
snapshot of myself at twenty. I don't remember, now, who took
the picture. Whoever, he or she stood behind me. In the photo I
am walking under shade trees on a buckled sidewalk. Grass sticks
up between cracks in the concrete. I am holding my two daughters' hands. The older—Rebecca—is three; the younger—Sarah
—not quite two. She has just learned to walk, is not yet
toilet-trained, and her rubber pants, diaper under them, bulge in
corduroy slacks. All three of us wear striped T-shirts, and we look
to me, now, like Christopher Robin, Pooh, and Piglet setting off
on a Honey Hunt. "Sing ho! for a Bear!"

The picture was taken during the year John Kennedy was

elected President. I wasn't old enough to vote, and had I been, I'm not sure how I would have gotten to the polls. Jack, the children's father, was in graduate school. We had a black 1947 Buick coupe he drove to school and work, a "hard-starting" and unpredictable car, more a wild angry animal than an assembly-line product. I never drove it. Transportation was an old stroller, its metal frame bitten by rust. I don't have photos of Sarah in the stroller. But I still see her, in my mind's eye, wedged among shopping bags, a big lopsided grin on her face.

Every penny counted. Some mornings we emptied the girls' piggy banks for gas money so Papa could get to school and to his job as a school-bus driver. The house we lived in when this photo was taken had belonged to a railroad worker and his wife. On the day he retired, they hitched a travel trailer to their pickup. By that night, both were dead, killed by a drunk in a head-on crash. Their son, stammering through tears, said he liked our looks and rented us the house for sixty-five dollars a month provided we'd keep up the yard.

Apple, plum, and pear trees ran along the property's south line. Half the huge back yard had been a garden the year before, and next to the garden, behind a tangle of blackberry vines, stood a toolshed in which I found two dozen boxes of dusty empty canning jars. The day I married, I had never cleaned a toilet or ironed a shirt. I could brew coffee in a percolator and toss salad. I could play the piano not very well, read French, set my hair in big rollers, trace the career of Billie Holiday, recite whole hunks of T. S. Eliot's *Four Quartets*, feel guilty, and make babies. So I took on the garden.

Determined to put by food to get us through winter and gifted with prodigious energy, I turned over soil, studied seed catalogues, planted, weeded. I hauled all the "fruit" jars out of the toolshed into the kitchen. Rebecca and I pushed Sarah in her stroller to yard sales and pushed her back home, surrounded by clattering jars I bought for a nickel apiece. I checked out cookbooks from the library, figured what I could do with the bounty of eight fruit trees. When August came, I borrowed a ladder, and with Rebecca and Sarah under the tree, shouting, "Don't fall, Ma, don't fall!" I picked plums, pears, apples. I canned fruit plain, and applesauce, preserves, conserves, chutneys, fruit butters. By evening Rebecca's bangs would be matted with pear chutney, and Sarah, like as not, would have a smudge of plum preserves dried on her upper arm.

Impatient and not very knowledgeable, I had terrific failures. As recipes directed, I cooked fruit butters on top of the stove. I stirred "constantly," per instruction. Still, several batches tasted scorched. By the time Rebecca was four, a year after the photo on my desk was taken, she accurately could weed out "intruders" from rows of seedling radishes, and both she and Sarah, by then three, gathered apples, plums, and pears—windfalls—that dropped into the grass under the trees. Out of those windfalls we made fruit butters.

The second August I learned from the elderly widow next door, whose husband's ladder I'd borrowed, that fruit butters could be "baked" in the oven without risk of scorching. Not only that, she said, if I used pears, half and half, with apples, my applebutter would have "a nice little grit to it." I did as she said: cored, chopped, cooked the fruit until soft, plopped it into my wedding gift Waring blender, added sugar and spices, whirred a moment, then poured the mixture into baking pans, and baked it over low heat until thick. No more scorched butter, and for a month the little house, and our clothes and hair, were perfumed with the sweet-and-sour tang of cinnamon, nutmeg, vinegar, sugar, fruit.

In late afternoon, in winter, with rain more often than not falling outside, we would make toast, heap it with applebutter (even when we used pears, we called it applebutter, one word), and sit at a table their father had made out of a door, eat toast (from bread I had learned to make), and drink cocoa.

This was Eden before the other shoe dropped. This is a mixed metaphor, but it's how it was. As years passed, we no longer needed what I "put by" to get through winters. We had plenty of money. But I continued to grow gardens, and in late summer and fall, at fruit stands outside orchards near Yakima, Washington, I bought apples and pears, apricots and peaches and plums, from fruit stands, and brought them home to can.

Convinced that Rebecca and Sarah needed to know something more practical than what I knew when I married, I insisted they help. During their junior-high years, they began to resent peeling and paring. But we'd still sit sometimes, the three of us, eat toast and applebutter, drink cocoa, giggle, talk, toss toast crusts to the bulldog, and wipe chocolate mustaches off each other's face. By high school, all hell broke loose in the kitchen. Made to wash, stem, seed, and quarter fruit, they rebelled: "I don't know why you can't just be satisfied with a goddamn jar of Sunny Jim."

Then, after Jack and I attended our second high-school commencement, the other shoe dropped. I left. Moved to California. Got a job. Felt fiercely jealous of women ten and twenty years younger than myself (women my daughters' age) who, unlike me, knew their way around the "big world." Realized I'd lost twenty years, wanted those years back, recognized that to "make something out of myself" was going to be a struggle. Got older. Looked at myself in mirrors, listened to myself, going off to sleep wondering, Was it worth it? Twenty years? Did it really make any difference to Sarah, to Rebecca? those twenty years? If I asked them, I knew—because they are polite and kind—their answer would be polite and kind. We saw one another at Thanksgiving, Christmas, a week in summer. They wrote, telephoned, mailed off perfume and blouses on Mother's Day and Valentine's and my birthday. I knew they loved me, and wasn't sure they should. That wasn't what troubled me. It was those twenty years.

This fall Rebecca flew to California for a long weekend. We hugged, kissed, at the airport gate. Around us, others hugged, kissed, and people hurried past us. I grabbed Rebecca's hand to lead her out. "Wait, wait," she said, "and close your eyes." " 'Beca," I protested.

"No," she said, taking her day pack from me, "close your eyes, Ma, and hold out your hands." I did as she said. Held out my hands. "Now, grab ahold," she said. And I did. "Now open your eyes." I was holding a pint jar of applebutter. "Are you proud of me?" she asked. "When we get to your house, we'll make toast."

MOTHER ON A SPOON

❦

FEELING LOW, I YEARNED AFTER ONE OF THOSE SOFT PUDDLY
custards or cool puddings I was fed as a child. I huddled under
my pale blue electric blanket, dial switched to a balmy maternal
4, and asked myself about the solace these humble, almost austere
dishes offer.

I thought how, as in my case (weak in the legs, woozy, and
easily weary), this even temporary loss of well-being drew me back
to earlier losses. That initial loss, for most of us, was the moment
when our mothers first left us with a baby-sitter or turned us from
breast to bottle or in some way frustrated one of what had become
our routine expectations.

Our entire world, back then, was Mother, our climate the
weather of her warm odors. Her milky breast withdrawn or her
actual solid presence gone out the door, our world dissolved.
Pudgy hands reached up and found no one. Wails, as far as we
knew, went unheard. Some of us sought comfort in a pacifier,
wildly suckling its rubbery teat. Others clutched the teddy bear or
anxiously twisted a worn, stained security blanket. These objects
reminded us of Mother; they substituted, momentarily, for her.

Of course we don't consciously remember any of this. We don't remember that first time when Mother did not unbutton her blouse to give us dinner. We don't remember that evening when Mother—lipsticked, smelling of Patou's Joy and wearing watered silk that rustled—hurried out the door and left us sobbing. But just as an old war wound acts up in damp weather, so when new losses occur, old losses reverberate through the psyche, echoing pain.

With this in mind, it made sense to me, ailing as I was, that I longed for one of those simple, pure dishes we call "comfort" or "nursery" food. What better stand-in for mother love (even if our mother never fixed us anything better than a fried bologna sandwich, with the bologna charred, because she was forgetful and impatient) than these mothering foods.

Specifically, I wanted rice pudding. I felt too ill, too shaky even to gather the ingredients, much less follow a recipe through to its end. So I got myself (weak-kneed and dizzy) to the supermarket. I rustled about in the dairy section, on shelves from which hung six-pack containers of vanilla and chocolate and tapioca puddings and red Jell-O. I found on a bottom shelf two 14-ounce cartons of Alex brand Rice & Raisin Pudding.

I got my pudding home, grabbed a spoon, returned to my spot under the warm blue cover, popped open the plastic lid, and dipped in. I'm not that picky, but Alex's rice pudding bears only a faint resemblance to homemade. Alex scrimps on rice, and if I'd gotten to the bottom of the gelatinous goo, where most the raisins had sunk, I couldn't have counted out more than a few dozen nasty sourish little things.

No sooner did I feel well again than a friend visiting for a week took sick. After twenty-four hours of tottering from guest room to bathroom, Ted was ghastly pale and fit to do no more than switch channels back and forth between Sally Jessy Raphael and Geraldo.

So I gathered the ingredients for rice pudding. The essentials are simple: rice, jumbo eggs, whole milk or half-and-half, sugar, butter (not margarine), golden raisins, vanilla.

Cookbooks offering rice-pudding recipes variously suggest long-grain, medium-grain, or short-grain rice, white rice or brown. Long-grain rice is fluffier and drier than the short chubby grain, which tends to get gummy. Medium-grain rice (about as thick as it is long), after cooking, retains a fairly distinct grain and also turns somewhat sticky, with individual grains that tend to be soft outside and firm at the core. I've made pudding with all three. Because one aspect of rice pudding of which I'm particularly fond is a bit of "bite" in the rice, a texture that contrasts well with the pudding's creamy consistency, I prefer the longer grain. Plus, this drier rice seems better at soaking up flavor. I've also used the slightly aromatic basmati rice, whose long, needle-like grains "cook up" dry, each grain remaining perfectly separate and distinct.

Brown rice is white rice with the bran left on; it is rice that has undergone less milling and polishing than white. (I find many people think bran is a grain all its own, like wheat or barley or oats. It isn't. Bran is the outer layer of any cereal grain.) Brown rice offers more fiber, has a chewier texture, and takes almost twice as long to cook as white. If your mom was a hippie (and your memory of her scent is patchouli) and cooked from Adelle Davis's *Let's Cook It Right*, she may well have made your rice pudding with brown rice and added chopped dates and coconut to the mixture and then baked it. She would have served it to you cut into squares so solid you could have used them as building blocks. The hippie and health-nut moms of my acquaintance were milky, splendid earth mothers, loving and lots of fun with their kids; their food was good for you, but bad flavor and texture were often the price of good nutrition.

White rice is what's left after milling and polishing: the starchy white endosperm, the plant version of a mammal's placental tissue. Most white rice, like white flour, is buttressed with vitamins and minerals to make up for the nutrients left behind in milling.

There are two basic ways of cooking rice pudding: on top of the stove in a double boiler or baking it in the oven. I'm not a fan of the latter method, which is usually served cut, like sheet cake, into squares. It's too dry, and many recipes turn out what looks and tastes like a gummy rice cake.

Making rice pudding gives you an excuse to buy a double boiler, a cooking utensil that comes in three parts: a lid and two saucepans, one small and one larger. You fill the larger, base pan with water and place it on a burner set to a medium flame. The second, smaller pan sits above and inside the bottom pot, surrounded by the water. When the water is brought to the simmering (not boiling) point, the steam rising off the water heats, at a constant temperature, the contents of the smaller top pan. So double boilers are helpful for any recipe that requires gentle and consistent heat. They do wonders when you want to warm up gravies, cream soups, and baby food, when you want to make the most delicate of scrambled eggs or melt chocolate or make sauces.

The nicest (and I suspect, priciest) double boilers are of tempered glass, such as Pyrex makes. A glass pan allows the cook to keep an eye on what's happening. With metal pans, there's always the worry that the water will start a dangerous rolling boil or boil down to nothing.

When I was learning to cook, much of what went on in pots and pans seemed an act of God. Why did cake rise or Jell-O jell or raw eggs thicken into scrambled eggs? I had no idea. Now I know that what causes rice pudding to thicken is the proteins in egg and, to a lesser degree, in milk. Both white and yolk are made up not just of protein in the singular but of proteins in the plural, and each type will coagulate at a different temperature in a zone ranging from slightly below 140 degrees F to slightly below 180 degrees F. A mixture like rice pudding, writes Howard Hillman in *Kitchen Science*, "reaches its full glory when it is heated to slightly below 180 degrees F, the temperature at which all the proteins have finally coagulated. Above 185 degrees F, some of the proteins lose their coagulating effectiveness and your pudding starts to 'weep,' either in the kitchen or eventually on the dessert plate. Prolonged cooking, even below 180 degrees F, does the same damage."

Ted lay ensconced full-length on the flowered chintz sofa, pillows supporting his head and a quilt my daughter had pieced sheltering his trembly limbs. He showed mild interest when I explained all this to him. "Semen," he said, pulling himself up a bit and scratching at his two-day beard, "is pretty much all protein." At the prep school from which he had graduated in the late 1960s, he said, boys in his house conducted an experiment designed to prove seminal fluid's high protein content. "They masturbated into pans of boiling water."

"My God," I said, covering my blush with both hands.

Ted and his sister, orphaned when their parents died in a car crash, were reared from babyhood by a prim grandmother, the widow of a Presbyterian missionary. I have seen the padded-leather albums of photos from early in the century in which Ted's grandfather, garbed in black except for the white ring of clerical collar, stands next to a thatched hut from whose door wide-eyed dark faces stare. Ted still seems amazed at what can be said in mixed company without God's striking him dead. My reddening was as much for his amazement as his words.

Ted pushed off the quilt and pulled his skinny self to a sitting position. "The semen, I was told, cooked up and looked like boiled egg whites. But the best thing I know about sperm is something my scientist sister, Lydia, told me, and that is that couples who have trouble conceiving are sometimes advised to use egg white as a lubricant during intercourse. The normal stuff people use can gum up the works by killing the sperm outright or keeping it from swimming to its"—Ted paused—"goal. Why egg white works better, says old Lydia, is that it's protein, and sperm has an easier time staying motile in fluid more like itself." With that Ted excused himself and went to take a shower.

I walked back into the kitchen, which by then was balmy with the sweet fragrance of cooking rice. The one-half cup of rice that an hour earlier I'd put into a quart of milk in the top of my double boiler had fluffed up to perhaps two cups of rice and the water in the bottom half of my double boiler was simmering. I lifted the lid. Steam rose. I added two tablespoons of unsalted butter and a half-cup of raisins to the rice-and-milk mixture. I broke into a mixing bowl two of the jumbo eggs and lightly whisked them— yolk and white—until they turned a pale lemony yellow. I added a half cup of sugar and whisked some more, but again, lightly, gently.

Then came, what's for me, the scary part: putting the egg-sugar mix together with the hot rice and milk. Why this always scares me is that if the rice and milk are too hot, over 150 degrees F, the eggs may curdle in the rice, leaving you with bits of scrambled egg in your still-liquid rice pudding. Or if you don't add the rice to the egg bit by bit, in small doses, you can also get this scrambled-egg effect. So I told myself to calm down and be very, very patient and began, gradually, to stir cooked rice into the egg mixture. Nothing bad happened. So I poured my big bowl full of rice and eggs back into the top of the double boiler. Stirring constantly, but again gently, with a big wooden spoon, I let the egg-rice fusion cook and thicken another five minutes or so.

While I stirred I thought about Ted, who was four when his mother died. How old Lydia was I don't know, maybe two years older than Ted. Neither has ever married. "I wouldn't want to," Ted said once, "and Lydia doesn't want to either. And even if we did want to, we both think it's too late. We're too set now in our own ways." Ted lives in an airy Manhattan apartment whose walls he papered forest green. A wedding photograph of his parents, smiling and soaking up each other's glance, sits on his parlor grand. He makes his living as an accompanist for singers. Lydia lives in Brooklyn. They see each other on weekends. Their parents were drunk when they died; Ted and Lydia never in their whole lives have drunk so much as even one beer. Their celebratory drink is Pepsi.

I took the top pan off the bottom pan and placed it on the countertop to cool. Some people like to add nutmeg or cinnamon to rice pudding. I don't. I don't like the egg and milk and rice, each tasting so strongly of itself, hidden under a blight of prickly spice. I want, at most, a muted, vanilla-scented background. I stirred in one teaspoon of vanilla and watched the dark brown extract disappear into the pudding. The egg yolks and vanilla turned the pudding the color fresh snow turns under an eleven-in-the-morning slant of sunshine.

Ted, after his shower, declared himself somewhat restored. But he felt rubbery, he said, in the legs. We wrapped him up again in the quilt and I brought him a bowl of the still-warm pudding. "Mmmm," he said, mouth full with his first taste, and then said nothing until his bowl was empty, when he said, "Thank you so much." Later that afternoon, apropos, apparently, of nothing, Ted said, "My mother would have turned seventy this year."

CRANBERRY BLOOD AND
A SAD MOTEL

Crabapples
ripen to rubies,
cranberries
to drops of blood.
ELIZABETH BISHOP

All the Indian huckleberry hills are stripped, all the
cranberry meadows are raked into the city.
THOREAU

IT WAS LATE OCTOBER, COLD, CLOUDY, WINDY, AND FOGGY
enough that we wouldn't see sun all day. Jack and I were in Pacific
County, the southernmost Washington State county that borders
the Pacific Ocean. We were driving along a bumpy blacktop two-
lane road, raggedly parallel to the ocean. We passed sand dunes
and heard waves boom and a foghorn. The ocean was sometimes
a quarter-mile away, sometimes no more than a block, but we
couldn't see it. Through the windshield we did see white gulls fly
toward us on big wide wings like the wings on angels in paintings.

We were glad we'd had the car heater fixed the day before in
a broken-down, almost abandoned mill town. We were glad, period. We'd escaped a fellow named Alvin and we were getting
along better.

An hour earlier, we'd eaten thick butter-soaked buckwheat pancakes, fried eggs, and sausage in a shack of a place so packed with
customers that you had to scream your order to the lone waitress.
We felt sorry for her; she was a broad-hipped woman serving ten
tables and a counter with half a dozen stools. The tables stood
close together and she had to turn sideways to squeeze between

them. Her customers were guys who kept up their stagged-off jeans with red galluses and called her by name. It was "Hey, Glenda, another cup of coffee!" and "Glenda, could we get some more syrup over here?"

After the place cleared out some, Glenda pushed her auburn-dyed hair up out of her pale pretty face and asked if we were just passing through. We said we were. She asked, "Where you from?" and when we said, "California," the men at the table next to us frowned and narrowed their eyes and looked us over.

One of the men, rolling a toothpick back and forth across his lips, picked up his check and put down his dollar tip. He hitched his jeans and said, "Not thinking of moving here, are you?"

We assured him we weren't, and he said that was good, because there was nothing here. Glenda laughed and told us not to pay ol' Alvin there any mind, he was "wore" out from working the cranberries.

"Cranberries?" we said, and Glenda said, "You bet! You're in cranberry country." She pulled in her stomach and pulled back her broad shoulders and smiled when she said "cranberry country." She went on to say that Ocean Spray had a big plant a few miles away and that picking would be finished in another week.

"Fuckin' A," Alvin said. "Another week."

Glenda said that right down the road there was a cranberry museum, but it wasn't open because the man who ran it was getting on in years and hadn't been feeling all that good. We said we were sorry about that but what we'd really like to see was cranberries growing. Glenda gave directions. She said we couldn't miss the bogs; that now, with the berries ripe, it looked like "running blood."

"Isn't nothin' to see," Alvin said, on his way out the café door.

As we left the warm café and walked across gravel to the car, the cold hit us, hard, in the sternum. The wind carried brine on it that settled on our faces in salty mist. Jack said it seemed to him, from our fellow eaters' pallor, that they never got much sun around here. He said he sure wouldn't want to piss off Alvin after Alvin had had a few beers.

Driving along, sausage smell perfuming our flannel shirts and our mouths shiny from sausage grease and egg yolk, we kept an eye out for Glenda's bloody field. A cranberry field, Glenda told us, started out pink in the spring, when the pink-and-white flowers bloomed, and then gradually, over summer, as berries came on, the field changed colors. Glenda said that they'd had cranberries around here in her grandfather's day, more than a hundred years ago. She said that when she was a kid—and she had to be fifty plus a few years—they picked berries by hand, using wooden scoops with long teeth; the teeth combed the berries off the vines into the scoops. She said the scoops were heavy and it took some doing to learn to comb out the berries. She said it was hard work, you bent over all day, and your hands got scratched. She did it for money for school clothes, and she used to think her back would break. In those days, they let the kids out of school to pick, but not anymore. "Everything," Glenda said, "has gone to machines."

When Glenda told us about picking cranberries, I was reminded of the painting I'd seen several times in the Timken Art Gallery in San Diego's Balboa Park: Eastman Johnson's *The Cranberry Harvest, Island of Nantucket.* Johnson painted a group of some forty cranberry harvesters in Nantucket in 1879. What you notice when you stand in front of Johnson's 54-inch-long painting and what you remember after you leave it is an autumnal light that gilds the pickers, as if someone had poured butter over them. The cranberry bog itself looks not at all like what I imagine when I hear the word "bog." When I think "bog," I think sinking into muck up around my ankles. In Johnson's painting the pickers variously kneel, sprawl, sit, and stand in a sedge-like growth that might be prickly enough to scratch your hands, and nobody's sinking. Nor does Johnson's field run bloody red, as Glenda suggested. Were it not for the painting's title, I would not have known what Johnson's Nantucketers were picking. Not until you look into several baskets set down in the painting's forefront do you see "red."

As we continued driving through the fog, what cued us to the cranberry field wasn't the color Glenda promised but rusty pickups fitted out with gun racks in the back windows. The trucks had pulled over onto the sandy shoulder next to a fenced field. We parked behind the trucks and got out. In the distance we saw men hauling sacks onto flatbed cars. Farther on, we saw men pushing what looked like an immense power lawn mower. At our feet, just beyond the fence, we saw a dense mat of vines off which grew narrow reddish-brown leaves and, above the leaves, at the ends of wiry stems, round blue-red cranberries. If you squinted a little, which I did, and looked straight ahead, the field itself might have been the field in Johnson's painting, minus, of course, that gorgeous buttery light.

More gulls flew over, their two-note squawks unnerving, and we stood there hugging each other in the cold wind blowing off the ocean. We were getting ready to go back to the car when a yellow Toyota pickup pulled in behind us. A tall, rangy fellow got out. He was maybe fifty-five and slightly bowlegged. He wore faded jeans and a jean jacket. His eyes were the color of his denims, and when I shook his hand, I felt calluses.

"She exaggerates a little," he said when I mentioned Glenda's promise of a blood-red field. He was from Ocean Spray, driving by to check fields for which his company had three-year contracts with the farmers. Ocean Spray, he said, had contracts on most of the cranberries in Washington State, about 1,500 acres of them.

While he stood with his back to the wind and tried to light his pipe, a corncob pipe like the one that Harry Truman's nemesis General MacArthur smoked, he told us that the cranberry is one of the only three fruits native to North America. The others are the blueberry and the Concord grape. A member of the heather family, the cranberry is a perennial, and some cranberry fields were still producing from vines planted over a hundred years ago. "In other words," he said, "we're harvesting vines older than any of us."

The cranberry, he told us, grew wild as far north as Canada's Maritime Provinces and as far south as the Virginia peat swamps and westward in the wetlands of Indiana, Michigan, Wisconsin, and Minnesota. He said the Indians on the East Coast used cranberries for all sorts of things, including food, but he didn't know what, I'd have to ask an Indian.

He asked if we knew how cranberries got their name. We didn't. The blossom, he said, reminded the Pilgrims of a crane's head and beak, so they called the berries "craneberries," but somewhere along in history the *e* got lost.

By then, the cold had gotten to us, and in the wind our cranberry expert couldn't keep his pipe lit, so we all sat together in our car. The cranberry expert settled into the back seat among heaps of *Seattle Post-Intelligencer*s and *Aberdeen World*s and a black crow with glassy yellow eyes that my husband had bought me in a taxidermist's shop in nearby Aberdeen.

Nobody, the cranberry man said, thought to try and plant cranberries until about 1810, because there were enough wild cranberries around to fill everybody's needs. But then a gentleman named Henry Hall, who lived near Cape Cod, figured he could farm cranberries and sell them to city folk. So he transplanted the vines, sod and all, into a field behind his house. They did so well that Hall soon had enough berries to ship to New York. Along in the 1830s, a fellow in New Jersey named "Peg-Leg John" transplanted vines into his fields, and pretty soon he, too, had enough berries to ship out to New York.

Our friend laughed, saying that the story was that Peg-Leg used his wooden leg to punch the holes in which he planted his vines. By the 1850s cranberry farming had begun to take hold in Massachusetts and New Jersey. While everybody else was heading out to California for the gold mines, our man said, people in Massachusetts and New Jersey caught what came to be called "cranberry fever." Everybody wanted to raise cranberries. "It seemed," he said, "like the perfect get-rich-quick scheme." He explained that cranberry fever was like that period during the 1930s when everybody decided they could become independent by raising chickens. A lot of these would-be cranberry farmers ended up, he said, like those chicken farmers did. "There was more to it than they thought, and they lost their shirts."

Did you ever hear the expression "Limeys"? he asked. We nodded, and I'm sure smiled, the way happy schoolchildren will when they know the answer to a teacher's question. "They were called 'Limey' because the English Navy gave sailors limes to keep them from getting scurvy, which you get when you don't have fresh fruits and vegetables to eat." But in America, he said, whaling ships took on barrels of cranberries, because cranberries have so much vitamin C and A that they keep you from getting scurvy and such a high acid content that packed in water they could last two years. He went on to explain that cranberries were also a big help to Union soldiers during the Civil War, to keep them from getting scurvy. (Later, talking to a well-read friend about cranberries, I learned that Melville mentions them in *Moby Dick*: "Go out with that crazy Captain Ahab? Never! He flat refused to take cranberries aboard. A man could get scurvy, or worse, whaling with the likes of 'im.")

So how did cranberries get to Washington? we asked.

"Not far from here a Frenchman planted about forty acres in vines that he'd hauled from New Jersey. He used Chinese labor that was already here with the railroad to plant them and then hired Indians to harvest. In 1912, Edward Benn started cultivating cranberries right around here. He's still got family in the area."

Cranberry farming, he said, "really took hold" out here. He thought, in part, that the fact that the cranberry farmers were mostly Scandinavian, Finns and Norwegians, the kind of people who knew what hard work meant, had something to do with it, along with the mild climate. There were now about 120 cranberry farmers in the Washington counties along the Pacific, and most of them pretty much supported themselves off cranberries.

What, we asked, was this business about bogs?

Cranberries, he explained, don't grow in actively wet bogs, but in *former* bogs that have either dried up or been drained. What a cranberry needs is acid soil, and if you have that, you can grow them. Why, he said, people tend to think of cranberries as growing in water is that we see photographs of East Coast berries being wet-harvested. The cranberry fields back East are built up so that they can be flooded in case there's frost and also for picking. The berries float up to the surface of the water and then mechanical beaters beat them off the vines, and eventually they're funneled into trucks. Ocean Spray uses wet-harvested berries to make sauce and juice.

"Here," he said, pointing out to the fields, "we dry-harvest. That machine you see the man pushing in the field strips the cranberries off the vines and knocks them into a hopper. And back in town there, workers sort them out and they're bagged to sell fresh in bags in your grocery stores."

I asked if there was any way a non-farmer could grow a tiny patch of cranberries in his yard. He'd heard of people doing that, he said, not as a food crop but as ground cover.

Before we left our cranberry expert that morning, he reached under the barbed-wire fence and picked a handful of the red berries and handed them to me. They were cool in my hand and plumper than the cranberries we buy at the supermarket, and each berry still had its minute wiry stem.

We said goodbye and drove farther along the oceanside blacktop. Back from the road, behind skinny alders bending under wind and evergreens not old enough to be even an efficiency-apartment Christmas tree, weathered houses stood raw in the fog. Woodsmoke rose out of chimneys; the wind took up the sulfurous yellow smoke and carried it inland through ragged scrub. We saw rusted house trailers, set up on concrete blocks, and garbage thrown underneath, and under one trailer an ugly dog. We wondered where Glenda lived, and figured back toward town. We wondered what it was like to live here, and figured lonely.

When we saw a FOR SALE stuck in sand in front of a motel, we pulled into the driveway and stopped. We got out. Nobody was around. Six cabins, each sharing a wall, leaned into each other. It was the kind of place that reminds you how much time has passed, and we stood there on the bald ground, as you'd stand in a great vaulted cathedral in Europe, and for a while, we didn't say a word. In the distance we could hear waves boom, and overhead we heard the squawking gulls.

The cabins were painted white and trimmed green. The paint had peeled off. Somebody, years ago, had tacked a metal number on each door. The numbers were long gone and we knew they'd been there only because we saw the 1's and 2's and 3's outlined in the flaking green paint. We pressed our faces against cabin 3's window and saw in the crack between the curtains a single iron bedstead, still made up under a spread printed with buffalo. We saw a picture on the wall, Gainsborough's sulky *Blue Boy*, and saw that what they'd done was to tack the Gainsborough print to the wall and then hammer strips of frame around it.

Out back behind the cabins next to a twenty-foot holly tree, wind making its leaves chatter and knocking off its red berries, was an apartment. "Probably," my husband said, "for the owner or manager." The door stood an inch or two open. We pushed it aside and shouldered in. We found ourselves standing in a small kitchen, next to a card table with a sugar bowl on it and two chairs that didn't match. The smell was rot and mildew. Brown grocery sacks stood in a corner, brown Olympia beer bottles, tin cans, and TV dinner cartons spilling out of them. "Somebody left here in a hurry," my husband said. He opened the refrigerator, which was dark inside, because the power had been cut off. He pointed out a package of turkey bologna with dried slices curling up under the plastic wrap and a head of lettuce dried down to the size of a big fist and slimy with rot.

The only other room was a bedroom, and beyond it a bathroom, dirty towel slung across the towel rack and a grimy bar of Lava at the edge of the sink. The faucet dripped. The single bed lay unmade; the sheets were filthy and the pillowcase stained brown where somebody's head had been. Empty hangers hung in the closet and, on a peg, a yellow baseball cap lettered *John Deere*.

Why we hadn't been getting along all that well is that although we were married, certain things had come between us. So we didn't live together. We hadn't for years. Yet we had never been entirely out of love. You can imagine the tensions.

We walked back and forth from kitchen to bedroom, and once we got over asking each other "What do you suppose happened here?" we began to say we could buy this place and fix it up. We'd quit our jobs and rent the cabins to tourists and dig a garden out back and maybe get a goat, for milk. Afternoons, we'd cross the road and climb down the dunes to the ocean and cast in the tide for dinner. We could dig clams in season. The children would visit on holidays. We didn't say "It wouldn't be like before," but I bet that for a moment we both thought it. We did laugh, and say, "And here we went and told Alvin we weren't moving here."

Pretty soon we got in the car, in which our cranberry friend's pipe tobacco had added its aroma to ours, and back on the road. I rolled the cranberries around in my hand and don't remember what was outside on the road, except for those screaming gulls and their wide angel wings. Eventually we passed a tavern and my husband said, "Are you hungry? I am." He made a U-turn in the empty road. Inside, a quartet of elderly men played cards at a back table in gloomy light. A woman who could have been Glenda's sister tended bar and made sandwiches on the grill. We sat at the bar and ate cheeseburgers with our elbows propped on the wood and drank beer and stared into the mirror. The glass wasn't clean and gave us back our faces blurred.

The other day, picking up a bag of cranberries at the supermarket, I thought about that deserted motel and what happened there, and why. I wondered if anybody ever bought it.

EATING PETER RABBIT

❦

PEOPLE WHO TRAVEL IN FRANCE AND ITALY, WHERE HARE AND
rabbit appear on family and restaurant menus, usually cheer a
rabbit dish. They tuck right into rabbit napped in a mustard sauce,
or rabbit sautéed with paprika and mushrooms, or rabbit stuffed
with wine-soaked prunes whose seed you replace with chopped
rabbit liver. Mafioso John Gotti, incarcerated now in our toughest
federal penitentiary, once regularly took dinner at a Manhattan
trattoria that accommodated his hunger for rabbit hunter-style in
an opulent tomato and black-olive sauce, served with bright yellow
polenta, or rabbit and mushroom casserole reeking of garlic. When
I see Gotti's name now in newspapers, I imagine him stretched
out on his back in his Colorado cell, reconstructing in his empty
mouth the taste of rabbit browned in olive oil, and then extending
that fantasy through the litany of possible sauces.

In Beatrix Potter's *The Tale of Peter Rabbit*, Peter Rabbit's
mother warns him, "Don't go into Mr. McGregor's garden: your
father had an accident there; he was put in a pie by Mrs. Mc-
Gregor." Anglophiles can be wooed with rabbit pie, composed
much as you would chicken pie, with potato, peas, diced carrots,

rich rabbit gravy, all enclosed within a sandy lard crust and served with Brussels sprouts, steamed only until fork tender, and a salad of apple, walnut, radicchio, and celery, dressed with sherry and lemon juice.

Southerners and Midwesterners, middle-aged or older, whose mothers and grandmothers fried or smothered or fricasseed rabbit, also applaud a rabbit dinner. For frying, rabbit is cut into six pieces—two front legs with rib sections, two pieces of loin or back, and the two hind legs. A small paper bag is filled with one-half to one cup flour, one teaspoon of salt, a pinch of black pepper. One piece at a time, the rabbit parts are put in the bag and floured. So easily does a cut-up rabbit reassemble itself in mind and admit of rabbit's familiar lineaments that one quickly wants to get the rabbit coated with flour and into the frying pan, which ideally will be a high-sided black iron skillet.

Exiles from the United States' culinary Old Country seem particularly gladdened when fried rabbit is offered as a centerpiece to mashed potatoes into which a fried rabbit's cream gravy can be pooled. Add to this nostalgic menu slightly bitter turnip and mustard greens or fresh green beans simmered all day with fatback and onion. Pass around a basket of corn muffins, Southern origin tweaked by cranberry and grated fresh ginger. Place on your sideboard, if you have one, a footed cake stand. On the cake stand set a lemon pound cake baked in a tube pan and drizzled while it cools with hot lemon syrup. No matter if you lack the sideboard or even the footed cake stand, as long as your cake sits in the background all through dinner, a Xanadu promising itself. The promise is what's important.

Americans, per capita, annually devour about 250 pounds of beef, pork, lamb, poultry, and fish. Of all that meaty poundage, Americans nibble an average of half an ounce of rabbit per man, woman, child. No dish I bring to the table causes such anxiety as rabbit. Taste isn't the problem. Domestic rabbit tastes not that different from the innocuous chicken breast. Nor is rabbit bad for you. The meat is lean and low in fat, cholesterol, and sodium; a four-ounce serving contains about 200 calories. The obstacle is mind, not mouth.

So many rabbit cultural artifacts clutter the American psyche that future anthropologists will consider us rabbit-obsessed. Rabbit fictions permeate childhood: Br'er Rabbit, Peter Rabbit and Benjamin Bunny, the Velveteen Rabbit, Hazel and Fiver and company in *Watership Down*, *Bambi*'s Thumper, *Rabbit Hill*'s Father Rabbit, *Alice in Wonderland*'s White Rabbit and March Hare. These fictional rabbits, turned to plush, comfort us in our cribs, soak up our nasty infant drool and insatiable infant grief. Add to these cartoon rabbits: Roger Rabbit, Crusader Rabbit, Ricochet Rabbit, Matt Groening's rabbits in *Life in Hell*, malicious Bugs Bunny with his annoying screech, "What's up, Doc?" The hand puppet Bunny Rabbit, who would do anything for a carrot, was a regular on Captain Kangaroo's morning television show. There is the song we sang as youngsters, "Here Comes Peter Cottontail, hopping down the bunny trail." The act in which the magician pulls a startled rabbit, often with fluttering chiffon scarves, out of his top hat is a standard, as is the cliché pendant from that act: pulling a rabbit out of a hat. For adults, Hugh Hefner's Playboy bunnies, breasts boosted agonizingly by push-up bras and bottoms punctuated by white bunny tails, dangerously sexualized the rabbit. John Updike's licentious Rabbit Angstrom, the rangy hero with the slight overbite who leched through four novels, from *Rabbit Run* through *Rabbit at Rest*, put a male twist on the sexualized rabbit. Conversations about sex use the rabbit. When we say, "She f——s like a rabbit," we mean she's an indiscriminate, lax slut. He who, however, "f——s like a rabbit" is a sexual marathoner, a fellow who never says die. Those who "breed like rabbits" tend to be people whose birthrate *we* believe needs lowering, which is anyone other than you and me.

But for Americans, what most likely deters a rabbit's transfiguration into dinner is cuteness. Cute is more difficult to lift from fork to mouth, to bite down on, to chew and swallow, than disgusting. We gag on cute. No animal whose telos is the dinner plate seems as cute as the rabbit. The pig, steer, chicken, even the waddling duck or ill-tempered but handsome goose can have the cute cooked out of them. The bunny rabbit, with its floppy ears, fuzzy tail, plumpish rump, twitching nose, Gene Tierney overbite, sensitive whiskers, and steadfast eyes is not so easily rendered into dinner.

Rabbit is not hare. Both rabbit and hare belong to the family *Leporidae*, order *Lagomorpha* (leaping animals), but to different genera. Rabbits are gregarious and dig burrows. Hares, except at breeding time, are generally solitary; rather than burrowing, they create shallow depressions for nests, usually among grasses. Rabbit young are born hairless, blind, and helpless; hare young are born furred, open-eyed, and minutes after birth are able to hop about. Adult rabbits are generally smaller than hares, their legs, feet, and ears shorter. Hares' coloring resembles their brownish surroundings. They tend to have very short upturned tails, a divided upper lip, and more powerful hind legs than rabbits, and are able to run faster and longer, which ability they need, since they can't, like rabbits, hide away in underground burrows. The domestication of hares has proved near impossible because, unlike the rabbit, the hare is reluctant to breed in captivity.

Popular nomenclature further confuses the rabbit-hare distinction. The snowshoe rabbit and jackrabbit are hares. The fashionable domestic breed known as the Belgian hare (the model for

Beatrix Potter's Peter and Benjamin) is a rabbit, not a hare. The cottontail, the most common wild rabbit in the United States, stands somewhere between rabbit and hare. It does not dig out burrows but rests and sleeps in slight depressions or the burrows of other animals. Like hares, cottontails tend to be loners, although when feeding or mating they will gather in groups. Cottontail young are fully furred within a week; their eyes open in six to nine days.

Rabbit, hare, and cottontail are herbivorous. They feed on vegetable matter, grain, grasses, roots, twigs, and strip bark from young trees. All are largely nocturnal. Unless startled, frightened, or injured, they are silent. They produce between four and eight litters a year, with three to nine young per litter. Although most die far earlier, all can live to their ninth or tenth year (the model for Peter Rabbit was nine when he died), and grow up to twenty pounds.

Rabbits and hares are indigenous everywhere but Australia, New Zealand, southern South America, and Antarctica. The rabbit and hare, aided by passionate fecundity, by adaptability, and by a gradual decrease in enemies other than man have proliferated across the world's temperate zones.

In Asia, the rabbit appears in myth and art, most often in stories, painting, sculpture, and ceremonial garb that make note of its fertility. Japanese wedding trousseaus, for instance, often feature rabbits, as do the small toggles of an elaborately carved ivory or wood called netsuke used to secure a purse suspended on a silk cord from the kimono sash. The Chinese 5,000-year-old lunar calendar, which assigns one of twelve animals to each year in the twelve-year animal zodiac, has as its fourth sign the Rabbit, a year characterized by elusiveness, cleverness, and fertility. People born in the Year of the Rabbit are considered ambitious, artistic, virtuous, and conservative, timid and easily led by stronger characters. In Chinese myth, the Moon Goddess, Heng O, or Ch'ang O, soars up to the moon after eating the "pill of immortality." On her voyage she is joined by a rabbit, which the Chinese and Japanese say can be seen on the moon's face.

Mayan and Aztec Indians linked the rabbit to the moon, fertility, and inebriation. Images of the rabbit were associated with Mexico's alcoholic drink pulque, made from the fermented juice of the maguey plant. The Aztecs fortified pulque with a root which, when ground, acted as an hallucinogen, and the visions that resulted, as well as the frenzied drunkenness, were associated with the rabbit and his procreative powers.

Rabbits and hares were widely present in the Old World. Egyptians, acknowledging the rabbit's breeding capacity, gave the animal an ideographic association with fertility. Rabbits are shown on Theban tombs, circa 1420 B.C. Rabbit and hare, lacking cloven hooves and the ability to chew their cud, were listed in Jewish food prohibitions.

Rabbit was a popular food in Greece and Rome. Romans captured and reared wild rabbits in *leporaria*, walled gardens that protected rabbits from predators. The Roman nobleman Apicius, who accumulated recipes some 468 of which have survived, recipes that make up what food historians deem the earliest extant cookbook, suggests a ground-meat patty flavored with pine nuts and myrtle berries. As to what kind of meat to use in the grind, Apicius writes: "The ground meat patties of peacock have first place if they are fried so they remain tender. Those of pheasant have second place, those of rabbit third, those of chicken fourth, and those of suckling pig fifth." Then he offers two recipes for hare—roasted hare with herb sauce and stuffed hare. Both accommodate hare and rabbit's lack of fat by wrapping the meat in pork. (Apicius's recipes can be found rewritten for the contemporary kitchen in *A Taste of Ancient Rome*, by Ilaria Gozzini Giacosa.) Both use the popular Roman condiment *garum*, a salty fermented fish sauce inherited from the Greeks and common throughout the Mediterranean by the time of the Roman Empire. (Some three hundred and fifty of Apicius's recipes require *garum*.) The Romans used the salty *garum* as regularly as Orientals use soy sauces or Americans use catsup and now salsa. *Garum* producers flourished in Pompeii, Libya, and southern Spain; the sauce was shipped throughout the Roman Empire in amphorae labeled with the manufacturer's name. Choicer brands of *garum* cost ten times as much as the finest wine.

Petronius (d. A.D. 66), a favorite at the court of the Emperor Nero and author of the *Satyricon*, offers a portrait of life in first-century Rome, and a reader can find rabbits there, too. "Trimalchio's Feast," a central section of the *Satyricon*, written after Petronius fell out of favor with Nero, parodies menus offered at the great Roman banquets. Four slaves carry in a tray and lift the cover: "Beneath it we saw fattened fowl and sow's wombs and a hare in the middle with wings attached to resemble Pegasus." As for Pliny the Elder (A.D. 23–79), in his 37-volume encyclopedia, *A Natural History*, he reported that Tarragona, in Spain, toppled as a consequence of rabbits' burrows dug beneath the houses of the city, and that many Tarragonans were buried in the ruins. This account, although considered vast exaggeration by later historians, indicates the prevalence of the rabbit as well as its pestiferous aspect.

In Western Europe, as early as 600 B.C., Celts believed that the rabbit spent so much time in its underground burrows because it was in secret communication with netherworld spirits and therefore privy to knowledge of the past and future denied to humans, living as they did aboveground. The rabbit's proliferative powers dazzled them, and wishing to acquire that power for themselves, they made a totem of the rabbit. While any part of the rabbit was believed to bring good fortune and fertility, the foot was the preferred body part. According to Charles Panati's *Ex-*

traordinary Origins of Everyday Things, how the rabbit, or more accurately hare, became associated with Easter can be traced to the origin of the word "Easter." He cites as his authority the Venerable Bede (A.D. 672–735), who suggested that Eastre, the goddess of spring, was worshipped by the second-century Anglo-Saxons through her earthly symbol, the hare. It is from the goddess Eastre that the words "estrogen" and "estrus" (sexual excitability, or being in heat) derive.

Accounts of hare hunting in Britain date from the Roman invasion. Introduced from Spain and Italy into France in the Middle Ages, the rabbit soon became acclimatized. On the Continent during the Middle Ages rabbits were domesticated in the monasteries, whose discipline forbade meat entirely or permitted it only rarely. The Church ruled that the flesh of newly born or not-yet-born rabbits was not meat, so the monks in such monasteries were permitted to eat rabbit fetuses. How these fetuses were prepared I do not know.

But Europeans considered wild rabbit's flavor far superior to domesticated; hare they found tastiest of all. (And beginning in the Middle Ages, hare's blood was one of the apothecary's most important ingredients.) Wild-rabbit meat offered a strong, gamy, rich "brown" taste; hare tasted even stronger. Hare and wild rabbit, foraging for food, of course exercised far more than did farmed rabbits and therefore had a darker, firmer meat than the caged rabbit's. Flavor differed from wild rabbit to wild rabbit and hare to hare, unlike the more uniform flavor of domestic rabbit. Particularly prized in France and Italy were wild rabbits who fed where thyme, rosemary, lavender, and other strongly fragrant herbs grew.

By the late 1700s, in the reign of Louis XVI, wild rabbits in France had become so destructive to crops that His soon-to-be-guillotined Majesty gave permission for anyone to hunt them. Louis XVIII was acclaimed as the canniest connoisseur of wild rabbits of his time. He could sniff aromas rising off a passing rabbit fricassee and declare, correctly, in which part of the country the animal had lived.

By then, most English estates kept domestic rabbits, and poulterers sold rabbit in towns and cities. Rabbit starred in stews and pies, was roasted with herbs and potted. Potting was a popular way of preserving foodstuffs. You baked the meat or fish in butter, drained it, and then sealed it under more butter, so that it could keep for up to a year. By the 1820s the two largest rabbit keepers in London had some 2,000 breeding does, from which they produced rabbits for home use. Mrs. Isabella Beeton, in her 1861 *The Book of Household Management*, urged householders to raise their own rabbits and proposed rabbit preparations with pungent marinades that returned to the domestic rabbit reminders of its wild cousin's fiercer flavor.

A preparation that appeared all across the Continent and in England was the civet, a thick game stew in which meat was marinated in a local wine, usually red, and herbs native to the region, and then cooked slowly until the meat fell from the bone. A civet could be made from any furred game—wild boar, venison, rabbit—but the most common meat was hare and, later, domestic rabbit. The civet takes its name from the French *civet*, small green onions similar to our chives, which have always been a prime civet ingredient, but what distinguishes the civet, however, is not the *civet* but that the sauce was thickened with the animal's blood and minced liver. Blood-thickened sauces were common in an era when slaughtering was done at home. (The traditional *coq au vin* uses the rooster's blood as thickener for its sauce.) Blood-thickened sauce is also used to prepare the traditional jugged hare, a hare baked or stewed in an earthenware jug. Now civets are most often prepared without blood.

When Dutch settlers to the New World in 1654 bought from

the Indians a piece of land along the Atlantic Ocean, they named
the land *Conye Eylant*, after the conies, or rabbits, that swarmed
through the area. But rabbit bones continue to be found in prehis-
toric American Indian sites, not only on Coney Island. Also, domesticated rabbit, like chicken, was brought to North America from
Europe as breeding stock, and German settlers who came to America in the 1700s and 1800s brought their celebration of the Easter
Bunny with them. Our ancestors, farmers and householders in
towns and cities, often kept a hutch of rabbits in back yards.

Yet by the twentieth century, rabbit was turned to only in bad
times. During the Great Depression wild rabbits were snared or
shot; the hutch reappeared in back yards. More recently, in *Roger
& Me*, Michael Moore's 1989 documentary about what happened
in Flint, Michigan, after the local General Motors plant closed,
Moore shows a woman named Rhonda supplementing her Social
Security check by raising and selling rabbits as "pets or meat."
Rhonda clubs and skins a rabbit. "First we were pets," says Moore
of G.M.'s laid-off workers, "then we were meat."

Jernigan, a recent novel by David Gates, depicted a contemporary rabbit rearer, Martha, with whom Jernigan, after his wife's
death, has moved in. In the basement of Martha's suburban New
Jersey home are rabbit hutches—"bunny hell," she uneasily calls
this arrangement. Jernigan notes: "I counted five cages, made of
two-by-fours and chicken wire. Each cage had three or four rabbits. White, black, piebald: bright, trusting eyes. Martha stuck two
fingers through the chicken wire and smoothed between the ears
of a chocolate-brown rabbit the size of a roasting chicken." He
gasps. Martha says, "It's actually more moral than going out and
buying chicken or something. Do you know how those chickens
live that you get at the store? You know how they die?"

Later, Jernigan kills a rabbit for dinner. "The gun went snap
and the rabbit gave a shiver and just turned to meat."

A BRIEF VACATION

&

I HAD TOLD MYSELF I WAS ONLY HANKERING AFTER A REAL SUM-
mer. But it was more than highs in the nineties, more than days
as slow as a low river, that had drawn me back.

Returning to Berkeley from the airport, the limo driver pointed
out the crowd walking up Telegraph Avenue. Derelicts were
slouched against the brick walls. Long-haired heads leaned on
graffiti and concert posters and indictments against the regime.
The driver said to me, "This used to be pretty live. I used to come
here. No more. Now they all jus' lookin' for their yesterdays."

So that was it! I hadn't known; then a limo driver told me. I'd
been gone two weeks from California, where I'd lived for two
years. I hadn't understood where I'd been. I hadn't known why I
went. I wish I'd talked to that limo driver before I left. I wish I'd
known.

We ignore the subject of returning. Nobody writes about how
to go back over old ground. Going back is a transgression; to return is taboo; prevailing wisdom focuses on the present. "Make a
fresh start. Forget the past." But there's always something or
someone "back there," niggling. There has to be. Anyone who

moves on has a reason to leave, even if that reason is nothing—
no work, no friends, no housing. You leave for a reason. Even if
something inside you sent you off, what it was still gnaws at you,
as a long-toothed rat gnaws at cheese parings. You can't go home
again. But you want to, and given the chance, you do. You may
still detest the local politics. You may hate the people, or a person,
or the climate. You may hate snow. You will have forgotten a lot.
But you don't get over the ground.

Before I pulled up in front of the two-story house I'd lived in,
stood on ladders by, and twice painted brown, I'd already driven
past the doctor's office where I learned I had a lump in my breast,
past the clinic where the lump was removed, past the gray shack
where I'd seen a porcupine throw quills into a yowling Irish setter,
past the streetlights where I'd watched a dozen season's snowfalls
sift down through the yellow light, where I'd watched ash from
Mount Saint Helens drift down, looking like snow but smelling
like sulfur. Sighting the doctor's sign, the Heavenly Blue morning
glories vining up the walls of the gray shack, returned the past.
Each memory came in an unbroken chunk.

Nobody tells you how to go back. When it first struck me out
of the blue California sky, the sudden, apparently spontaneous
inclination which felt like falling in love but wasn't, I told myself
it would pass. I said I was tired. I needed a vacation. I told myself
I was only looking for, hankering after, real summer of the old-
fashioned heatwave variety. But I was hungry for more than watermelon so ripe the first stab cracks it. I was about to become
another one of those derelicts, hair wild, dragging a bedroll, looking for yesterday.

It happened fast. "Celebrate me home," Kenny Loggins sang
one morning on KBLX. I couldn't believe what I'd heard. I bought
the cassette. I played, studied, then replayed that one song. Then
I bought the ticket, shaded my eyes from the brass-band glare of

the California sky, and scuttled gratefully into a DC-8. I had Loggins playing into my ears, and I felt happy.

What was I leaving as I flew north? Well, it won't seem like much to you. Two years before, I'd rented a room with two windows to the west and one to the south. For the first time in my life I was by myself. I liked it. I bought a cheap radio and turned it on. I tried all the stations. After the first year I bought bamboo shades. But it still wasn't much. Someone opened my door, looked in, and said, "This is a Bedouin's existence." It is. Hot plate. Cup-of-Soup. Change of clothes. But it had the virtue of being a life I could walk across without every square block emoting memories, a life whose store windows didn't show me back a three-act play starring myself.

Two hours after I left California, the Washington coast came up in the window: Seattle and the San Juans; Bainbridge and Vashon Islands. It was late afternoon. The rain had pulled back into the sky and off to the east; out of Elliott Bay, by God, a double rainbow arched up.

At the airport, meeters and greeters, wrapped in still-damp steaming rain slickers, grinned and waved and kissed. Soon I was driving past Seattle, heading into central Washington. I–5 loops through the Cascades, a range of picture-postcard mountains. The traffic was light. I rewound, replayed Loggins across Snoqualmie Pass. There, at 3,500 feet, I–5 begins to drop down the eastern Cascade foothills into Kittitas County. At the county line, an aw-shucks Western movie vista, you'd swear you've driven into Montana six hundred miles too soon.

Black basalt lies right under the tufted bunchgrass that grows through the gray ash blown out of Mount Saint Helens's first big one. The hard dense volcanic basalt stands vertical, ebony and dramatic and looming: a badlands.

I'd packed up and gone off. I'd left the pantry, there in that

brown house in the middle of black basalt and ash, stacked with
bread-and-butter pickles and peach preserves and applebutter
pressed from apples from the front-yard trees. I had not replanted
the dahlia tubers or separated the peonies or bent the stems of
white cosmos down for winter. I had not mulched. I had taken a
few suitcases, books, and walked away from twenty years.

I was five miles out of town on the rise. The seven o'clock
westering sun hit the brick facings on the four-block downtown
and the one-hundred-year-old university buildings. I slowed my
rented Toyota to a putter. What had been only a blurred memory
for me in California was now out there. This was the real thing.
My eyes ate it up. It burned going down, like whiskey. Driving
downhill, I peered farther out over the green valley, twenty-five
miles long and ten miles wide. I looked past the town water tower
thick with the numbers of years—1983, 1976—high-school classes
had painted on it, past the clock tower, past the old city hall to
Manashtash Ridge, a cordillera of hills forming the valley's south
and west walls. I felt home begin to melt in my mouth. I'd go up
there tomorrow. I'd take a six-pack. I'd stretch out. I'd play Kenny
Loggins. I'd walk under the Douglas fir and cottonwood and alder.
I'd walk under the shadows that dapple the ankle-deep carpeting,
and I'd sink into the mulching, moldering evergreen needles, the
damp leaves and dry lichens. I'd be careful not to slip on the soft
moss.

Even if I was quiet, I'd probably not see the elk and deer scuffle
down below the timberline. But I knew, from rare times having
seen them, that the dark-chocolate eyes look up and the thick
movie-star lashes blink when they hear the flapping overflights of
redtail hawks or the occasional vulture.

I could cool the beer in the creek where, after coming down
over a shallow riffle, the cold water makes a hard right turn and
runs against a basalt cliff, forming a narrow, deep slot. Then the

water fans out into a broad flat, twenty feet wide and a hundred feet long. I could watch as fifty cutthroat trout methodically nip insects out of the surface film during a late-afternoon mayfly hatch.

I could sit on the same rock where for the first time I'd had blood on my hands that wasn't from raw hamburger or a paring-knife cut. I had held the trout's slippery throat tightly, then knocked its head on a rock jutting out over the noisy creek. The eye looked up. I rapped the head on the shiny hump of granite, rapped it repeatedly, fiercely. The water plashed down over the glinting rocks, gurgled, made swallowing, gulping, choking sounds.

Another two miles east, I–5 follows the Yakima River downhill between West Manashtash Ridge and Horse Heaven Hills. I was closing in. The sun was inching down. Then through the two-lane aperture into the valley proper, past the Kiwanis sign, past THE EPISCOPAL CHURCH WELCOMES YOU, past the Pautzke Bait Company's billboard, I rounded the curve into a moment that was like opening a Hallmark card. Grief rose up to meet those three cottonwood trees, drooping after the long day's heat, leaning over at the turnoff to the tire-rutted county road.

I would not go around that corner. The rutted road led to a riverbank beach, to my husband's favorite takeout for rafts, to the gray fist-sized and smaller rocks I had portaged the children across, summer after summer, to sit in shallow water, sunsuits stripped off, where I splashed them carefully to cool them off (and where, I believe, had I sat and listened carefully, I could have heard, again, their delighted shrieks of "Oooh, Mama!"). The road led down to where I had unrolled Great-grandmother Moore's Star of Bethlehem patchwork quilt and angrily, almost defiantly, been "adulterous."

It's a small town this river runs through. I had paddled the river in my canoe through other July hot spells, through humming bugs and breeding insects, through murmurous rutting July heats. My paddles had slapped the green water smartly, and skittered the flies. I had carried brush for campfires along both banks. I had tossed cans of water to douse them. I had dumped a kayak and struggled, caught in the cottonwood roots growing down along the sides of the bank. The force of the river and the tangled roots had held me. I had almost drowned. My husband yelled, already down-river from me, "Don't lose the goddamn paddle."

It's a small town this noisy river runs through. Perhaps your town is large. Size and population don't matter: one spot waits for you where the centrifuge of memory will drag you down. Or you wouldn't want to be there.

Bring something to catch the drippings. The memories serve themselves up to you in the flesh, smelling fresh and still quivering. My husband's multicolored hair—red, blond, gray, white—wild on weekends, his small tough hands reeking of surgical soap . . . My little girls, tousled and tan and red-cheeked, who grew up to have magnificent bosoms and minds of their own . . . My lover's anguished face, his blue eyes filled with a past that wouldn't let up, his long cool hands, cool like trout, white at the knuckles when he gripped my arms. The bruises he left I would touch the day after, would examine with the awe of a child who's finally found proof. His long thin back, which he carried slightly off-center, taught me, finally, that when it came down to it, no one would save me. I would have to save myself. Saving myself, I left all of them, left behind my pickles and applebutters, left without mulching the cosmos or dividing the dahlia.

In my yesterday's small town, the spires and steeples cast long shadows. You shiver under them. After one of those patchwork-quilt afternoons, someone—who? will I ever know?—sent me a white sweatshirt with a ten-inch-high red A, an athletic letter meant for a bowling shirt.

I drove fanatically, as if my flesh were studded with iron filings attracted to true north. The wind rushed in through the car windows, blowing the sweet smells of new-mown timothy hay and alfalfa into the car. I drove straight into the aroma of dinners and the spray of lawn sprinklers circling above fresh-cut grass, and saw, replicated in the sprays' fans, more double rainbows. I drove into town at seven-thirty in the evening, not even six hours after leaving California. It hadn't been enough time. I was, by then, living downhill on roller skates, with neither a guide nor my guard up.

All at once there I was: back home. I walked by the forsythia, past the apple trees and the peonies. I opened the screen door. Hugo was running toward the sound of my feet on the cement.

I had two fears: that after two years my eleven-year-old dachshund would not remember me and that he would. He remembered me. He skittered on the rug inside the front door. He skidded. He moaned repeatedly, the sound a siren makes whining through city streets on its way to a crime. A long, sustained cry, like mourning, rose up through his long throat. Then he jumped. He bounced. His tail whirred.

I sat down, hard. I threw my purse on the floor, and my hands and arms went out to him. He licked my nose, cheeks, mouth. His breath, hot and sour, had not changed. Nor had the smell of salty buttered popcorn that his body gave off. He pushed his wet nose into my hair, my ear. I kissed him. I grasped his strong wriggling trunk. His muscles rippled and quivered under his rich red coat.

What I discovered then, sitting on the rug by the door, hugging a dog who repeatedly licked my nose, had not been part of my fear; I was empty of feeling for my dog. During two years of telling myself, "I miss my dog," the statement had ceased to be true.

I wanted to push him away. I forced myself to hold him, to smile, to say his name. I smoothed his already smooth coat. His tongue hung out, dripping saliva. His muzzle had grayed. His eyes were cloudy.

I stood up and straightened my skirt, brushing his red hair off the black cotton, feeling all-business and unemotional. Hugo danced around my ankles. He leaped to my knees and yapped. I could hear, in memory, the echo of my calling him, through the house, crying out, "Hugo, Hugo," waiting to be met, greeted, coming home from the store. Well, that's over, I told myself, brushing more fallen hair from my skirt.

I picked up the note my husband had left on the table: Be back at eight. Love.

I walked through the living room, through the dining room, into the long kitchen, indifferent to the objects that over two decades I had put on walls, floors, and shelves. Hugo jumped beside me, encircled me, and when he bumped into a chair that had stood in the same spot all his life there, I realized how blind he had become.

I said, "Oh shit," and kicked the same chair. I asked myself, sweating now and angry, Will all of being here feel this way? Will I not care any longer?

The first night in my old bed I lay gripping my favorite pillow, trying to go back to the unhappiness of the earlier years. I tried to reconstitute, whole, my wakefulness, my terror, my anguish. I tried to bring back the grand operas of emotion that had blown through me. I couldn't. I couldn't even remember the person I had been then. I could only recall what I had worn. Right down to which perfume.

Over the next week I visited old friends. I drove out on country roads. On hillsides I stopped the car and left the motor running and jumped out to look out over the valley. I took my canoe down to the river and slid it into the water and floated. I had my teeth cleaned. I sat on the rock where I had killed my first fish. And I did play Kenny Loggins. It sounded thin there, and didn't get me off. I ate apricots off the neighbor's tree. I played my old records. I rummaged through my old journals. I even cooked a meal.

I had expected the aging of my peers, what shocked me was the aging of our children's friends. The little redhead Moira, with whom Sarah, our younger, had been friends since junior high, walked past me on Main Street, carrying a year-old baby in a backpack. We talked. Her face had wrinkled. Her eyelids drooped. Her stomach, which I could recall flat and lovely in a purple bikini, now pouched out, her breasts drooped under her T-shirt.

A boy our older daughter had known since sixth grade—"Little Joey Bach," we called him then—was sitting at the Crossroads bar. He had delivered our morning paper until he was in the ninth grade. Now he wore a hat that read *Coop Feeds*, his neck had thickened, and his hands, once barely large enough to heft the paper onto the porch, went all around a chunky old-fashioned beer mug. At twelve his pale skin had been fine enough to show blue veins beneath his cheeks, his hair a blond thatch slicked down with water. Now he had a thick Buffalo Bill mustache, and the bristle of his light-red beard shadowed sun-toughened, work-hard cheeks. He talked with the bartender in a booming voice, kept saying "Shee-it" this and "Fug-ck" that, and when he turned on the bar stool and saw me in the booth with Don, he blushed as he nodded hello.

I like Don. I went to his house one morning. You can do that, because Don doesn't work summers. He mostly stays out on the river. "It's my god, the river," he says. He goes downriver at least once, every month of the year, even in winter. One summer *Sunset* magazine came to town, took his picture, and wrote him up.

Don is almost sixty now. We sat together in his kitchen, our feet up on the chairs. Outside, his son-in-law climbed up and down a ladder propped against the garage.

"Don is drinking too much," someone said to me. I searched his tan face for the briar patches of broken capillaries that come from too much alcohol. All I could see was the beam off his face, the big light. "But you look so wonderful," I said. He pointed to the back yard. His five-year-old grandson was playing tetherball. "It's that little fucker," he said.

When Don stood up to walk through the kitchen and open the back door, his glasses slipping down his nose and his blue eyes looking out over the top of the frames, he did what Hugo did. He bumped into a chair.

Arlene was my best friend. She sat against a redwood wall whose wide windows look out onto the willows, alder, and evergreens that fill up the gully. Outside, the temperature was in the nineties, but the air-conditioned house was cool, almost chilly. While we talked, perspiration stains grew under the arms of Arlene's lavender gauze smock. I always thought she was the prettiest woman in town: tall, honey blond, oval-faced and lightly freckled, with aqueous blue eyes under thick mobile bangs. At parties I would watch her, wishing I could dance as easily as she did, laugh as melodiously, lob tennis balls as fast and as far and as accurately, that I could buy the right blue for my eyes.

She told me everything she had done in the past year. The news was the same as in the mimeographed Christmas letter she had mailed me. "Well, I guess, huh, that your life in California's pretty wild. Isn't it?" she said.

When you go back, almost no one will want to know what you really do, what it's really like, where you've gone, where you left them to go. You left them. You broke it up. Remember too: they're afraid they're missing something. What's out there. They don't want to know what it is. Once you believe there's something or someone beyond Eden, you've already lost Eden. They don't want to have to go. So they will not ask.

When Arlene and I parted that first afternoon, she hugged me lightly, tenuously, held me at a distance, as if I were a sick person and she might catch the illness.

Remember, going back, you said something was missing. You said there has to be more.

Friends, even acquaintances, will tell you what they normally keep to themselves, for they know you'll go away again. Leah, in her early fifties, had been widowed ten years before. Last year she remarried. Over breakfast, almost as an aside, she said to me, "He hits me. And he's taken my money. All of it." Tears squeezed out and she bit her lip. "I don't know," she said, "what to do."

Roger, standing by the bank while rain began to fall, talked to me rapidly, as if I were a spy sent to town to carry his message to the outside world. "I want to leave my wife," he said. "I no longer love Alice. But I feel guilty. She hasn't done anything."

Three men I knew whose livelihood depended on crops told me they were worried about the corn. "It wasn't even ankle-high by the Fourth of July." But I knew they would not tell each other.

So it is with returning. In the two years, or ten, or the month you've been gone, you have changed. Falling over, bumping into, trying to find, wringing the last drop of grief from your yesterdays, you find how much and how little you have changed. You ask yourself, standing on old ground, who you are now. Circling back, you are asking the past to tell you. But none of them—not the people, not the place—ever will.

The last night I was in town Don took a dozen of us out on the river. We lit a fire on the narrow inlet where, in February, we once cooked mushrooms over a bonfire blazing on top of snow. We sang, we drank until we were unsteady. We talked. Before we doused the fire, we stood holding hands around the circle of rocks that held wood and flame, crackling in the chilly and swift off-river breeze.

We circled idly, swayed around the campfire. I had one hand around Don's waist, up under his jacket, and the other on Arlene's shoulder. Sparks flew up from the wet wood. The paper cups we'd tossed were burning, turning blue in the flame. I looked around. Flames lit the faces. Eyes met across the circle. I smiled into faces opened up by liquor and cool air and fire and long, complex, outspoken knowledge of one another and one another's company. For the first time no one was smiling back at me. Two years ago, three, Don would have winked. Someone would have invited me to lunch. Another would have told me, "I have a book for you." Not now. They were smiling at each other. They would be there, together, Monday morning, downtown, at a dance class, at the clinic, over at the school. Then on Monday night, they'd swim laps at the pool and then sit in the Jacuzzi and sweat and visit.

I wouldn't be there. I'd be driving back to Berkeley from the airport. The limo driver would point out the long-haired heads leaning on graffiti and concert posters. He would say, "They all jus' lookin' for their yesterdays."

SPRING HERO

❦

SOMEBODY I LOOK UP TO ONCE TOLD ME I SHOULD ALWAYS TRY to write as if writing to someone who had only six months to live. Think of your reader, I was told, as a person like yourself on her or his deathbed. Don't imagine a romantic death. Imagine the real thing. Death that devours, eats, and chews away at flesh. Death that hurts and smells bad.

"Somebody like you." My friend nudged me. "Somebody in pain," he said, "for pain does more than hurt flesh, pain cuts you off. Lead with your heart, not with your head." He laid his hand on my wrist. The light glimmered on the hairs on the back of his arm. We were in a crowded restaurant, but a hush seemed to have fallen across the tables. "Facts, how many missiles we have tucked away in Nevada or what makes the internal-combustion engine work, a reference librarian can tell you that." He took a sip of the dark resinous wine he had ordered, made a few smacking noises, took a deep breath. "You should always try to tell something true about yourself." I know that I flinched, that some muscle in my arm, on which his long fingers lay lightly, must have fluttered, and I guess I frowned, because he went on to pat my arm and say,

"Don't be embarrassed. And," he added, beginning to laugh so wildly he choked for a moment on the wine, "give hope."

This talk (it was a "talk," a speech, not conversation) came back to me when I was trying to write about how happy I'd been out in the patio under bright spring sunshine, dribbling white pebbles into six big new red-clay pots, filling them with gritty sand and soil, sowing three of them with okra seed, two with yellow crook-neck squash, and fitting two cauliflower plants into the sixth. I admired the buds emerging from the pots in which last fall I'd tucked hyacinth bulbs. I'd also repotted the bushy Christmas tree, three Christmases old and so badly rootbound that it has been unable to grow. Not only have I never gotten around to buying a star for its tip, but I don't know whether it's pine, spruce, balsam, or some other evergreen. I never can keep straight the names of trees with needles rather than leaves. "Christmas tree" will have to do.

I'd wanted to make the point that spring's return offers hope, and that working in a garden, however small, helps that hope along. I was having trouble.

That's because I had left out something. I'd left out the man who seems to have taken up residence on our block. He's maybe sixty, maybe as old as sixty-five, white-haired, blue-eyed, sturdy, and muscular. He always wears the same navy-blue slacks, a tan windbreaker. He carries a plastic garbage bag. On different days the bag's a different size, depending, I guess, on what he's gathered and been given. Unless you'd seen him, as my next-door neighbor and I had, rising early on several mornings from the matted vines along the side of my neighbor's house, leaning against the red bricks, hunching over to drink water from the hose, you'd not identify him as a person who lives on the street. He doesn't seem to drink; at least we never see him with one of those paper sacks wrapped tight around a bottle. I'm scared of him. He looks angry, like someone whose mood might change on you any second.

When I went out to the patio to begin work that morning, the old man had come out from behind the seven-foot-high board fence that separates my patio from the next-door house. His windbreaker and trousers were soaked from his drinking from the hose, and a thin veil of pinkish blood, oozing out a cut on his forehead and diluted by the hose water, fell over his face. I had walked quietly. I'm sure he'd not known I was there until he saw me. We stared. We did not speak. His eyes blazed. He rushed past me down the street. For a moment I felt sick to my stomach.

I had also left out my father.

I never wear gardening gloves, and out in the patio that morning the soil under my bare hands felt busy. When I was a child, my father, turning the plot for his Victory gardens, used to tell me that were I to put an ear tight against the ground and listen very hard, I would be able to hear, through static, all the way to China.

What would I hear?

"Chinese music."

Well, what would Chinese music sound like?

Rolling his eyes, my father would recite on a singsong atonal spiraling: "Chop Suey. Chiang Kai-shek. Chow mein. Shanghai. Madame Chiang. Foo-yung." He would be huffing and puffing from the effort of breaking rough dirt and bursting clods. He'd put his red rubber-booted foot up on the turning fork, grip the fork's handle, and then, throwing back his head the way opera bassos do when they're ready to belt it out, he'd toss aside the turning fork, throw out his arms, and from deep in his belly sing, "Mary had a little lamb, little lamb." Then he'd laugh and laugh.

My father said that the static through which I had to listen so hard was the sounds growing made—that, and worms wriggling. So when I've got my hands down in the dirt. I hear, as if I were

an aural hallucinator, the underground suckling and sobbing of
tight corn against grains splitting open their yellow skin, sprouts
breaking out of lima beans, wispy new radish roots coaxing up
deep waters.

For me, my father was spring's hero. Yearly, he planted huge
gardens, and after he retired he built a greenhouse in which he
started flowers and vegetables for bedding out in his gardens. I
think of his body underground—he'd always said he wanted his
body to be worm food and he'd left a letter of instruction, ordering
that no autopsy be performed or any embalming (in the state
where he was buried, not to be embalmed was not illegal). His
doctor, a close friend, took him out of the gardening clothes he
died in and dressed him for burial. He was buried in a pine box.
By now worms and beetles will have eaten his fine features down
to bone and his hands and toes, chewed his navy-blue suit to rags,
chewed his made-for-him-in-England shirt, his socks. The shoes
may still be there.

I can't seem to tell anyone, with the ardor to match my feeling,
how much I miss my father. How much, even after years have
passed since he dropped dead, I still want to show him this or tell
him that, though the longer he's been dead the less I remember
what I liked, admired, loved about him. He did the best he could.

Nothing that might come out of my mouth equals what's in my
heart.

Back to that morning. I hustled the half dozen small hyacinth
pots into the house, two at a time. Last fall I had lined up the
clay pots, filled them with soil mix, and buried one hyacinth bulb,
nose up, halfway into that mix in each. Now, ten weeks later, green
leaves and pointed buds were swelling out of the dirt.

I'm particularly fond of hyacinth for its colors (I prefer Delft
Blue, Pink Pearl, and the white L'Innocence) and perfume, which
is strong and sweet, also fleshy and musky, even unpleasant. There

is something vulgar about hyacinth. A teenager who's picked up a few Freudian clichés might observe that this vulgarity follows from the phallic shape the flower takes, as hourly in a warm sunny room the flowered spike rises up and swells between the thick, blade-shaped leaves.

Greek mythology has it that Hyacinthus was the youngest son of a Spartan king, and his great beauty attracted Apollo. The god killed him accidentally when teaching him to throw the discus. Another version has it that Apollo's rival, the wind god Zephyrus, out of jealousy deflected the course of the discus in such a way as to strike Hyacinthus and kill him. In both versions Apollo, sick with grief, caused a hyacinth to grow out of the pool of Hyacinthus' blood. (Similar stories have violets, roses, and anemones growing from the blood of the dead.)

I'd had to ask my neighbor to help me transplant the rootbound Christmas tree. I knew better than to ask him if this was pine or spruce, because he's one of those entirely urban types whose expertise has little to do with botany. While he held the tree in a horizontal hip hold, rather like the hold one uses to carry a toddler on one's hip, and I examined and then pulled apart the tree's hairy roots, we talked about the man. He looks healthy, we said. We agreed that somewhere he was getting meals and haircuts and shaves. We thought he probably was not a mental case.

My neighbor, still balancing the tree across his slim hip while I separated the last of the tightly entwined roots, said he wasn't scared of the man, though he was annoyed by the man's urinating against his house, because his own bed, he snorted, was right above the vines where the man slept. So he knew it was this man who did this, late at night, maybe three in the morning. "A cataract of piss against the wall. Like a stallion pissing. And when it gets hot out there, it's going to stink like a pissoir."

But what can we do about him? I asked, helping my neighbor

tip the tree into the hollow I'd made in the soil of the new big pot. We sank the tree's roots into the billowy humus. I got on my knees. I patted down the soft dirt around the trunk. The scratchy bark, oozing drops of black pitch, scraped my cheek. I was thinking maybe I should have bought a bigger pot, but it was too late.

My neighbor brushed dirt off his hands into the air. The dirt flew off in the breeze, vermiculite chips sparkling as if someone had tossed out a confetti of minuscule diamonds. He looked up at the sky, across which wind was blowing puffy white clouds that broke up the sun. He eyed a sooty-headed Steller's jay, which screamed down at us from the rooftop. "Hush," he shouted at the jay, and then, lowering his voice, he said maybe there was something—but what?—that we could do about this guy.

The Christmas tree looked awkward in its new pot. My neighbor tweaked the topmost branch, pulled off a tinsel strand, worried the silver between his fingers. "Something other than call 911. Because the police wouldn't, couldn't, anyway do anything." We considered various scenarios. None was practical. The solutions we came up with were more about us than about the man, were more about what might make us feel less selfish for at least a few hours. "Maybe," my neighbor concluded, "we have to accept that there's nothing we can do."

When writing's not going well, it's true that you do well to look for what you're leaving out. There is also the opposite, more obvious tack: you may need to cut part of what you've already composed. Trying to write about how happy I'd been out in the patio, I hadn't wanted to write about my father, because I don't enjoy feeling how much I miss him, but at least he fit into my scheme. I didn't want to write about the old man in the vines, because I didn't want to face how much his presence clouds the pleasure I take in my garden. I didn't want to see in my own words my lack of generosity, my increasing hardness of heart toward people who have no home. The old man didn't fit in the story I was telling; the scaffolding of text was not strong enough to make me do what's right. I know what's right. I do not do it.

So I took out the old man.

Writing about spring, I had wanted to allude to the cycle of dying and rebirth, reference to which shows up regularly in greeting cards and hymns.

I put the old man back in. He had made himself part of my garden. Nothing that comes out of my mouth equals what's in my heart. The crookneck squash seed I planted will be droopy with yellow fruit by July. The okra stems will be fat with pods. By next Christmas the Christmas tree will have grown a foot. I will learn its name. I will buy a star for it. My father, beetles perhaps even now are chewing your shoes. I am remembering you, planting and hoping.

SPUDS

❧

JACQUELINE KENNEDY ONASSIS WAS BURIED AT A TIME WHEN I was thinking about potatoes. Potatoes and death, burial and resurrection, rising from the dead and returning to life, for me seem linked. To think of that homely edible tuber that swells at the end of an underground stem of the green plant *Solanum tuberosum* is also to think of all my beloved dead and my hope for our eternal life.

This connection may seem bizarre, even macabre, if the way you see the world does not include belief in life after death, as resurrection or reincarnation. But even the most apparently rational view will admit that when you bury a potato in the earth, you are burying hope for the future.

Potatoes are one of the most dependable crops a home gardener can grow. Buy a bag of seed potatoes from your garden center, choose a planting method, pop the potato into soil, and three or four months later your one seed potato may yield ten or more pounds of potatoes.

Planting potatoes does not necessarily demand digging deep trenches or holes that go through to China. If your soil is loose and loamy, set your seed potato atop the ground and cover it with five or six inches of compost, hay, or even old autumn leaves. As weeks pass, this blanketing will settle and more hay, compost, whatever, will have to be added. When harvest time comes in the fall, pull away the mulch and pick potatoes.

In the southern United States I have seen gardeners plant potatoes in old car tires. As the potato plant grows, more tires are added. I've seen as many as four bald Michelins surrounding one potato plant.

Even if all you have is a patio, you can grow at least one potato plant. Fill a whiskey barrel or pressed-paper pot the appropriate size of a whiskey barrel with potting soil. Wet down the soil. Bury your potato six inches beneath the soil in the middle of the pot. Keep the soil moist but not soggy. Depending on the weather, a green sprout should rise within a few weeks. Aboveground, the bushy potato plant's dark green leaves will provide a foliage display. Down in the pot's dark interior the tubers will quietly lead their own genetically encoded potato lives. Blessed by stubborn and powerful instinct, they push aside soil to make room for themselves; they grow and grow, filling themselves with what later will be our digestible, sour-cream-topped, buttery joy.

A seed potato, or mother tuber, doesn't look much different from potatoes you buy at Safeway. There's nothing to keep you from planting a Safeway potato. But the problem with a grocery-store potato is that it may have been given a bath in sprout retardant and therefore won't put out the sprouts you need to get your plant growing. Also, the seed potato will have been dusted with fungicide to prevent the rot and diseases to which potatoes are susceptible whereas the grocery-store potato won't.

Home gardeners and commercial potato producers rarely plant potato from seed. Dr. Herman Timms, a retired University of California–Davis professor whose entire professional life concentrated on the potato, explains that the potato plant can be reproduced either sexually, by planting potato seeds, or through vegetative, or asexual, means, by planting the seed potato or mother tuber. The seed potato will reproduce the same plant that grew one year or even one hundred years ago, depending on the age of the variety.

Potato flowers appear near the stem's end among the plant's coarse green leaves. The wind-pollinated potato flower is a pretty little yellow, pink, or white blossom, depending on the variety. The fruits that develop from the flowers resemble tiny green tomatoes and are poisonous. The seeds within these fruits, says Dr. Timms, do not "always breed true. You can have ten to fifteen thousand variations within one seed ball. So many different combinations of genetic material are in one ball that each seed in that pod likely will produce a different potato. Because the potato tends to revert to its wild ancestors, the offspring that come from a sexual union might go back a thousand years to potatoes growing wild then in Peru. You might get a potato plant that would set a tuber that weighs three pounds and has yellow flesh or a plant that would set a tuber that is long like a snake and has purple flesh. You are rolling the dice. You don't know what you're getting."

Also, your potato flower may not get around to producing a seed pod, says Dr. Timms. "In California the temperature sometimes rises so high that the flowers are aborted. Along the coast where the temperature is lower you are more likely to get flowers that stay on the plant."

Should the flower produce seed and should a gardener want to plant these seeds the next season, harvesting the seed is fairly simple. When the seed ball begins to soften and seems ready to fall off the plant, pick it. Bring it indoors and break up the pod into a pan of cool water. The seeds will sink to the bottom of the pan and the pulpy mess will float. Skim off the pulp, lay the seeds out on a paper towel to dry, and when they are dry, store them in a closed jar. Along in January you can plant the seeds indoors in a flat filled with moist potting soil. When the seeds germinate and the plants sport three or four leaves, put out the plant into your garden and grow as you would any potato. The result will probably be at least one terrifying monster potato, perhaps, as Dr. Timms says, a throwback to one of the Peruvian originals.

The potato, taxonomically a member of the nightshade family and a relative of tobacco and tomato, first grew wild as many as eight thousand years ago from the southern United States to the tip of Chile. More than ninety wild species are still found there, together with several hundred cultivated varieties. Although food historians disagree by as many as four thousand years as to when the potato was first domesticated, certainly by the time Plato was memorializing Socrates' chitchat, the Incas in Peru, Ecuador, and northern Chile had lined up the wild potato into rows and tamed it. "I think," says Dr. Timms, "that someone stumbled on the potato tuber and asked themselves, 'I wonder if this is good to eat,' or someone saw an animal eating a tuber and decided, 'Well, I'll try a bit of that. If the animal can eat it, I can sure as heck eat it, too.' That's usually how plant domestication first happens." The potato became a staple of the Inca diet and so central to Incan life that the Quechua language has a thousand words for different kinds of potatoes. The Incas measured time by how long it takes potatoes to cook and used potatoes for divination. An even number of potatoes was a good omen and an odd number a sign of trouble ahead.

After Spain's conquest of Peru in the 1530s, potatoes were packed on board returning conquistadors' ships as food for sailors and thus made their way to ports where the Spanish ships stopped. Europeans initially regarded the potato with suspicion, even terror, in part because of the poisonous alkaloids present in many nightshades, including belladonna, potato, and tomato. "You don't want to make yourself a salad," says Dr. Timms, "from potato and tomato leaves."

This poisonous alkaloid, solanine, is present throughout the plant. Dr. Timms suggests that solanine protects the potato greenery and underground tuber from insects, which find the alkaloid's bitter taste disagreeable when they chew a leaf or potato tuber. Potato tubers exposed to light develop solanine, which gives a green tinge to the tuber's skin and its flesh directly beneath the skin. That's why potatoes should be stored in a dark place and why green portions on a tuber should be pared away. Solanine is destroyed by cooking, but it can turn a potato bitter. Sprouts that form on stored potatoes also contain solanine and should be cut off before cooking.

Legend has it that Sir Walter Raleigh tried to tempt Queen Elizabeth I with potatoes, managing on one occasion actually to get a dish of boiled potatoes placed before her at the royal table. Apparently, she refused them. Many years later, Louis XVI of France, to encourage potato growing at a time when wheat suffered repeated crop failures, ordered the royal fields planted in potato. He set his troops to guard the fields, hoping that this would both provoke public interest and make the crop seem particularly valuable. He sported a potato flower in his buttonhole and served banquets in which potatoes featured prominently.

Not until the mid-eighteenth century was potato regularly planted as a food crop in Europe. In Ireland, it quickly became the most important crop. Ireland's mild damp climate and the "lazybed" easily encouraged an increase in potato acreage. To prepare a lazybed the farmer had merely to spread a plot with manure, seaweed, rotted turf, or dry peat, dig a ditch on either side for drainage, throw dirt from the ditch atop the plot, tuck in seed potatoes, and, when fall arrived, dig up his tubers. By the early 1800s potato and milk were the principal food of more than 40 percent of the Irish population, who ate an average of seven pounds of potatoes each day. Thus, when the fungus *Phytophthora infestans* struck Ireland's 1845–47 potato crops, it caused what came to be called the Great Hunger, the worst European disaster since the Black Death of 1334–50. In 1840, with 8.5 million people, Ireland was one of the world's most densely populated countries; during the famine that figure fell, through death and emigration, by 2.5 million. The Great Hunger brought a million Irish to the United States, among them Patrick Kennedy, the thirty-fifth President's great-grandfather.

Potato was first grown as an American commercial crop in fields around Londonderry, New Hampshire, in 1719. Europeans as they were, the colonists were suspicious of potatoes. They fed them to cattle and sold them to West Indian planters, who bought them as an inexpensive food for slaves. But this suspicion ended when the Irish arrived in great numbers. The next important actor in the American history of the potato is Luther Burbank (1849–1926). Born in Massachusetts, Burbank was an indifferent student who through his mother became interested in plants. When Burbank's father's death left his mother a dependent widow, Burbank gave up plans to attend medical school and took up truck gardening. Market success, Burbank realized, depended on his producing earlier, bigger, and more attractive vegetables and berries than did his older commercial rivals. Without training and only a slight understanding of scientific theory, Burbank taught himself plant crossing, selection, and hybridization.

While cultivating bigger, earlier Hubbard squashes and tomatoes, Burbank also turned his attention to potatoes. During the 1850s, *Phytophthora infestans* had begun to turn American potato crops to slime in the fields. Horticulturists believed, correctly, that sexual rather than asexual propagation might well keep America's potato crop from the fate of Ireland's.

Dr. Timms explains: "You can carry any number of diseases with seed potato. All seed potato is loaded with viruses. The viruses are latent, sitting there, benign, really not doing any damage. Just as we carry bacteria and fungi around with us in our bodies and don't die from them, so does the seed potato. And as with the human body, all the seed potato needs is some environmental factor to trigger the bacteria or fungi, and damage can then ensue."

During the 1860s a New York farmer who acquired wild potato plants in Panama developed, through crossing, a potato he named the Early Rose. The Early Rose appeared resistant to *Phytophthora infestans*, but its tubers were smaller than most housewives preferred and they stored poorly, not lasting over winters. "It required no genius to know," Burbank later reflected in his autobiography, "that if a large, white, fine-grained potato could be produced, it would displace the other varieties and give its discoverer a great advantage over his competitors." In the summer of 1872 Burbank's Early Rose potato plant produced a seed pod, a rare event. Every morning when Burbank went to his seventeen acres, he checked the pod for readiness. And then one morning the pod had disappeared. "Day after day," Burbank later wrote, "I returned and took up the search again." When Burbank finally found the missing pod, only a few feet from its parent plant, he preserved its twenty-three seeds for planting. Next season he carefully planted all twenty-three seeds, one foot apart. All twenty-three seeds produced plants and tubers, but only two of these plants produced tubers that Burbank believed were a genuine improvement. "These," he wrote, "were as different from the Early Rose as modern beef cattle were from the old Texas Longhorns."

The next year, 1874, Burbank planted the seed from his two plants. "It was from the potatoes of these two plants, carefully raised, carefully dug, jealously guarded, and painstakingly planted the next year," wrote Burbank, "that I built the Burbank potato." In 1875 Burbank sold for $150 all but ten of the tubers from his new potato to J. H. Gregory, a Marblehead, Massachusetts, seedsman. Gregory named the potato Burbank's Seedling.

"Perhaps one of the first words I ever heard was California," wrote Burbank. With his $150 plus $500 from his inheritance, ten mother tubers, and as it happens, a broken heart, Burbank headed to Santa Rosa, California, to make his fortune. The ten tubers led to the Burbank potato's introduction to the West Coast. Although Burbank for the rest of his life continued to experiment with potatoes, he never had another success with them. He did, however, go on to develop the Shasta daisy, Santa Rosa and Satsuma plums, the plumcot (a plum-apricot cross), the July Elberta peach, the thornless blackberry, spineless cactus, and white blackberry, and made improvements on various tomatoes, corn, squash, and peas.

When I ask Dr. Timms about Burbank, he replies enthusiastically, "Oh, he was spectacular! No one has ever been able to duplicate what he did with the potato. He went out there and made sexual crosses by transferring pollen from one flower to another. But no one to this date has ever been able to duplicate what he did to get the Russet Burbank.

"He did it by chance alone. If you try to put this on a computer and figure out what the chances are, it's astronomical. We've never been able to find a potato that's better than the Russet Burbank for the general purposes we want. No one has been able to duplicate it. I've had requests from all over the world, from China and India, for seed with which they could do again what Burbank did. But no one knows. He either had a Midas touch with plants or he had a secret no one else has ever been able to uncover."

Potato now is the fourth most important food crop in the world, after wheat, maize, and rice. Potato, which yields more energy per acre than do cereal crops, grows well in all temperate climates and in many parts of the tropics. Because the potato tuber grows underground, says Dr. Timms, potato tends to be considered a root vegetable like carrots or beets or turnip, which technically it's not. The potato tuber is the swollen tip of an underground stem that serves as reserve for excess products of photosynthesis and stores those products as starch. A large portion of the photosynthetic product is used in respiration and photosynthesis itself, the activities required to keep the plant factory operating. The excess that goes into the tuber is for the most part acquired in the evening and night, when temperatures go down and the rate of respiration diminishes somewhat. "Then," Dr. Timms says, "the excess carbohydrates are translocated down, in sugar form, and enter the tuber, where they are converted into starch."

A potato tuber is not just a potato, says Dr. Timms. Potatoes come in hundreds of varieties, classified into four basic types. Until recently potatoes in grocery produce sections tended to be identified by the place where they were grown rather than by variety. Some 75 percent of the United States' annual potato crop can be traced back to the Burbank Russet. The russet is distinguished by a thick brown skin, an oval shape, white flesh, and a high starch content. Grocers often identify this potato as the "Idaho," even though other states grow them. Russets are the ideal baking potato, although they can also be used for mashing, frying, or potato soup. Among popular varieties are Russet Arcadia, Centennial, Lemhi, Norgold, and Norkotah, all closely related to Burbank's original.

Second is the round white, with a light-tan skin and round shape, white flesh, and a medium starch content. This is an all-purpose potato, good for cooking in any way. Popular varieties include Chippewa, Irish Cobble, Kennebec, Katahdin, Monona, Norchip, Ontario, Sebago, Shepody, and Superior. Third is the round red, with a red skin and white flesh, a medium to low starch content, best used for steaming, salad, and fried potatoes. Popular varieties include La Rouge, Norland, Red La Soda, Red McClure, and Red Pontiac. Fourth is the long white, with a thin tan skin, white flesh, an oval shape, and a medium to low starch content. It is recommended for salad and scalloped potatoes. A popular variety, grown in California, is the White Rose.

Among the horrors that the Second World War brought us are boxes of instant mashed potatoes. Reconstituted potatoes were developed during the war and served in K-ration meals. The best use I know of for potato flakes is to drizzle them over Christmas tree branches and pretend they're snow. They're not fit to eat.

If you want to eat potatoes and don't want to go to any trouble, buy a clutch of small red-skinned potatoes. Scrub them clean, pop them into a pot of cold water, bring the water to a boil, turn down the flame, and let the potatoes simmer. When you stick a fork gently into one of the potatoes and the flesh meets no resistance, the potatoes are cooked. These red-jacketed potatoes remind me of a choir of homely grade-school boys singing slightly off-key. Serve them in their red jackets and, if you wish, sprinkle them with finely chopped fresh parsley, chive, or cilantro. When you spoon one or two of these potatoes onto your own plate, you can break the potato apart with your fork and mash in a little unsalted butter. Some words give off taste in my mouth. The word "earth" tastes sepia brown, deep, serious. When the first forkful of a boiled potato arrives in my empty mouth, the taste of that potato is the taste I associate with "earth."

Mashed potatoes say home cooking even if you never had much of a home and your mom couldn't boil water without scorching the pan. To make good mashed potatoes you've got to "take pains." First of all, you want to begin with a floury or mealy potato. Dr. Timms explains why. Potatoes are 80 percent water. Of the remaining 20 percent, 85 percent is starch, 5 percent sugar, and the rest fiber, mineral salts, and vitamins. Potato starch is in the form of granules contained in starch cells. Some varieties of potato have inside these cells one big starch granule, while others have many starch granules. As an example, Dr. Timms cites the Kennebec, the potato often used for potato chips. The Kennebec has one large starch granule per cell. The Russet Burbank and its near relations have within each cell anywhere from five to thirty starch granules per cell. The more starch granules per cell, the more floury or mealy the potato will be.

What you want to avoid, when preparing mashed potatoes, is breaking the cell walls that contain the starch granules and, says Dr. Timms, "getting that loose gelatinizing starch all over the place." Therefore, you must not overcook your potatoes, which will break down those walls.

Cooks disagree as to whether potatoes should be cooked whole, in quarters, or in two-inch cubes. I prefer working with potatoes peeled and cut into quarters, put into a large saucepan, and covered with cold water. Bring the water to a boil, then lower the flame and cook over medium heat until the potatoes are tender when poked with a fork, about fifteen to twenty minutes.

What one mashes potatoes with—butter, margarine, milk, cream, half-and-half—is a matter of taste and depends, too, on what else one is serving. For mashed potatoes that will be sluiced with gravy, I use no salt and little butter. For mashed potatoes served without gravy, I depend on unsalted butter and plenty of it. The French think nothing of adding one-quarter pound of butter for every two to three pounds of potatoes. I am with the French here.

By the time your potatoes are tender, you want to have your milk or cream warmed. Butter or margarine, ideally, will be at room temperature and cut into small bits. Some cooks melt butter in the milk or cream. The only reason I don't do this is that I enjoy watching butter melt into the hot potatoes.

Drain the cooked potatoes in a colander. Return them to the pan. You are ready now to mash. Remembering that what you want to avoid is breaking the cell walls that contain the starch granules, mash carefully. "What you want to do," says Dr. Timms, "is fluff up, not break down. You want as much as possible to keep those cell walls intact."

James Beard recommended using an electric mixer to mash potatoes. But an electric mixer is too rough on the cell walls. For the same reason, don't toss potatoes into the food processor: the sharp, rapidly turning blades will atomize cell walls. Use what your grandmother used, an old-fashioned heavy wire potato masher. (My grandmother's bicep bulged when she mashed a huge vat of potatoes for her hired hands' dinner, in those days, the noon meal.) And mash using an up-and-down motion: the potatoes will be airier that way. Plan your meal in such a way that this is one of your last acts before putting dinner on the table. You can keep mashed potatoes warm for a few minutes over a very low, low, low flame but the likelihood of their scorching scares me so much that I never do this.

Although mashed potatoes need nothing more than themselves, they take happily to additions. Before adding milk and butter, you can include, at a ratio of no more than half and half, other cooked vegetables: carrots, turnips, parsnip, rutabaga, onion. You can toss in minced fresh herbs—chives, parsley, savory, or tarragon—or dashes of chili powder. For a garlicky flavor, toss peeled cloves of garlic into the water when cooking potatoes.

Dinnertime wasn't far away when Dr. Timms and I chatted about potatoes. We talked about meals our mothers and grandmothers had made, with which they served mashed potatoes. Fried chicken, of course, served with Kentucky Wonder green beans, snapped and simmered all day with fatback and onion, bright yellow roasting ears bathed in sweet butter, huge meaty slices of a big tomato like Mortgage Lifter, and then the meal's crown: gravy made with milk, flour, and the crunchy drippings the frying chicken left behind in the high-sided black iron skillet. You took your teaspoon and made a crater in the miniature mountain of mashed potatoes on your plate. You carefully filled the crater with gravy. What you had was a gravy lake, a calm surface speckled with gold chicken fat. Sunday summer sunshine, streaming through polished dining-room windows, might catch at a speck of that fat and make it glimmer. You wanted to keep that lake for as long as you could, so you picked with your fork at the potato mountain's base. When you took your first bite, you savored the earthy potato flavor, but you also tasted mountain. "It was," I said, "like eating scenery."

GOING HOME

❧

YOU LEAVE A LITTLE TOWN, AND THEY SPEAK OF YOU—IF AT all—as if your departure, like hailstorms or miscarriage, were an act of God. Not always understandable but certainly part of a providential design whose immediate scribbles—however elusive—work out, eventually (a blessing in disguise), for the benefit of all.

"Who can know?" said my mother-in-law, venting opinion on my leaving for the city. "Perhaps it's best for everyone concerned." And I can't tell, although the town believes it knows but doesn't quite, why her son stayed and I went.

Perhaps you're like me. Perhaps some little town draws you back from the big city, where you sit, reading this, as a dog is drawn back to his buried bone. If not, you can still think about your past, your relation to it.

My heart hankering for it, my head saying, "Forgive and forget," saying, "Don't go," I return, again and again, to land settled more than a century ago by Midwesterners, originally German, Scandinavian, and Scotch-Irish; in the main, Protestant and pietist. The Indians, as elsewhere, had to move on.

The Thursday before Labor Day I unpack city clothes into country bureau drawers; (my gray-muzzled dachshund leaps, leaps, at my feet. Framed photographs line the mantel: the night our older daughter graduated from high school; her sister, hair flying, riding her bicycle through a mud puddle. There are more. You can guess them.

(Think, too, of what no one took pictures of. The screaming in the kitchen. You, leaning out its window to conjure heartrending sunsets, loathing the real horizon.)

This time, I tell myself, look at it straight on, without music.

Bloodlines intertwine like the creeks that run into the river and produce a physiognomy—short neck, brutish chin, thick torso, and sloped belly—that makes half the population appear to be first cousins. No local family tree doesn't have its poison apple and expurgated branches. Behind the lace curtains, what goes on here goes on everywhere. A "good face" and "best foot" are kept forward. Appearances are everything. What you don't know, well, maybe it didn't happen.

The return ticket sits out on the dresser. I am just passing through.

(Maybe it didn't really happen. Mr. X of the pioneer X'es, no more than usually inebriated, began the drive home from the club. The roads were icy. Mrs. X, beside her husband in the Chrysler, may have suggested he slow down some. He didn't. He swerved and hit, head on, a "clunker," killing the driver outright and injuring a passenger. Neither X was hurt. Mr. X moved to the passenger side and put Mrs. X, a teetotaler, behind the wheel. When the highway patrol arrived, Mrs. X reported herself the driver. Eventually Mr. X's insurance company settled. A decade later, another snowy night, the X'es stood in the club cloakroom, bundling up against a blizzard.

Mr. X's son, noting his father's uncertain gait, said he'd drive his parents home. Mr. X argued: "Hell, I'm fine." The son reminded Mr. X, "My God, Dad, you killed one woman and crippled another for life." Mr. X, blinking: "Fer Crissakes, it's not like we knew them. They were just passing through.")

Unpacked. Drove to the country to visit Delia. Whom for years I had envied and tried to imitate—even her bashful lisp, her cheerleader high spirits. Whose apparent contentment eluded me, even when I, like her, wore myself down with what were, after all, superficial good works—knitting mittens for the Christmas bazaar, one afternoon a week pushing a trolley of games and toothbrushes through hospital corridors.

The rich soil that drew early settlers lies in dark strips between fields of hay. A red barn stands, its doors open. SMILE, JESUS LOVES YOU in white letters arches above the doors. Far afield, corn harvesters drive down rows. Dust rises. Russet cows graze the green pastures—not one green but hundreds. If no one irrigated, by July these myriad greens would be busted back to straw.

Orchards ridge the hills. Through drooping cottonwoods, you can see to the river. It sparkles.

A tankful of gas and no destination: years ago, I made this six-mile drive, tape player bleating Rickie Lee Jones's paeans to Los Angeles. Something ought to happen, I thought, looking toward the horizon to see if a rescue team had appeared between the sky and the last black ridge, to see if a lone eagle, flying over, would drop down a rope.

Bang the brass knocker. Delia greets me, her arms out. Only her legs, in striped shorts, have aged. Her face could be her college-age daughter's. She hands me a frosty long-neck Lone Star. "See?" She fills up her brown eyes with meaning. "I don't forget." We settled back into needlepoint pillows (each one takes a year to stitch).

She wonders aloud, "Will we see you at the brunch?" An annual function, the pre-rodeo parade brunch.

"I've promised to make at least a cameo appearance," I say.

"There are days," she sighs, and her voice trails off: "Larry, he's doing well." Carefully shaped eyebrow raised: "Are you still happy there?"

❦

On the first evening home, my husband takes me downtown to dinner, in the only restaurant that uses tablecloths at noon *and* night.

My husband has not suffered an "identity crisis." He is indifferent to dislike. He casts for trout in the same streams where his great-grandfather cast. In the eighth grade he used a desk into whose wood his father had carved initials. Nights, under a lamp that was his grandfather's, he ties deer hair and rooster-neck feathers into Joe's Hoppers and Royal Wulffs. If you ask, "What are you thinking about?" he says, believing he tells the truth, "Nothing." His hands rarely tremble.

Although I know people like him, what he has isn't catching. I tried.

The salad plates are taken away, a nearby winery's white is poured, and we talk. The hot and rainless summer, the subsequent fire danger in forests. The "sex crime" I'd read about in the letters between us. "*Technically*," my husband says, "'sex crime' is a misnomer. He panicked and dropped her before he could get to that."

One of Jack's old girlfriends from high school, cluttered by a silk print, strides toward us across the low-lit room. She tilts her head to one side, as if that tilt makes her query casual. "Are you back for good?" she asks, and when I say I'm not, she shrugs and returns to her table. Jack circles the pink linen with his index finger. One arm is larger than the other from years of fly casting.

Out of the corner of my eye, I see a silk print sleeve planted on the table. "At least my claim to fame isn't that I fucked all the Seahawks except Jim Zorn," I mutter.

Chicken reduced to bone, dessert and coffee brought, a friend opens the restaurant's heavy front door, hurries to our table, kisses the hollow of my temple. Then, holding me off from his seersucker jacket, says, "You always look the same. Lovely."

"Well, yes and no," I say, "yes and no."

Tomorrow night—Friday—is family night at the county fair. Saturday morning, the pre-rodeo parade brunch, and then the parade. A Saturday-night dance at the club, and on Sunday morning "Cowboy Church."

Oh, how I sleep! Our doors unlocked and open on that hot, windless night. The dachshund wanders in and out at will. His toenails click.

Friday morning. "Not a cloud in the sky," my husband proclaims.

A resonant tenor drawls the going prices for pigs, milk solids, feed grains, and soybeans over the 50-watt station. Kenny Rogers and Dottie West sing "Don't Fall in Love with a Dreamer."

Out at Hazel's on the south fork interchange, Hazel herself arranges the breakfast on oval meat platters. She shreds hash browns from potatoes boiled that day, hand-cuts her fries, and doesn't charge for coffee past the first cup.

Barb and Joe and their grandson Gable push open the door. Big woman, big-busted, Barb is wearing a nursing-home uniform that pulls at the seams. Joe behind her, his belly riding his low-slung belt, yells out "Hi there!" to the wide backs leaning over the counter. The men and women swivel on their stools and return greetings. Eight-year-old Gable's black hair is wet-combed off his

broad brown forehead. Below the waistband on his Little Man
Levi's, the size tag reads 32.

A hundred years ago, the town creamery churned a high-fat
butter that commanded a heftier price than was obtained for butter in any other section of the United States. Not just at Hazel's
do bodies thicken early. We joked, "Our principal product is fat
cells."

Hunkered over his stool at the counter, eggs shaded green by
his visor, Big Roy, jack-of-all trades, asks the man at his right
elbow, "Didja hear the one about? . . ." and the man, in brown
Sansabelt slacks, owner of the Downtown Office Supply, slathering
catsup on steak, is cut off, openmouthed, by Big Roy's wife (clerk
at Mode O'Day), who asks, "Anybody know the condition of the
preacher's little girl, now she's home from the hospital?"

By a Yuban can, slit across its plastic top, Hazel has propped a
newspaper photograph. The child, wearing white-collared plaid,
grips a panda and holds her mother's hand. Hazel has taped a plea
over the Yuban: HELP THE REVEREND WITH MEDICAL EXPENSES.

What they talk about—while Hazel turns behind the counter
and refills coffee cups, while her daughter-in-law fries onion rings
two inches from the pancakes, empties ashtrays, and swats flies
come in from the slaughterhouse down the road, while satisfied
eaters lay down money on green receipts and go out the door and
soon-to-be eaters push open the door and come in, while the day's
heat sends the thermometer on the downtown bank up seven degrees—what they talk about is how the three-year-old daughter
of the Nazarene preacher was abducted from where she played
one weekday morning near her front yard, the so-called sex crime.

"That long-haired kid plucked her up right off her yard, threw
her over his shoulder like a croaker sack, and run off," Big Roy
tells me.

Downtown Office Supply's owner: " 'There but for the grace of

God goes my kid,' we were all saying." He folds a ten-dollar bill and slips it into the Yuban can. Hazel thanks him.

Hazel: "It wasn't minutes before police got the neighborhood cordoned off."

"Neighbor lady found her," says Big Roy's wife, "forty minutes after he got her two blocks from home, in a runoff from the crick. He'd stripped her of her play shorts and a little ol' Minnie Mouse T-shirt. She was layin' facedown, all underwater, except a foot. It was stickin' out."

"Woman that found her," says Barb, "she was up visitin' the nursing home and told the gals that child was totally limp. Whole body was blue, even her eyes, is what she said. No way did she think she could live."

"You know what he was wantin' to do with her," says Big Roy, wiping his mouth.

In the stockyard, cattle bawl.

"The guy that grabbed her," offers a retired rancher, "he sure musta wanted to get caught, way he left his shirt near where he dumped her."

"Trouble is, I can think of any of seven or eight guys right around here strange enough to have grabbed a kid," says Hazel's daughter-in-law.

The retired rancher: "A neighbor knew the shirt. Police knocked. Kid didn't resist or nothin'. Said, I did it, said he grabbed her and then panicked an' tried to kill her."

"I tell you"—Big Roy worries a toothpick under his bottom denture—"police were all over that kid like a coat of paint. In a city, the crime would never've been solved."

"Here," notes the loan officer, his thumb on the counter, "you can put your thumb on perpetrators and press down."

Hazel offers the fly-swatter to the black-haired boy, fidgeting and restless, and says, "Give you a penny for ever' one you smash."

The conversation drifts to the county fair and rodeo. I finish my coffee and surmise that local history—oral, compulsive, revisionist, always in flux—is right now growing by several pages. That I was seen today laughing across pink linen, that "He's never divorced her, now can you tell me why that is?" Rumor will have it that I'm at work on a novel set in Coraville. It will be said, "She has been a cross, God knows." To which the reply will come, "He has not, you know, worn himself out, carrying it." The man who says this will snicker.

Downtown proper is only four blocks: two banks, the telephone company, the real-estate office, two diet-center franchises, one movie theater, a barber, a Christian bookstore, small businesses that come and go, cafés, the "tablecloth-at-noon" restaurant where I will be reported (incorrectly) as sipping iced tea and "scribbling fast in her notebook," when in fact I am dropping my husband off at the back door of his office, one story above the office that for years was his grandfather's. We plan to meet at the fairgrounds after he finishes work.

Fifty-year-old Sandy Biddle, Jr., owns the men's clothing store founded between the wars by his father. Sandy helps his twenty-five-year-old son, Little Sandy, carry a card table out onto the sidewalk and stack straw cowboy hats. "So," Sandy asks, "back to settle down?" His teeth gleam out of an ingratiating but abject smile. "Look at the highways! Look at all those cars and campers! You don't see them driving to the big city. You see them on their way here. Hills here"—he points to the ridges outlined against the sky—"they're like having walls of your house around you." He hitches up his trousers and motions me to follow him into the store. On a shelf among the work shirts a radio plays Hank Williams, Jr.

Little Sandy, rusty thick hair like his father's, goes back to knocking flies out of the air with a rolled-up copy of *Parade*. His

father says, "Here you know everything that's going on. That con-
trols a lot of how you act and react in relationship to the mores
of the community. That boy that grabbed the preacher's daughter,
now he got put away." He snaps his fingers. "Toot sweet. In cities,
those guys can get done what they want to get done and then run
hide."

"Gettin' ready for rodeo?" Sandy asks a customer.

"No, for winter."

"It's comin', winter is," says Sandy. "Comin' like everything
else."

A philosophy professor and I eat lunch in a café opened early
in the century as a curtained tearoom for ladies. Vico is fifty-five,
full head of hair, tall and stooped, too thin. Cigarette burns on his
slacks. Two decades ago Vico and other men in their late twenties,
early thirties took jobs at the local college, planned to stay a few
years, then move on. They have been here ever since. "When my
wife left me," says Vico, "a friend advised, Get out of here, change
your name, go to Paris. When he was here last week, he said,
You're like an old used teabag, steeped in grief."

I quote a Jungian: "You may have escaped death in a holocaust
or war and not yet have inwardly escaped."

Vico looks at me hard. "You're just begging to be taken pris-
oner." When I tell him not to look at me so mean, he laughs and
fishes out a clean, unironed handkerchief, blows his nose, asks how
my hay fever is, and says, "Nobody here ever forgives anyone
anything. But over the years, almost no one isn't guilty. It evens
out."

My hay fever, I tell him, is worse here.

"It's the despair." He giggles. "It's thick. A delivery boy for the
pizza place told me, 'As soon as we open, at eleven in the morning,
I begin taking pizzas around.' He has to bang at doors. Game
shows and soap operas are booming. People in the underwear they

slept in. Days here are long, and the nights, too. But years speed by." He asks for the check, pushes my money back. "Keep your money. I hope to outlive my scars."

Outside, thickly leafed maples hang heavy and motionless over the sidewalks. The sun presses the buildings down. On the corner the tavern, open since eight this morning, keeps its doors ajar. Pool cues clack against balls.

"No," Vico says, he won't go to the fair with us. "The minister who studies ventriloquism so that some Charlie McCarthy he sets on his knee can recite Bible verses will be there, selling barbecue beef and throwing his voice into corn on the cob. The emphysemiac with oxygen tanks strapped to his back will be there. Fatties wearing dangling earrings to distract your eye from their grinding behinds. Your in-laws and your friends will be there. Your husband," he snarls, "is violently anti-intellectual. He and his friends talk of nothing but trout. Hell, no, I won't go to the fair with you."

We walk off in opposite directions. I pass two old men who lean against a brick wall. Vico and I are twenty, thirty feet apart. He calls my name. I turn, smile, am smiling as he yells, "The past is a hiding place."

I always felt like a blasphemer, the years here. Always, deep down, waiting for the villains to ride in and take over the town.

Standing in what was my front yard, I hear hammers ping five blocks away at the fairgrounds. The forsythia shadows a four-foot circle. I had taken for granted, when I dug out a hole for the three-branch seedling, that I would live here my whole life. I expected to go gray-haired in this house. To tend my lilies and tight-budded peonies, put in chunks of potato in spring, and wait for my Cuthbertson sweet peas to climb up a permanent string.

Look at it this way: When you're eighteen, there's the novel you like so much, which ends too soon. You're forty when you read it again, and what you thought went on wasn't it at all. Had the story gone on longer, it wouldn't have kept on seeming true.

The first of us fairgoers, shouldering through the perspiring melee, walk onto springy grass as green as movie lawns. Hay bales and picnic tables sit opposite a long row of booths selling curly fries, hot pepper jelly, and pickled garlic, tacos, barbecue beef (served by the members of the Assembly of God, who have painted on their booth that message again: *Smile . . . Jesus Loves You!*), chili dogs, caramel corn, candy apples, pie à la mode.

Squeals stop me in my tracks. Inside a chain-link fence, as if in a theater in the round, eight piglets look out at us, sharing their arena with uncountable children and a half dozen adults, one of whom grips a microphone in one hand and cups his other hand to his ear, like an old-time radio announcer.

"In this event, one team member has to control a pig without hurting it, then the other team member has to put three articles of clothing on this pig. One's a pair of shorts. One's a shirt. And one's a bib. Bob and Carol will give us a trial run."

Outside the fence, hurrahs. Inside, Carol carries the shorts, shirts, and bib to centerfield. Bob rushes the pigs, and they run, short legs blurring, to one end of the arena and then, like swimmers doing laps, turn and run back. Bob reaches down to a piglet barreling toward him and nabs it by its hind feet.

"This is a timed event," says the announcer. "Six-minute limit. We would like to have everyone compete, but if a pig gets tired or overheated, we won't let that pig compete anymore."

Seven uncaptured pigs, shoulder to shoulder, press their buttocks into the fence.

My husband touches my bare arm in greeting and says, "The pigs know something bad is going to happen." He hands over an aqua Sno-Kone. Grateful in this heat for cool wetness, I suck ice while Bob dangles his piglet upside down. It squeals. Carol, grinning, slips the piglet's back legs into red boxer shorts, forces ears, snout, and wriggling foretrotters through a polo shirt's neck and sleeves. Bob tosses the dressed pig snout-first onto the grass. Peculiarly humanoid in its shorts and shirt, the pig circles—once, twice—bib flapping beneath its snout.

In the poultry and rabbit barn "Orval Orpington," a nine-pound, smooth-feathered giant crowned by a serrated red comb, scratches at his wire cage, tosses back his head, and crows. A stooped stick of a man, old, filling Orval's water cup, tells us, "It's his third time at the fair. People make him nervous."

"Well, I guess Orval'll be glad to get home when the fair's over," I say.

"Naw, forty-eight hours from tonight he'll be foreign to the flock. When I take him back, the flock won't remember no more. He has to fight all over again to get back his place. I've had 'em killed that way."

Just past jars of pickled okra, we find ourselves boxed in a crowd intent upon a plumpish woman who squeezes frosting dollops from a pastry tube. With frosting she "dresses" a cake that's cut to resemble a cartoon mouse in red Western shirt, blue jeans, and boots.

"Is that butter-cream frosting?" someone asks.

"Yes, but we make it with Crisco because of the heat and compensate by using butter flavoring. So you get that wonderful butter flavor. Yum, yum." Above her head a large sign is affixed to the wall: GIRL SCOUTS DIAMOND JUBILEE—OUR GIRLS ARE OUR JEWELS.

Nearby, a white frame building houses fine arts, crafts, and photography exhibits. Painted on canvas or paper and framed behind glass: sunsets, fruit-heaped bowls, sad clowns, happy clowns,

cocker spaniels, more sunsets, many sunrises, frothing oceans, bal-
lerinas, a palm tree, pensive doe-eyed girls, and a white church
with a gray gouache storm cloud stippled behind its steeple. Unlike anything that ever was, these paintings. What is here, exqui-
sitely alive behind the glassed frames, is longing.

Crafts are for sale. Wooden ducks dressed in checked gingham,
candleholders shaped as sitting hens, Pennsylvania Dutch hex-sign
refrigerator magnets. "Isn't this darling!" a woman says, pointing
to a black rag doll, body made of overstuffed brown cotton, covered in a print shift covered by a white apron. Painted onto the
brown cotton, an outsize half-moon smile shows white teeth. Yarn
curls rise out of a bandana. The feet are bare. The tag attached
to the doll reads: "Pickannini $19." Next to the "pickannini," a
black man and woman jiggered out of wood: their lacquered lips
have been set with the same half-moon, bright white teeth; they
are joined together by a slice of watermelon. On the stand to
which their feet are glued is printed WELCOME.

Light gilds the hilltops. So many people line up at food booths;
so many eaters stroll between the booths. We take small steps,
not to bump anyone. The carnival riders scream, cattle moan, the
rooster crows, and barkers outside the food booths call out, "Burgers!" and "Corn!" From the adjacent rodeo arena, calves bawl
and cheers soar. A barbershop octet harmonizes "You Are My
Sunshine."

Two teenaged couples, both women hugely pregnant, try a pin-
toss game. One husband—shirtless in the heat, his hairless chest
sunken and pale—has just won a stuffed panda, which his wife
holds atop her bulging stomach. The other husband lunges forward to spin the bowling pin through the hole marked PRIZE.
When he wins, he asks for Spuds Mackenzie. "The party dog!" he
cries, handing the stuffed dog over to his wife.

Blue smoke haloes the stand selling "elephant ears," wide

wedges of fried sweet dough dipped in sugar. At a picnic table
near the elephant ears, my husband's sister and her husband sit
next to Sandy Biddle, Jr.'s wife, Janey. Sandy, his cowboy boot
propped on the bench, talks to a man who recently bought a farm-
equipment dealership at the edge of town.

"Years ago," says Sandy Jr., "there was lots of jackrabbits around
here. They'd come down at night and eat their way into the hay-
fields. My gramma had some summer fallow up above the ditch
line. So some of the guys, we got in a car and drove up there, up
above the ditch, and we found that, gee, you could take a .22 and
drive along and shoot jackrabbits—they'd be right there, in the
headlights."

A story I've heard before. Janey pleats and unpleats a paper
plate.

"Real fast," continues Sandy, "that got too easy. We'd kill off
twenty or thirty a night. One night we run out of shells, and someone said, 'Next time let's get clubs.' So we got a bunch of big
flashlights, and we got clubs. We clubbed 'em. That was okay, too."

My husband's sister, elephant ear wrapped in napkin, mimes,
"Want some?" and Jack reaches across the table to take a portion
of the pastry.

"But after a while we got pretty good at that, and so it was
pretty tame. One night a rabbit tried to run between one of the
guys' legs, and he reached down and grabbed it by the ears. So,
what are we going to do with a live rabbit? 'Hell, throw it in the
trunk,' somebody said."

Three days from full, the moon is out: bumpy on one side, the
deep orange of fertilized yolk. Across the way, at the carnival, a
sound system pours out Jimi Hendrix's "All Along the Watch-
tower." The line for curly fries extends to the edge of our table,
and in that line, a shirtless boy, face contorted to anguished intensity, strikes invisible guitar strings, sings, with Hendrix, " 'Isn't

there a way out of here?' said the joker to the thief." Shrieks crescendo as the Super-Loop's cars ascend, looping the loop. Its lights flash color across our faces.

"It right away got to be one of those things. 'Well, if he can do it, I can do it, too.' Took no time before we'd caught a trunkload of jackrabbits."

I say to Jack, "I see a thousand familiar faces." (Matched sets of kitchen canisters: grandmothers, mothers, daughters.) A few feet from us, a tall blonde in blue denim crop top, blue denim miniskirt, even high heels made out of blue denim, leans over and pulls up a lace-trimmed anklet. Her naked rib cage glows.

By the time Sandy finishes his story, its climax the setting loose of the jackrabbits at a dance, the sky has turned navy blue. Thousands of feet up, a plane's lights twinkle.

Kiss of breeze, and Janey, shuddering intermittently, asks, "Aren't you cold? Where you live is so much warmer." Each word trips her tongue as neatly as I remember she dices carrots.

For all that, I scarcely dream all night, and what I dream, I don't remember.

❧

To get to the brunch, we must park a block away (unusual here). At our host's two-story white house, guests crowd the front verandah (by which the parade will pass at noon) and call out, "Hiya, you two."

Cowboy hats, each with its own "signature" crease, litter mahogany tables. "Bloody Marys, champagne, or orange juice?" I'm asked, while one of my husband's fishing buddies grips his shoulder and screams, "Why not have a wild pig feed and call it fun? Ay?" His eyes check me out, from flat-heel shoes to mouth, where he stops.

(Someone, hidden by a fissure in the black basalt across the river, squinted through the lens. When the photo was blown up, you could see how the slanting light picked up the riffled water. In the city no one would have even noticed, or given a second thought to the two people on the opposite bank.)

The dining-room wallpaper depicts a Venetian canal. The blue-lidded wife of one of the town millionaires addresses our hostesss, pointing to a chafing dish set round with Wheat Thins. "How did you make this?"

"Two packages frozen chopped broccoli and Cheez Whiz." She smiles, showing lipstick on her teeth.

(Loose gravel litters the riverbank. You have to put down a blanket. "I have a terrible need for affection," he confessed. To which I, putting up naked arms, said, "The flesh is willing, but my spirit has been flogged.")

Rex Barber, real estate and insurance, salacious slow dancer, in high school called "Mule," wriggles a finger to greet me, then quickly reassumes his serious mien. He says to a bald dentist, "You have the candle burning at both ends. You got to blow one of them out."

Jack is lost in the crowd.

(Think, however, of what no one took pictures of. Think of what someone said, when the pictures were shown round: "He picked her up, you know, out of the gutter.")

Across the outsize Sony, baseball players run bases (sound low). I lean against antiques, answer no when my mother-in-law's friend, who has said I am "looking lovely," asks if I am "back for good."

Rex cups my bare elbow in his palm. "It's been so long. Last year this time? Listen, I miss you."

I hear my father-in-law's voice, hear women with whom I served in Altar Guild. Over Rex's shoulder I meet my mother-in-law's eyes. She lifts her eyebrows in hello.

"Must be pretty wild there," says Rex, who claims he doesn't believe me that my life in the big city is mostly hard work.

At my right, as the high-ceilinged living room heats up, the middle-aged daughter of a third-generation family purrs to the inheritor of an early-century real-estate stake, "He told us, you have to own your own ecstasy! Well, Jerry about died . . ." At my left, a man is protesting, "It's instinct, something like what that kid did to the preacher's child. C'mon, a wolf doesn't learn to kill a sheep. You're being suckered by those for-the-underdog types."

"But do you feel fulfilled there? In your new life?" Rex asks, leaning over, gripping my wrist. His question lifts stray hairs across my forehead.

Delia's voice trills in from the porch. Excusing myself from Rex, who holds my wrist tight enough to leave marks, I find her. Violet silk. Off-white linen trousers. Mauve toenails.

A kiss. A hug.

She goes in to grab a drink, whispers, "Stay here. I'll be right back." It is hot and windless. Sun almost at noontide; spectators on the sidewalk across the street await the first band and seek the shade of overhung branches.

On the porch two of my father-in-law's hunting buddies—Joe and Matt—tell a third man about how in the old days "us boys" would pile up the pickup with ducks, then drive by and leave off the birds for the "colored boy," who plucked and cleaned ducks for a dime a carcass. "Ol' Black Jake," says Matt, "he'd pluck and clean ducks for a dime a carcass. Ol' Black Jake," says Matt, "he'd pluck those suckers clean."

"Oh yeah," adds Joe, slurping his Bloody Mary, "he shined shoes down at the Deluxe Barbershop."

"He had him a goose dyed purple that he walked, every year, in the rodeo parade. The goose and Ol' Jake, they went every-where together."

"I always thought that was some strange niggerish thing to do,

havin' a pet goose." Joe chortles. "But who knows. When did Ol'
Jake leave town?"

"Fifty-six or '55, mebbe."

The trio drinks in silence for a few moments. "This is the best
damned rodeo parade I ever saw," Joe says.

"It hasn't even started yet!" comes Matt's reply. (It's about to.
From a distance, snare drums clatter out a beat.)

"By God, you're right." Joe laughs hard enough to loosen
phlegm in his chest. So he coughs before he says, "The goddamn
street is empty."

Drums. Piccolo. Trombones. Brass slides vigorously drawn in
and out. The Sousa march emerges in a disconcerting unison.
Everyone hurries out front onto the porch, down to the sloping
lawn. The women's high heels dig into the sod.

The color guard, heavy uniforms bunched at the genitals, red
faces streaming sweat, pass by. Cowboy hats go into hands, hands
go to hearts. Faces slack from Bloody Marys stiffen to attention.

High-school band. Golden plumes on crimson shakos. The rodeo queen and her princesses bounce atop creamy Appaloosas.
Goose-stepping Shriners, yellow and green ribbons striped around
massive bellies, the sweat sticking white shirts to their backs, are
cheered. Indians, their feathered headdresses limp, straddle skit-
tish roans. Their women walk, papooses on their backs. Round-
faced children in fringed hide hold one another with a hand,
clutch a paper Coca-Cola cup in the other.

"The booze is getting to me," I tell Jack.

He leads me inside to the air-conditioned den, draperies pulled
closed, ice tinkling in glasses, odor of bourbon deep as shame,
where a home movie of this same parade flitters on the screen.
"How long ago did you take all this?" my husband asks our hosts.
The film is forty years old. An out-of-tune band passes. Shriners.
Golden plumes. Indians. Jake. The purple goose.

Late in the afternoon, at home and fanning myself with a newspaper, I ask, "Before we left, did I tell Delia goodbye?" I did. I ask then, "Can't we skip the dance, go back to the fair, and walk around the carnival? Maybe ride the Super-Loop?"

Which is what, after dark, we do. A blue haze hangs over the grounds, "because there's no wind to take off cooking grease," Jack says.

He nods toward the darkening sky. He says, "Moon one day closer to full." He adds, "Don't you ever wish . . ."

". . . that things had turned out differently?"

Cowboy Church. The sun pours down on the rodeo arena's north bleachers over several hundred worshippers—locals, rodeo participants (from among whom the morning's preacher will come), a few carnies—who sit on risers, frowning into heat. "Everybody's got a talent," a young cowboy is saying as we take a seat. "My talent just happens to be trick ropin'. But God's chosen you, too, plucked you into special areas of life."

Bibles lie open across denimed knees. Here and there are red eyes, dolorous with hangover. Several heads are bowed, lips moving. Others stare past the roper onto empty bleachers across the field.

"Just like the guy who is captain of his ship," warns the roper, "you'll see, out there in the ocean, that you gonna have to confront some maybe very adverse and stormy weather."

Under the bleachers, calves bawl. Out in the arena a truck, a tank fixed on the back, sprays water onto the dusty ground.

"Life's like that," says the trick roper.

Down several rows, Rex Barber ties a handkerchief over his bare head. Ranged next to him, his three towheaded boys sit straight. "I don't see Delia and Larry," I whisper to my husband.

"But if you man that ship, you're gonna get where you need to go."

Carrying a portable cassette player, two petite blondes in pink jeans, pink-and-white-checked Western shirts, pink boots, step into the spot vacated by the trick roper. "My sister and I are gonna sing 'Can You Reach My Friend?' and our mom's gonna harmonize on it." Their mother also wears pink. While they sing—tones nasal, querulous—a cowboy hat is passed for the offering, "for medical expenses for the three-year-old little child of our brother in Christ."

Squared shoulders made squarer by the red-and-black-plaid flannel shirt tucked into his faded Levi's, big silver belt buckle, ruddy skin redder in the heat, the preacher thanks the singers, bows his head, pulls down one side of his black handlebar mustache, and squinches his eyes closed. "Let us pray," he urges, then intones rapidly: "I just turn myself over to you, Lord. I just pray that every need is met, Lord. Lord, I just give you the praise and the glory. I just pray in Jesus' name, Lord."

"Amen" from the bleachers.

"Bulldoggers," he drawls looking out at us, "we cain't be very smart. We get on a nice quarter horse and ride forty miles an hour and jump off it. But me and my wife, Samantha, we've made ourselves available, on the rodeo circuit, to serve Him.

"I'm not no way a Bible scholar, but I'm gonna share with you what the Lord has shared with me, and He's gonna anoint it. If you come to hear God, you not gonna be let down. I'm just an instrument He's usin'. Let God be liftin' us up."

"Amen."

"This is Satan's world. You've got to abide in the Lord. He's gonna tell us how to get out of every circumstance.

"Through my and Samantha's eyes, just this year, God has answered prayers. One night we left Casper, Wyoming, and we had to be in Dodge City next day, and it's a long way we had to drive. Got twenty-five miles out of Cheyenne, traveling in our motor home. Blew out both tires. I got 'em changed hour and a half later. Two o'clock in the morning. I was tired. I was mad. I jumped in the motor home, turned the key on, battery was dead."

"Ohhhh's" of disappointment drift across the bleachers.

"I messed with the battery. I turnt the poles. Our battery was ruint so bad, it wouldn't hold a charge. Wouldn't even run lights, wouldn't even honk the horn.

"Samantha was sittin' there on the other seat. She said, 'Why don't you just pray?' An' I said, 'What do you think I been doin?' Whenever I said that, the Holy Spirit sorta tapped on me and said, 'Hey, He'll do it, if you'll ask Him.'

"I reached over and took Samantha's hand and said, 'Father, in the name of Jesus, start this thing and get us out of here, and we thank you for it in Jesus' name.' I reached down and turned it over, and we had a new battery. That was an answered prayer."

"Hallelujah!"

"Isn't nothin' anybody can say: it was God fixed that battery. He can work miracles today."

The cows low. A rooster—Orval?—crows.

"The second way he answers prayers is delayed. I give you an example out of us. I used to have to just give examples out of the Bible. But God has let me live so we can share His words, and I know for a fact it works, because I been through it.

"Samantha and I went out on the road in January. We got down to the end of February and our money was all gone. We hadn't won a thing. Things were tough. We'd been prayin' all winter, God, let us win a rodeo. Let us place. Just give us money to keep goin'.

❦

"We got to Houston, Texas, down there to the world's biggest rodeos, one of the richest rodeos. I had my first steer, and I didn't come close. Friday night is when I had my second steer. Friday morning I got in prayer, and God spoke to me, 'Watch the 700

Club.' I was watchin' it, and it was real good. But toward the end of it I said, 'God, this was real good, but there wasn't nothin' here for me, though. What did you tell me to watch it for?'

"You know, we got a knower down in deep. In my knower, I knew that God told me to watch that. But it didn't seem like there was nothin' there.

"Toward the end of the program a guy on it started givin' words of knowledge and prophecy, prayin', and he said, 'God, You're showin' me something right now about a rodeo. I don't know where it is. I cain't see it.' He raised up, and he looked at the camera, and he looked me in the eye. He said straight to me, 'You're sittin' watchin' this program, and you've got a problem on a rodeo circuit. God wants you to know right now. He's in control, He loves you, and He's gonna take care of everything tonight.'

"We went to the Astrodome that night, an' Samantha tol' me she wanted somethin' to eat. We put ever' bit of money we had left, $257, for an entry fee an' had to borrow that and had bills at home, and we were way down in the hole. Samantha wanted a caramel apple. They cost a dollar. I had eighty-six cents. I bought a bag of potato chips, an' they cost seventy-five cents. I had eleven pennies in my pocket.

"I went in there into the arena. I said, 'God, all I am is yours.' We won $4,700 that night. God, He made my time into His time."

"Praise the Lord!" the congregation shouts. And even Jack (who does not believe in God—what's here, he says, "is enough") raises a fist and says, "Praise Him!" with the crowd.

"That was a delayed prayer.

"The third way God answers prayers is to just say no. Not a cowboy here right now that hasn't rode into this box and got into a chute down here and said, 'God, let me win,' and then went out there and fell off on his face. God does the way He wants to, not the way we want to.

"It's tough. I know. Because things hadn't been the way I wanted them all year. I'm a rookie this year, and I wanted to have a chance to win Rookie of the Year, but things got to be the way God wants them to be.

"There's one prayer God always answers. It's the prayer that asks God into your heart. If you never done it, He's available this mornin'. If any of you never opened the door and let Him in, do it. I don't know what's in your heart, but do it. Say, 'Here I am, Lord, take me.' " The bulldogger spreads out his arms.

Rex Barber hurries to catch up with us as we leave the arena. "Where were you guys last night?" he asks. "Talk about your bacchanal! Like my Greek?" He bows at me, then nods toward Jack. "Your folks, your dad, was dancing like he was all new." About Delia, he tells me, "I bet that gal hasn't moved a limb yet. An' I wouldn't either, except the wife had me bring the little tuckers here." He points then to the bulldogger preacher, kneeling in an aisle at the edge of a riser, hands cupped on a weeping man's head.

Leaving the fairgrounds, I say, "Every year I wonder if grass will grow here again."

PICNIC

❦

MORE THAN ANY RESTAURANT MEAL I LOVE PICNICS. TOSS INTO a basket almost any sandwich, chicken leg, deviled egg, celery blade (with its pale hollow and strings to pull), and cool juice to sip, take me away to loll somewhere quiet, green, and shaded, and I'm daffy with pleasure.

Picnics are a relatively recent development. Western man had to put many centuries between himself and his Paleolithic forebears, had to suffer increasing formality at the dinner table, before he could permit himself to carry food outside in pretty baskets.

Pique-nique first appeared in a French dictionary in 1692. The word then referred to what we would call a potluck. It was a meal eaten indoors to which everyone present had contributed food or paid a fee to attend. Jean Anthelme Brillat-Savarin, who died in 1826, wrote about hunting luncheons in *The Physiology of Taste*, the first book that treated gastronomy as Art. Most often these luncheons were men-only affairs. But occasionally ladies ("our wives, our sisters, and our pretty cousins and their equally pretty friends") were invited. Brillat-Savarin's ladies, "decked with feathers, and with flowers," arrived at the hunting site in "light carriages with prancing horses."

At these hunting lunches, wrote Brillat-Savarin, "the world is our dining room and the sun itself is our light." As for food and drink, "everything that can well be carried away from the most knowing culinary laboratories" (plates of turkey in transparent jelly, pâté, salad) was served, together with "potent champagne."

The change in the meaning of *pique-nique* from "everyone bringing food" to "everyone eating out-of-doors" was not completed until the 1860s. By then, the French Revolution was almost a century past, and the great days of restaurant dining and the rise of great chefs and Grand Cuisine were in full bloom. Only then was it perhaps possible for society to allow itself the transgressive act of eating out-of-doors, casually, with fingers rather than forks.

Paris, between 1830 and 1880, grew in population from 576,000 to almost 2.3 million people. There is the suggestion that the increase in popularity of the *pique-nique* was also related to this increase, as city dwellers sought out rural or park settings as relief from urban crowding and squalor. Indeed, so filthy was Paris that beginning in 1853 Napoleon III put his master planner, Baron Georges Haussmann, to work supervising demolition of its slums and building wide, straight boulevards and the great park at Bois de Boulogne, where picnickers dappled the grounds. At about the same time, the invention of the collapsible tin paint tube and portable easel made possible landscape painting in the open air. Painters began to fill canvases with picnics and picnickers. The most infamous of these picnic paintings was Edouard Manet's huge *Déjeuner sur l'herbe*, or *Luncheon on the Grass*. Set in a wooded park, the painting shows four figures: two clothed men and two women, one entirely unclothed and one in a gauzy slip. The men wear dark jackets, light-colored trousers, and black caps. The woman wearing the slip recedes into the painting's distance, where she bathes in a shallow stream: she seems more lawn ornament than picnicker. The second woman—she was the model Victorine

Meurent—situated to the left of the painting's dead center, sits next to her pale blue frock and straw skimmer. Near her bare hip are an open picnic basket, and peaches, cherries, and a round loaf. The beautiful Victorine, wearing only her opalescing birthday suit, stares out boldly at the viewer, her smile ironic, amused. (Not long after posing here Victorine served as model for Manet's *Olympia*, where again she gazes out at the viewer with this self-assured, mesmerizing calm.)

Viewers considered *Déjeuner sur l'herbe* scandalous when it was exhibited in 1863. Victorine's nudity was not specifically the issue. Parisians easily accepted studio-made allegorical history paintings aflutter with half-clothed mythical subjects and summing up a moral lesson. And in his picnic painting Manet "quoted" older, long-accepted paintings by Giorgione and Raphael in which nudes were focal points. But Manet's figures were out-of-doors, and the men were garbed in contemporary clothes and the women in next-to-nothing and nothing at all—that is why the public declared itself shocked and disgusted. There was nothing to be learned here, no battle between Spirit and Flesh in which Flesh is over-come. There was only flesh and the peaches and cherries, which next to Victorine's milky skin appeared rather shopworn.

While poor Manet suffered his critics' lashings, picnics were becoming popular across the Continent, in England, and even in America. Mrs. Isabella Beeton's *Book of Household Management* offered a picnic menu for forty: cold roasts, chicken and duck, lobster, salad, Christmas pudding, pigeon pie. Here in the United States, during the Civil War, families were seen picnicking on biscuit and sausage, apple cider and apple pie next to a battle-field.

We were not a picnicking family. I first learned about picnics when my father read to me from *The Wind in the Willows*, *Winnie the Pooh*, and Johanna Spyri's *Heidi*, the story of the little orphan sent to live with her grandfather in a hut high in the Swiss Alps. It is Heidi's first day in her new home. Peter the goatherder is to take her with him while he moves goats to new grass. Grandfather packs Heidi's food into Peter's leather bag: bread and crumbly goat cheese. He adds a bowl, telling Peter, "The child cannot drink the milk as you do from the goat."

Heidi, Peter, and the goats reach pasture. "Peter takes up his quarters for the day at the foot of the high rocks . . . Heidi sits down next to him . . . the goats climb about among bushes overhead. Heidi had never felt so happy in her life before . . . and wished for nothing better than to remain there forever." At noon, Peter arranges the bread and cheese on the ground. "Then he took the little bowl and milked some delicious fresh milk into it from the white goat."

Heidi asks, "Is the milk for me?" "Yes," replies Peter. Ever since, I've been half in love with Peter, although I've assiduously avoided tasting goat's milk.

When I made imaginary picnics for my childhood dolls and actual picnics for boyfriends and then daughters, it was Kenneth Grahame's *The Wind in the Willows* picnic from which I "quoted":

> The Rat brought the boat alongside the bank, made her fast, helped the still awkward Mole safely ashore, and swung out the luncheon-basket. The Mole begged as a favor to be allowed to unpack it all by himself; and the Rat was very pleased to indulge him, and to sprawl at full length on the grass and rest, while his excited friend shook out the tablecloth and spread it, took out all the mysterious packets one by one and arranged their contents in due order, while gasping, "O my! O my!" at each fresh revelation.

This shaking out of the tablecloth—what a lovely sound, that sharp starchy snap!—these mysterious packets whose unwrapping brings forth one after another fresh revelation are what I hope for in a picnic. And when I went back recently to a book of paintings and looked at Manet's picnic, I had this sense of his milky-skinned Victorine as being lifted out of a basket, like a high-sided angel-food cake, and unwrapped and revealed.

But to get down to business, what must you have to go on a picnic? A basket. Food and drink. A friend or friends. A place. The basket need not be one of those thousand-dollar fitted Fortnum & Mason wonders. Even a good-size Easter basket will do, lined with one pretty cloth napkin and covered over with another. As for food, a picnic can be as simple as good bread, sweet butter, nice cheese, fruit, and a sweet. But it's not a matter of tossing peanut-butter sandwiches and diet Fresca into a paper sack, although it can be when two people are newly in love.

A picnic rule that I think makes sense is that one should be able to eat the lunch picnic with fingers; the dinner picnic may require silver. Lunch can be narrow finger sandwiches, roast-beef-wrapped gherkins, deviled eggs, stuffed celery sticks, cornichons, radish roses, olives green and black, lemonade, iced tea, or iced coffee, and oatmeal cookies. Dinner is poultry, white soft rolls, rice salad with ginger and chopped Brazil nuts and green onion and tiny chunks of dried apricot, a green-bean and button-mushroom vinaigrette, or papaya-and-asparagus salad. For dessert pack berries or melon balls or Bing and Queen Anne cherries, lemon-curd bars, pecan squares, or lacy cookies.

For me, any picnic, lunch or dinner, must include deviled eggs. I am all for the simplest preparation: halve the boiled egg on the horizontal, mash the yolk with good mayonnaise, bright-yellow mustard, a pinch of celery seed, and no salt at all. I have tasted deviled-egg fillings mixed with deviled ham, liverwurst paste, chopped chives, green olive, even vile curry powder. Pure egg taste, particularly now that eggs are forbidden in so many diets, seems the best. Each egg half can then be cradled in its own lettuce or spinach leaf and packed tightly into a dish, like candy in a candy box.

The picnic feigns informality. Like a pretty woman who gives her blond hair a windswept tousle with careful blow-drying, the picnic strives after the appearance of casual aw-shucks ease. But as the blonde would tell us, it's not so easy to appear gorgeous and casual. Everything—linens, china, glasses, food—should be delicately pretty. If you pack baked or fried chicken or game hens, ask your butcher for white paper ruffs and fit them around the poultry's legs. Buy your loaf uncut, so you can slice the bread thin. Trim the crusts. The meat, too, you want to slice so thin that it's almost transparent. "Waterproof" the bread with a light haze of butter or mayonnaise. If you bring a thermos of lemonade, pack see-through lemon slices to float in glasses. For champagne, bring champagne flutes (wrap them and all your breakables in napkins). Use napkin rings. For evening, include a small broad-based vase and a handful of pink cosmos or one big white deliciously smelly lily, a stubby candle, and a glass candleholder.

Any more than four people seems too many for a picnic. The farther you take your picnic from civilization, the better you must get along. If only two of you go, one must be strong enough to carry the basket.

There should be a rise toward which you walk, not a huff-and-puff hike, but enough of a walk that you feel accomplished upon arrival. Unfold your blanket beneath a large shade tree with spreading boughs the sun can stream through. Ideally, there will be grass that crushes lightly under bare feet and a vista onto which you look down, perhaps a river unwinding.

Then, as did Mole, shake out your tablecloth and spread it, take out all the mysterious packets one by one and arrange their contents in due order, while gasping, *"O my! O my!"* at each fresh revelation.